The Post-Bubble US Economy

The Post-Bubble US Economy

Implications for Financial Markets and the Economy

Philip Arestis
*University of Cambridge and
Levy Economics Institute*

and

Elias Karakitsos
*Global Economic Research and
Associate Member of the Cambridge Centre
for Economic and Public Policy
University of Cambridge*

First published 2004 by
PALGRAVE MACMILLAN
Houndmills, Basingstoke, Hampshire RG21 6XS and
175 Fifth Avenue, New York, N.Y. 10010
Companies and representatives throughout the world

PALGRAVE MACMILLAN is the global academic imprint of the Palgrave Macmillan division of St. Martin's Press, LLC and of Palgrave Macmillan Ltd. Macmillan® is a registered trademark in the United States, United Kingdom and other countries. Palgrave is a registered trademark in the European Union and other countries.

ISBN 1–4039–3649–8 (hardcover)
ISBN 1–4039–3650–1 (paperback)

This book is printed on paper suitable for recycling and made from fully managed and sustained forest sources.

A catalogue record for this book is available from the British Library.

Library of Congress Cataloging-in-Publication Data
Arestis, Philip, 1941–
    The post bubble US economy : implications for financial markets and the economy / Philip Arestis and Elias Karakitsos.
        p. cm.
    Includes bibliographical references and index.
    ISBN 1–4039–3649–8—ISBN 1–4039–3650–1 (pbk.)
      1. United States—Economic conditions—1981–2001. 2. United States—Economic conditions—2001– 3. Financial crises. 4. International economic relations. I. Karakitsos, Elias. II. Title.

HC106.83.A74 2004
330.973—dc22   2004056083

Printed and bound in Great Britain by
Antony Rowe Ltd, Chippenham and Eastbourne

This book is dedicated to our children Natalia (and to her husband Tom) and Stefan (Philip Arestis), Nepheli and Eliza (Elias Karakitsos)

Contents

List of Figures

List of Tables

Acknowledgements

We would very much like to thank Amanda Watkins of Palgrave Macmillan, and her staff, for the encouragement and efficiency throughout the duration of this project. We would also wish to thank colleagues at the Cambridge Centre for Economic and Public Policy, University of Cambridge, and at the Levy Economics Institute, New York. We are grateful to Michael Hanes, John Mather, Warren Mosler, Farhan Sharaff and Andrew Thornhill for helpful comments. We are particularly grateful to all we have mentioned for their continuous support throughout the period of writing this book. Without their support this project would not have been completed.

We are also grateful to the journal Public Finance and its editor for permission to draw on material published therein from the following: Frowen, S.F. and Karakitsos, E. (1998), 'A Strategic Approach to the Euro Prospects', Public Finance, 53(1), 1–18.

Foreword

'When solving problems, dig at the roots instead of just hacking at the leaves.'

Anthony J. D'Angelo

This fascinating book could not have been better timed as there is a need for clear vision in dealing with the development of client's economic well-being.

As a financial planner and wealth manager, there seems little point in creating good order in clients' affairs if we are to entrust funds into the hands of those who do not understand the fundamental concepts contained in this book. As Marcus Tullius Cicero put it: 'Wise men are instructed by reason; men of less understanding, by experience; the most ignorant, by necessity; the beasts, by nature.'

It is gratifying to find a book that seeks to understand the levers of economic change and then to explain the observations to the reader so clearly. The authors have identified the important drivers and the weighting of them in this multi dimensional space. The resulting model, correctly applied, identifies solutions and routes through to deliver value paths of assets.

Having worked with Elias for the past few years the education has been a truly rewarding experience and his work deserves to be read more widely. This book will ensure that that happens.

JOHN MATHER
London

Foreword

What is now known as the K-Model started with an informal chat I had with Elias in London, in November 1987, on the causes of the stock market crash. His answer was simple enough: 'market discounting of a policy induced recession, as investors lost hope that the dollar could correct the then US current account deficit'. My next question was: what drives asset prices? His answer was: 'news on economic fundamentals'. I was again in total agreement, so, I then asked: can one systematically beat the market? The answer was: 'yes, because markets pay too much attention to short-term news, but systematically miss the medium term'. Finally I asked: what you need to create a better forecasting methodology and put this in practice? The answer was: 'I have a macro model, but I would need to develop the financial model, all I need is money!' The money enabled Elias to develop the financial models and the results are what you see in this book.

Through the years the methodology has been vastly improved. As the CIO at Citibank, it was my job to challenge the analysis, the adequacy of the framework and pose the questions. As the methodology improved I was able to sharpen the questions. Elias has a highly analytical approach to markets, he is able to model new ideas, and immediately integrate them into his full macro and financial model thus creating a different perspective on markets. The back testing of such new models enables him to verify the trading potential in the 'real' world. This approach is of great help to portfolio managers and traders who are able to link economic theory to their intuitive and technical approach to markets.

This book exemplifies this methodology. There are four features that set it apart from traditional ones that are widely used in the Street.

First, traditional models of short-term interest rates are backward looking as they purport to project central bank actions on how it has behaved in the past. In contrast, the K-Model is forward-looking, as it is based on an optimisation approach that projects short-term interest rates on how the central bank *should* respond to the problems facing the economy, given its stated policy objectives in the current state of the economy in the business cycle.

Second, traditional valuation models of bonds and equities and commodities provide a buy or sell signal that follows the random-walk model. Investment decisions based on such models can be very misleading because the fair value of the asset is changing as its market value is changing so that their co-variation is purely random. Hence, knowledge that the market is, say, currently overvalued bears no prediction on whether tomorrow the market would be more overvalued, undervalued or fairly valued, because both the fair value and the market value will change randomly so that mean reversion cannot be guaranteed. In contrast, the K-Model is guaranteed to provide a buy or sell signal that does not follow the random-walk model. It does so, by an explicit modelling of the persistency effect (momentum or greed that drives the market away from equilibrium) and the equilibrating effect (mean reversion or fear that drives the market back to equilibrium). Whether the persistency or the equilibrating effect drives the market depends on news on economic fundamentals and the market intrinsic dynamics (i.e. time series analysis or technical analysis). The K-Model, therefore, integrates fundamental with technical analysis into a coherent whole.

In computing fair values, the K-Model makes a distinction between short- and long-run fair (or equilibrium) values. The long-run fair value is a pure measure of fairness based just on economic fundamentals. The short-run fair value takes also into account the reaction of the market to news on economic fundamentals.

Third, traditional models of risk are based on the correlation of historical returns captured in the historical variance–covariance matrix that is both backward looking and extremely volatile. ARCH-GARCH models that purport to model the volatility of the historical variance–covariance matrix are usually poor models of risk that lead to poor investment decisions because they are backward looking and therefore they systematically miss the turning points of the variance–covariance matrix. In contrast, in the K-Model risk is forward-looking stemming from the probability that the forecast may be wrong. The risk arises from two sources – the forecasting accuracy of the model and the validity of the assumptions in predicting the correlation of future returns. Moreover, the K-Model allows for an explicit decomposition of the forces that comprise risk. This provides a systematic analysis and monitoring of risk that leads to better investment decisions.

Fourth, the investment strategy is determined through an optimisation approach based on Optimal Control Theory (OCT). The problem can be stated as one of maximising the portfolio objectives subject to the financial markets model over a given time horizon and for a given degree of risk aversion. The optimisation determines the optimal investment strategy in terms of asset allocation parameters. The portfolio objectives can be taken simply as the maximisation of a convex linear combination of the portfolio expected return and the risk attached to that return.

The above approach has a great advantage over Modern Portfolio Theory (MPT). The latter is using as a measure of risk the variance–covariance matrix of historical returns. The difference is that MPT would select an optimal strategy on the basis of what happened in the past. In contrast, OCT would select an optimal strategy on the risk that the forecast is wrong. A corollary of this difference is that whereas according to MPT international asset diversification provides a hedge against risk, according to OCT it does not necessarily provide such hedging.

The book is an illustration of the thinking process in market analysis and investment strategy. I hope that the readers would find it as interesting and challenging and extremely beneficial to the task of managing money and greatly enhancing performance as I found it in practice working for nearly fifteen years with Professor Karakitsos.

Farhan Sharaff has held a number of very senior positions in the Investment world including the CIO of the Private Client Group of Citigroup, Global Chief Investment Officer of Zurich Scudder Investments and the CIO of Cigna Corporation.

FARHAN SHARAFF
New York

Prolegomena

The issues covered in the book

The recent US recession was very mild, in spite of the burst of the 'new economy' bubble, which was one of the worst in monetary history. Equity prices fell precipitously, yet the consumer remained resilient. The burst of a typical bubble implies retrenchment by the personal and corporate sectors, as falling asset prices create a gap (i.e. an imbalance) between the assets and the liabilities of the private sector. In the euphoria years in which the bubble balloons, both companies and households accumulate disproportionate amounts of debt, induced by rising asset prices. Once the bubble bursts and asset prices collapse, the high level of debt is incompatible with the new low level of asset prices. Once companies and households accept that the new level of asset prices is permanent rather than temporary, they try to repay their debts and rebuild their wealth by saving more, thereby dragging the economy into a severe recession characterised by asset and debt deflation.

This process of asset and debt deflation is long and painful, as it usually infects the balance sheet of the commercial banks, which respond by cutting new credit (credit crunch), thereby accelerating the bankruptcies in companies and households. The experience of the Great Depression of 1876–90, of the Great Depression of the 1930s and of Japan in the 1990s shows that the burst of every bubble has had exactly these characteristics and policymakers had little scope in soothing this process. Yet, the US experience of the 'new economy' bubble was very different. Asset prices fell as in a typical bubble, yet the economy had the mildest recession. The personal sector continued to accumulate debt, while the corporate sector reduced it only slightly. Two factors may account for this experience and emergence of imbalances. The first is that monetary policy may have achieved a soft landing of the economy. The second is that investors regarded the burst of the bubble as a temporary rather than a permanent phenomenon. These are key questions addressed in the book.

The lower geopolitical risks after the end of the Iraq war, coupled with the subsidence of the governance crisis and the perfect timing of yet another fiscal package in 2003, as well as the accommodating stance of monetary policy in the last three years, have combined to create a booming economy in the last nine months which may have put it on a sustainable path to recovery. A US-led world recovery, and signs that deflation in Japan is coming to an end, is surely boosting hopes that the worst is over. The last three years look like a nightmare that belongs to the past. Confidence is high among consumers and companies not only in the US, but also in the world at large.

Would the scars of the imbalances, to which we have referred above, disappear? What are the prospects of the US economy? These are further key questions that are addressed in this book. Financial markets have recovered in the last nine months and optimism is running high that the rally in the equity market has a new upside. But is such optimism justified? What are the prospects for bonds, equities and the dollar? Which are the risks that investors should consider when working their investment strategy for the next few years? Should they overweigh equities and dumb bonds in their portfolios? What about the dollar? In the last three years it has fallen a great deal, but disproportionately with respect to some currencies, like, for example, the euro and the pound sterling. Now that the economy is recovering is the dollar near its bottom? The prospects and risks to financial markets is yet another issue that is addressed in this book.

The policy debate on how to deal with bubbles centres around two polar views. The first is that central banks should leave financial markets to function freely on their own and asset price inflation should not be the concern of a central bank. However, a central bank should deal with the consequences of the burst of a bubble. The opposite view is that asset price inflation is as bad as inflation in goods and services and as the latter is in the realm of a central bank so should be the control of asset price inflation. Thus, the policy debate can be summarised as dealing pro-actively and pre-emptively with bubbles, or reactively with their consequences. The Fed has clearly played with the pro-active approach in the early days of the bubble with the familiar 'irrational exuberance' remarks. But in the event it opted for the reactive approach of dealing with the consequences, as it cut the Fed funds rate aggressively in the last three years in a way that was not justified by the depth of the recession. Such policy seems to have paid off and it has done a great deal to restore the tarnished reputation of the Fed in the aftermath of the burst of the bubble. Only time would show whether the pro-active or reactive approach is preferable.

The difficulty with a pro-active and pre-emptive approach stems from what should be the target for monetary policy, as it would be inappropriate for a central bank to have a target for one of its stock market indices. The book addresses this issue and makes appropriate recommendations, crucially net wealth targeting, which deals with the consequences of the bubble on the spending decisions of households. This can provide the basis for pro-active monetary policy on asset price inflation.

How this book should be read and its potential readership

The book is particularly relevant to investors in world financial markets, as it addresses the prospects and risks to financial markets emanating from the post-bubble US economy. Although it is confined to the US economy it has implications for global markets, given the leading role of the US. The book is not just a narration of events and prospects as well as risks to the economy and financial markets, but offers an in-depth analysis of the thinking process that underlines the sophisticated formation of the investment strategy of major financial institutions. The methodology, therefore, of the book is that it begins with the realities of the US economy, where the factual analysis makes good use of available data, fully cited and explained, before the analysis builds upon them to articulate the theoretical background involved in each case. The more empirical aspects of the book then follow.

This thinking process is based on a top-down approach, which formalises the view that asset prices, at any point in time, reflect market discounting of how the central bank should respond to the state of the economy, as judged by the latest available information. This thinking process is encapsulated in the macro-financial model, which is an integrated system for analysing systematically macro and financial data that leads to an informed investment decision-making process. The book effectively describes that process by analysing in every chapter one constituent component of the macro-financial model, to which we have just referred, that leads to a synthesis in the last chapter that deals with bonds and equities. The structure of the book follows the rationale of this top-down approach of the macro-financial model.

The book, therefore, may be extremely relevant to Chief Investment Officers, portfolio managers, traders and individual investors, who may be interested in the state-of-the-art methodology for the analysis of financial markets and the process of investment strategy. From this point of view, the emphasis in this book is not on the conclusions of the current investment strategy, which, by definition, would be obsolete by the time the book is published. The emphasis is, rather, on the methodology underlying the analysis of financial markets and investment strategy. However, the book is not written just for the benefit of the sophisticated investor. Indeed, it is written with the economist also in mind, along with those non-economists that are interested in understanding the causes and consequences for the economy and financial markets of the 'new economy' bubble. Policymakers may also be attracted on the issue, since there are serious policy implications involved.

The book has been structured in such a way so that it can embrace such diverse readership. The reader can get a quick first impression of all the issues covered in the book by reading the summary and conclusions at the end of each chapter. All chapters have a similar structure so that an approach to reading the book can be formulated. Every chapter begins with the issues that are explored subsequently. It then offers an analysis of the relevant statistics that form the basis of the analysis. This does not require any prior knowledge and provides easy reading. Yet the analysis is deep enough so that the alert reader can guess the model behind the thinking process. Next follows a lengthy explanation of the parts of the model that are relevant to the issue in hand. The purpose of this section is not to provide a textbook treatment of, say, investment or consumption, but a formal description of the variables that should be monitored in order to form an opinion of how, say, companies or households reach their decisions on spending and investment and the risks in the current economic climate. A flow chart explains the interrelationship of the key variables in each chapter, which can be read independently of the rest of that section by the interested reader.

Reference to the work of others is given so that the reader can put the model in perspective, without burdening the book as if it was a review article. We have avoided mathematics, as they are not appropriate for the general readership we have in mind, although the more mathematically inclined economists should not be disappointed by its absence. We have attempted to describe in words formal mathematical relationships and simply summarise the functional forms that hold in the long-run equilibrium, so that the interested reader can form an opinion of the depth of the analysis. Even that simple functional form should not frighten the general reader, who can skip it without missing anything from the relevant sections. For the mathematically inclined reader, though, it might summarise in a succinct way, the verbal arguments and avoid the confusion that usually arises in verbal explanation. Only our readers can say whether we succeeded in this difficult task.

An analysis of the prospects and risks for the relevant section of the economy or financial market is provided in every chapter. It does so by simulating the macro-financial model underpinning our analysis under two scenarios. These scenarios are the same in each chapter so that the reader can appreciate the prospects and risks and enable a synthesis at the end of the book for bonds and equities. Although one may think that in the subject matter of the book there are thousand of assumptions that can be made and that the conclusions follow from the choice of these assumptions to suit the arguments of the analyst, we have attempted to show that there is a logical way of conducting an analysis of prospects and risks. Once an assumption is made about the growth of the economy, the implications for all the other variables, like inflation, interest rates and equities, can be derived. We have, therefore, simulated the macro-financial model employed, under the alternative scenarios of (i) slow growth in 2004 and 2005 at around potential output; and (ii) fast growth in 2004, above potential output, but lower growth in 2005. However, the average for the two-year period is the same under the two scenarios. This effectively means that we are interested much more in the volatility of growth rather than the level of growth itself in gauging the implications for the economy and financial markets. We believe that this volatility of growth is likely to arise from the strong possibility that fiscal policy may turn out to be easy in this election year. This is clearly inappropriate as the economy is on the recovery path, so that fiscal policy may be pro-cyclical rather than counter-cyclical, which is what its role should be.

We believe that simulation analysis is more appropriate than direct point-forecast. This, we maintain, is because we do not think that, given the margins of error in any model, point forecasting can be useful and reliable, neither in working out the prospects nor the risk to any economic or financial variable. In fact, investment decisions do not require and do not need to rely on point-forecasts. Investment decisions are about risk management and simulation analysis is very appropriate. Throughout the book we have tried to show that this is the case. The simulation analysis is intentionally very detailed. We believe that an in-depth analysis differs from a journalistic approach in this respect. The value of the simulation analysis in evaluating risk is in identifying the levels that critical variables should reach before they trigger a change in the investment strategy. Readers who might be interested in those critical values should, therefore, read these sections. However, even these readers should be warned that by the time the book is out such critical values might have changed. Hence, the essence for including them is mainly for methodological reasons.

Two final comments are pertinent. The first is that in every section that deals with simulation analysis we also undertake sensitivity exercises that complement the former in risk analysis. The second comment is that although in every chapter we describe the appropriate part of the macro-financial model utilised, we do not offer the numerical values of the relevant equations. Instead, we provide a graph that depicts how closely the model can explain the relevant variable and offer the forecast error. We believe that a detailed analysis of the numerical values of the model and its statistical properties would not be satisfactory in view of space limitations. In any case, such an attempt would have detracted from the main analysis, purpose and focus of the project, without adding significantly to the book.

Data series

The data used throughout this book cover the period 1947–2003 and they are either quarterly or monthly as indicated. The data are the official figures as made available by EcoWin live databank (see www.ecowin.com).

1
Introduction

1 The purpose of the book

The US economy has gone through a very interesting period over the last twenty years or so. There was a period of expansion that lasted for ten years, the largest ever recorded by an industrialised country. So much so that allegedly a 'new economy' emerged with rules, which were different from what, traditionally, had been known. The stock market produced enormous gains, especially so in the areas of Technology, Media and Telecommunications. Beginning March 2000 the stock market simply collapsed. The optimism surrounding the 'new economy' vanished with it, followed by pessimism. In fact, beginning March 2001 the US economy entered a period of recession. This prompted the Fed and the US fiscal authorities to pursue expansionary policies. There were no less than 13 reductions of the Fed Funds rate between the early parts of 2001 and mid-2003, along with expansionary fiscal measures. The surplus in the government budget, created during the expansion, turned into a deficit and a higher government deficit is expected in the near future, especially in the second half of 2004.

The purpose of this book is to investigate the causes of the burst of that bubble and its consequences, with the focus being on the post-bubble era. It is also to examine closely the recent experience of the US economy and its financial markets along with their prospects and risks from a short- and long-run perspective. We are keen to study closely the prospects of the post-bubble period, but also the risks, which we believe are serious enough to justify undertaking a project on this aspect of current US economic developments. This examination is particularly pertinent once we have reminded ourselves that the 2001 US recession was unusually mild along with unemployment and inflation both remaining at relatively low levels. It is also worth pointing out that the subsequent recovery has been anaemic, especially so in view of the unsatisfactory pace of job creation and slowness in investment pickup.

In the sense to which we have just alluded, the current recovery is different from previous ones. Normally, investment expenditure declines in recessions and expands in recoveries, while household and government expenditure does not fluctuate as much. The current expansion has produced the opposite. Investment has been weak, which has resulted in reduced job growth well below what is normal at this phase of the cycle, while consumption has been strong and the government sector turning into a large deficit. Mankiw (2001b) puts it slightly differently but in essence the same point is made. He observes that the US boom of the 1990s appears to be the 1970s in reverse. The 1970s were characterised by adverse supply shocks, steep fall in stock-market capitalization relative to GDP, decline in the rate of productivity growth, and rising unemployment and inflation; exactly the opposite of what happened in the 1990s (see, also, Temple, 2002). It is clear from this short resume of the realities of the current US economic realities that the study proposed here is timely.

The introduction purports to give a flavour what is to follow in the book, but also what has been achieved in the book. The next three sections provide a brief resume of where we think the US economy stands at this juncture. This is followed by a brief description, chapter by chapter, of the contents of the book, along with what we have achieved in each chapter. A brief explanation of the macroeconomic model we have utilised throughout the book to back up propositions made and hypotheses postulated.

2   The current state of the US economy

Growth accelerated sharply after the end of the Iraq war (see Figure 1.1). In the third quarter of 2003 the US economy grew at a staggering 8.2% quarter-on-quarter (q-o-q), from a 3.1% in the second quarter and 1.4% in the first quarter. Real GDP increased 3.5% year-on-year (y-o-y) in the third quarter, compared with 2.5% in the second quarter and 2% in the first quarter of 2003. The recovery came earlier and was stronger than had anticipated. This induced the consensus to revise upwards growth forecasts for both 2003 and 2004 and raise hopes that the economy is at last on a sustainable path to recovery. However, the stunning 8.2% growth in the third quarter was due to one-off factors and the economy decelerated in the fourth quarter of 2003 to 4%.

Real final sales (GDP less inventories change) confirm that the strength of the economy in the aftermath of the Iraq war surprised not only financial markets, but companies, too. In the second quarter of 2003 the real change in private inventories subtracted 0.9% from the change in real GDP. The buoyancy of final sales suggests that the strength of demand was unexpected and had to be met by running down inventories (see Figure 1.2). Consumption also accelerated in the last three quarters, although it decelerated in the fourth quarter from its torrid pace in the third quarter of 2003 (see Figure 1.3). The superb performance of consumption in the third quarter was due to the income tax cuts that were introduced in that quarter.

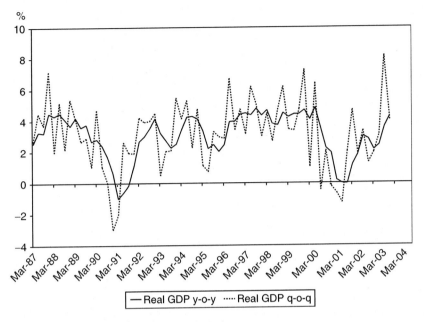

Figure 1.1 Real GDP in the last business cycle

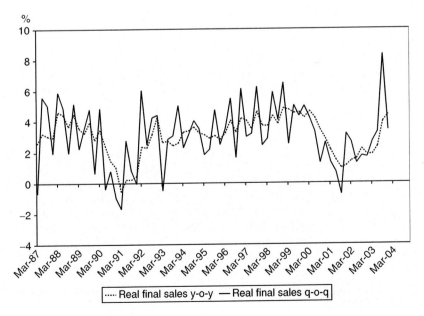

Figure 1.2 Real final sales in the last business cycle

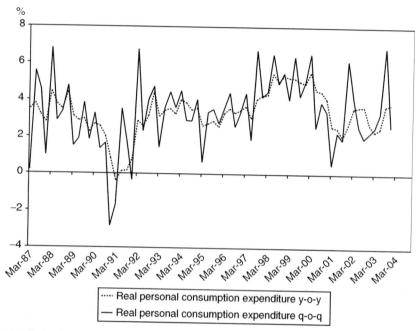

Figure 1.3 Consumption in the last business cycle

But hopes that the recovery may have finally become sustainable are pinned on the performance of investment in the last three quarters of 2003. Fixed investment soared from 1.1% in the first quarter of 2003 to 15.7% in the third (see Figure 1.4). However, the spectacular recovery of investment is, partly, due to one-off measures related to the depreciation incentives provided in the second quarter of 2003. These measures came at the right time because investment would have increased anyway, as companies had managed to restore profitability. However, the recovery of investment is not uniform amongst its constituent components. Investment in structures is the weakest component of fixed investment. It jumped in the second quarter of 2003, as companies rushed to take advantage of the tax measures, but decelerated in the following two quarters showing that there is no underlying strength (see Figure 1.5). On the other hand, investment on equipment and software soared from 0.5% in the first quarter of 2003 to 17.6% in the third and the deceleration in the fourth was very mild, indicating its underlying strength (see Figure 1.6). Residential investment is the most buoyant component of fixed investment, as the housing boom has continued uninterrupted since the beginning of the recession, fuelled by the falling interest rates (see Figure 1.7).

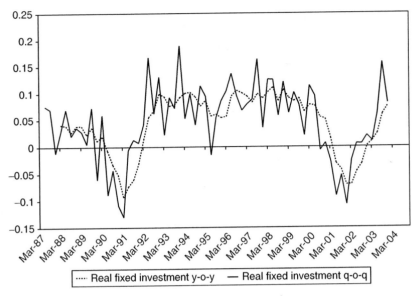

Figure 1.4 Real fixed investment in the last business cycle

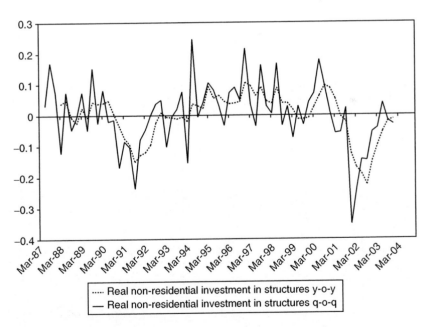

Figure 1.5 Real investment in structures in the last business cycle

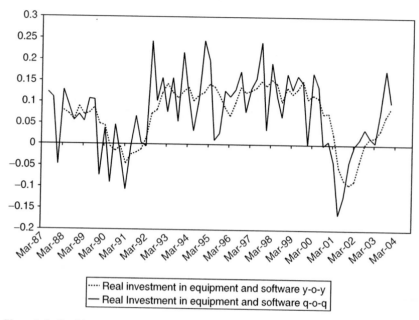

Figure 1.6 Real investment in equipment and software in the last business cycle

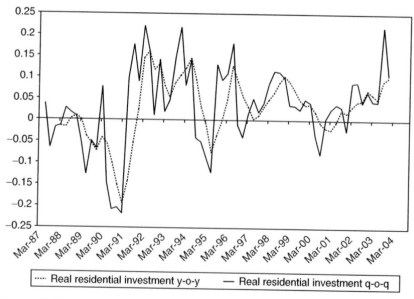

Figure 1.7 Real residential investment

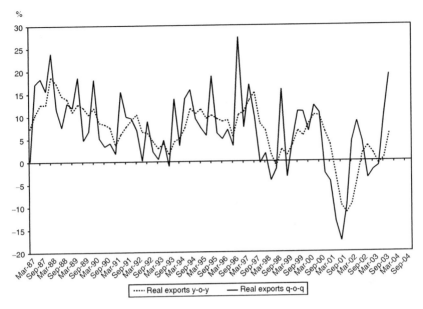

Figure 1.8 Real exports of goods and services

Finally, exports have also registered a stunning recovery. They bottomed in the fourth quarter of 2002 and hit 19.1% within the following 12 months (see Figure 1.8). This shows that the US has a lot to gain from a US-led world recovery.

3 The forces that shape growth

The forces that shape growth with a yearly view are fiscal and monetary policy, confidence and private sector imbalances. Monetary policy was eased once more at the end of June 2003 with the Fed funds rate cut to 1%. Figure 1.9 shows the stance of monetary policy, which is a weighted average of domestic and external monetary conditions, with the weights being the importance of domestic demand and exports to GDP. Domestic monetary conditions are measured by the deviation of the real Fed funds rate from its neutral level, while external monetary conditions are measured by the deviation of the real effective exchange rate from its neutral level.[1] Domestic monetary conditions have been eased with the real Fed funds rate been cut by 3.9% since December 2000. External monetary conditions have also been eased with the real dollar falling by 14.4% since February 2002. Consequently, overall monetary conditions (i.e. the stance of monetary policy) have been eased by 4.8% since November 2000. This is a huge monetary

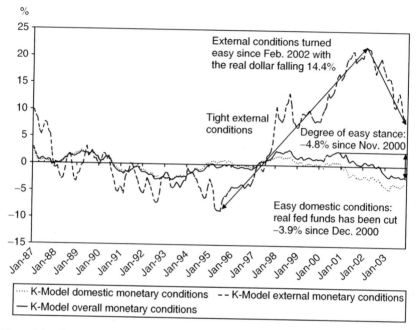

Figure 1.9   The stance of monetary policy

stimulus, which until recently has been shrugged off as confidence was low and the companies' priority was to restore profitability and healthy balance sheets. Now that all these factors have improved the easy monetary conditions are expected to provide a boost to domestic demand.

The stance of fiscal policy (Figure 1.10) turned 1.6% of GDP easier with the 'Jobs and Growth Tax Relief Reconciliation' Act of 2003. The act provided for an additional first-year bonus depreciation write-off, increasing the immediate depreciation write-off from 30% (provided for in the 'Job Creation and Worker Assistance Act' of 2002) to 50% for property acquired after 5 May 2003, and placed in service before 1 January 2005. The additional depreciation provided by the 2003 act is estimated to have increased depreciation expenses in the second quarter by $83.7 billion and by $30.9 in the third quarter. In addition, the 2003 act provided for a reduction of $100.9 billion in July in personal tax and non-tax payments. The act reduced withheld federal taxes $45.8 billion as a result of new marginal tax rates, the expansion of the 10% income tax bracket, and an acceleration in 'marriage-penalty' relief. Federal non-withheld taxes (payments of estimated taxes plus final settlements less refunds) were reduced by $55.5 billion because of advance payments of the child tax credit that began being mailed out 25 July 2003. The fiscal stimulus provided through the depreciation incentives and

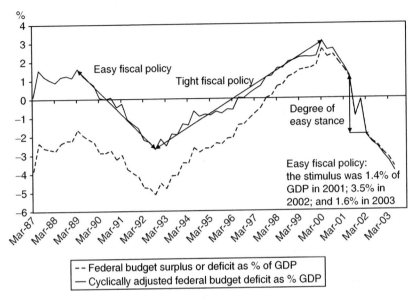

Figure 1.10 Stance of US fiscal policy

tax relief, ignoring the additional measures on dividend income, as they are controversial with respect to their effect on demand in the economy, is estimated to be 1.6% of nominal GDP. This huge fiscal stimulus accounts for the better than expected performance of the economy since the end of the Iraq war and is expected to continue boosting domestic demand in 2004.

The imbalances of the personal, corporate and federal sectors will shape the effects of fiscal policy in the long run (i.e. the fiscal multipliers in the second year and beyond). These imbalances will affect the speed at which the positive effects of fiscal policy dissipate, and therefore they are more relevant in 2005 and beyond. Other short-run factors will determine the extent to which fiscal policy creates growth over the next 12 months.

4 The case for a strong cyclical upturn in 2004 and long-term risks

The combination of easy fiscal policy with easy monetary policy and increased confidence, due to lower geopolitical risks, should lead to higher than potential output growth in 2004.

The surge in investment in 2004 will depend on industrial production, capacity utilisation, the real interest rate and corporate profits. The prospects for these variables are good. The unexpected strength of the economy in the second quarter of 2003 caused inventories to run down. Hence, industrial production should increase with a six-month view to replenish inventories. It should increase even more with a twelve-month view to provide for higher level of inventories in anticipation of stronger demand, as a result of the fiscal measures.

Even more important is that the corporate sector retrenchment between July 2002 and April 2003 has come to an end, as its objective of lowering unit labour cost has been achieved. The unit labour cost bottomed six quarters earlier and increased for the first time in the first quarter of 2003 thereby contributing to the poor performance of corporate profits in the same year. Since the recovery was the worst ever, cost cutting was the most important way in which companies attempted to salvage profits and remain in business. The bottoming of the unit labour cost prompted a second round of retrenchment with investment slashed, along with deep layoffs. This retrenchment would have continued until unit labour cost began again to fall. In the two quarters to September 2003 the objective of lowering unit labour cost was achieved, thereby bolstering profitability. Moreover, the stronger growth and the depreciation incentives fuelled a surge in corporate profits, which actually lessens the need for further retrenchment. As a result, the second round of retrenchment that began in early 2003 has come to an end, paving the way for increased investment spending in the course of 2004. The end of the second round of corporate retrenchment would favourably affect the fortunes of the personal sector. As the pace of layoffs is coming to an end household real disposable income will be bolstered and consumer confidence will increase, thereby prompting consumers to finance current expenditure by running down their savings. Hence, the savings ratio should fall once more. The tax relief will further boost real disposable income and consumption will increase in the course of 2004.

Hence, both consumption and investment should contribute to growth above potential in 2004. The buoyant recovery of the US economy after the end of the Iraq war and the spectacular performance of G-3 exports in the third quarter of 2003 has raised hopes of a strong US-led world recovery. The OECD index of leading indicators, which precedes changes in world demand by six months, bottomed in April 2003 and has continued to rise, until November (the last month for which data is available), thereby suggesting further improvement in G-3 exports over the next few months. But over a longer horizon the conclusion of a US-led world recovery depends on the strength of the US economy and the extent of previous changes in G-3 competitiveness. The depreciation of the dollar in the last two years has led to gains in US competitiveness. Despite the roller-coaster of the yen in the last three years, Japan's competitiveness has also improved. However, the euro area has suffered significant losses in competitiveness because of the strong appreciation of the euro, especially during 2003, and its slow adjustment of competitiveness to changes in the nominal exchange rate. These developments in G-3 competitiveness augur well for a rise in US and Japan exports from a world recovery, but they cast doubts on whether the euro area can benefit from it. Nonetheless, strong growth in the US would also offset the losses in competitiveness and even the euro-area exports would recover. The recovery in the world economy will give a further boost to US growth. So that consumption, investment and exports would be strong in 2004 boosting GDP growth above potential.

However, there are long-term risks to the economy and financial markets stemming from fiscal policy. The current Administration has submitted in February 2004 a neutral budget, which however may turn out to be easy. The Administration has called for the temporary tax cuts to become permanent and to be financed by spending cuts. The two houses are likely to resist pressure to cut spending, and the President is unlikely to veto the spending bill in an election year. Hence, an intentional neutral budget is likely to turn easy. Burgeoning budget deficits and faster economic growth would in the long run lead to higher bond yields.

The rise in government bond yields in the third quarter of 2003 was very abrupt and reversed itself in the fourth quarter when the economy weakened. Although in the short run (six months) bond yields may fall even more, if the deceleration were to continue and inflationary pressures abated, the medium-term trend (twelve months) is up. Soaring budget deficits, faster economic growth and a rekindle in inflation later on will lead to even higher government bond yields. Corporate bond yields will rise with a lag as investment picks up and the economy accelerates. The higher bond yields would lead to retrenchment by the corporate sector and business investment would be affected as a result. Falling profits because of rising unit labour cost would lead to layoffs that affect, in turn, the fortunes of the personal sector. Consumption would therefore be infected.

In the current environment higher bond yields pose an additional risk to the personal sector, as they threaten to prick the property bubble. The resilience of the personal sector in the current downturn is to a large extent due to huge profits in the property market that have more than offset the losses in financial markets in the last three years. However, the price of these profits from the property market has been a continuous accumulation of household debt. Falling bond yields, as a result of the deflation of the last three years have fuelled the property bubble, and have encouraged the surge in household debt. Low bond yields have made easier the debt service, but this may become a problem in 2005 if economic growth increased in 2004. In fact, the more buoyant the growth in 2004 is, the softer the economy will be in 2005. Consumption will not be the only victim in 2005 of higher bond yields. The corporate sector debt is still very high, in spite of a small decline in 2003. Higher bond yields would cause deep cuts in investment. The extent to which bond yields will rise with the boom of 2004, depends to some extent on monetary policy. Its objective is to moderate the rise in bond yields by being accommodative. The Fed has threatened to buy government bonds of various maturities, if bond yields rose sharply.

A recent study by McConnell *et al.* (2003) downplays the danger of pricking the property bubble. The argument for the possibility of pricking the bubble rests on the premise that the pace of mortgage refinancing reached a record level in 2003. Refinancing, therefore, enabled borrowers to take on new mortgages for larger amounts than the loans paid off. This extracted equity boosted household spending in general and property spending in particular. As the refinancing comes to an end and interest rates begin to rise, this household ability is eroded and a significant retrenchment in household spending would ensue. The study by McConnell *et al.* (op. cit.) suggests that this is unlikely to materialise because 'households are quite sensibly using low-cost, tax-advantaged mortgage debt to make many of the same purchases that they otherwise would have financed by drawing down their financial assets or incurring non-mortgage debt' (p. 2). Indeed, the authors argue that over this period there has been 'a slowing in the rate of increase of non-mortgage household liabilities, an increase in the personal saving rate, and a reduction in a comprehensive measure of household debt service burden relative to disposable income' (p. 2). In other words this study claims to have produced evidence that shows that since the 'aggregate household balance sheet' has not deteriorated by the boom in home equity withdrawal the danger of household retrenchment has disappeared. Recent relevant data, however, dispute rather dramatically this contention, as we believe we demonstrate strongly in Chapter 7.

5   The structure of the book and what we have achieved

Chapter 2 is devoted to the causes of the bubble and the consequences of its burst for the economy and financial markets. The bubble is compared with previous ones and the 'new economy' paradigm is analysed critically. The debate of whether monetary policy should also include asset price inflation targeting is discussed and a proposal is put forward on how this can be made possible without interfering with the free function of financial markets. In this post-bubble era, the long-term risks to the economy and financial markets stem from the fact that the current US Administration is not willing to take the risk that the economy would only be growing at the rate of potential output in 2004 as employment growth may not be robust. It is, therefore, considering yet another fiscal package to stimulate the economy in the run up to the presidential election. Although such package would ensure that the economy is booming at the time of the election, it will raise long-term interest rates even more and will foster the forces that would ultimately weaken investment in 2005 and beyond. High long-term interest rates may also prick the property bubble and weaken consumption. In the face of a slowing economy and high bond yields equity prices would dissipate rapidly.

To analyse these risks and assess them quantitatively we must first evaluate the conduct of monetary policy. The extent to which inflation will rise in the next two years will ultimately determine the degree of monetary tightening. This is one of the reasons Chapter 3 is devoted to wages and prices. Allegedly the Fed policy actions affect inflation with a long lag of approximately two years. It is this consideration that has led us to choose a two-year horizon in analysing the prospects and risks to the economy and financial markets. Inflationary pressures can be gauged before they surface on Consumer Price Index-inflation (CPI-inflation) by examining producer prices of finished goods, intermediate supplies and crude material prices. The latter are influenced by commodity prices and the price of oil. Moreover, the labour cost is the most important determinant of producer prices. This, in turn depends on employment wages and productivity. Hence, an assessment of future inflationary trends requires an analysis of the whole wage–price nexus. But there are two more reasons why we study inflationary pressures thoroughly in Chapter 3. First, wages and prices determine the pricing power of companies, profit margins and overall corporate profitability, which affect investment and equity prices. Second, inflation is also a major determinant of bond yields.

Chapter 3 shows that with steady growth around potential output over the next two years inflation will dissipate for most part of 2004, but will rise sharply in 2005. With faster than potential output growth in 2004, but slower in 2005, inflation will remain muted. For reasons explained in that chapter the Fed would have to tighten more aggressively with slow growth than with fast growth.

The inflationary pressures and the likely conduct of monetary policy set the scene for the rest of the developments in the economy and financial markets. Chapter 4 analyses thoroughly corporate profitability by breaking it down into unit profit, volume of sales and profit margin. Corporate profitability depends on the entire wage–price sector and in the simulations conducted to assess the risk the profit model is run simultaneously with the wage–price model. Profits are a major determinant of investment and equity prices. Chapter 4 shows that profits are likely to decelerate from their torrid pace at the end of 2003. The rate of deceleration, though, depends on the pace of job creation. If confidence in the economy continued to be high and companies relaxed and hired many people, which is what the current Administration wants, then profit margins would decelerate rapidly and this would pose long-term risks to investment, the economy as a whole, and equities. The faster the growth in 2004 is, the greater the risk that the economy will soften substantially in 2005. From this point of view easy fiscal policy in 2004 is not desirable as it involves the risk of a boom and bust mini cycle. Easy fiscal policy in the upswing of the cycle is most likely to be destabilising the economy and the equity market.

Chapter 5 is devoted to the analysis of investment. Corporate profits as well as wages and prices are key determinants to investment and hence the analysis of the previous two chapters is pertinent. However, in addition, industrial production, capacity utilisation, interest rates and expectations, what Keynes called 'animal spirits', play a significant role in investment decisions. A full model that incorporates these additional factors is presented and analysed in order to assess the prospects and risks of investment. Therefore, the investment model is simulated simultaneously with the wage–price model and profit model to assess quantitatively the prospects and risks of investment. Investment plays a key role in business cycle analysis and any long-term weakness of the economy, and decline in equity prices, is likely to come from investment. The conclusion of this chapter is that fast growth in 2004 will pose long-term risks to investment. Therefore, this provides yet another reason of why another fiscal package in 2004 may be undesirable and destabilising to the economy and equity prices.

Chapters 6 and 7 focus on the consumer. Chapter 6 analyses the housing market and residential investment, an important component of personal sector wealth. The role of the housing market in contributing to the consumer resilience in the aftermath of the bubble is analysed thoroughly. A model of the housing market is then presented that enables the quantification of the prospects and long-term risks of the housing market. Chapter 6 shows that long-term interest rates are the single most important determinant of the housing market; thus the importance of running the housing market model simultaneously with the wage–price model. Chapter 6 reinforces the argument that fast growth in 2004 poses risks to the housing market. This risk is exacerbated if the excessive growth stems from yet another fiscal package, as long-term interest rates are likely to increase more than otherwise.

Chapter 7 is devoted to consumption, which is the biggest component of demand in the economy. The fortunes of households depend on the corporate sector and fiscal as well as monetary policy. Consumer decisions on how much to spend depend on wages, employment, inflation, taxes and subsidies, interest rates, the net wealth of the personal sector, unemployment and confidence. Hence, the analysis of all previous chapters is important in analysing consumption. A full model of consumption is presented and is run simultaneously with all other models to assess the prospects and long-term risks of consumption. The conclusion that emerges in the preceding chapters is again reinforced, namely that fast growth in 2004 poses long-term risks to consumption, and especially if that growth emanates from easy fiscal policy.

Chapter 8 is devoted to export demand as another determinant of growth in the economy. This involves an analysis of the world economy, which we highlight by considering the role of a US-led world recovery. This chapter investigates the determinants of exports in the euro area and Japan and the feedback to US. Competitiveness plays an important role in exports and the chapter analyses its gains and losses and the consequences for G-3 exports. Strong growth in the US in 2004 is likely to boost exports in the rest of the world, including the euro area, and despite serious losses in the latter's competitiveness. The chapter concludes that a US-led world recovery would boost US exports, scant evidence of which emerged with the release of the fourth quarter NIPA data, rather late to be taken into account not only in this chapter but in the entire book. Strong US exports further diminish the need for yet another fiscal package to boost the economy. Chapter 9 considers the implications of the economy for the dollar. Both a theoretical and an empirical model are put forward to analyse the dollar trends. The theoretical model is based on earlier work by one of us, which emphasises the role of the US as a leader in a game theoretic framework. This framework provides new insights for dollar trends. It asserts that none of the variables of the small open economy model or the two-country model are relevant in the dollar determination. The empirical model is based on the theoretical model and is part of the K-Model that predicted in 2002 the collapse of the dollar in the last two years.

The analysis of all previous chapters culminates into an investigation of the prospects and long-term risks of the bond and equity markets in Chapter 10. The models for bonds and equities are presented in some detail so that the reader can appreciate how they are expected to perform and why. But the emphasis is again on the risks to financial markets from fast growth in 2004. With growth at around potential output, bond yields are likely to rise gently in 2004, but sharply in 2005 to the critical levels that threaten to tumble the property market. Such accident, though, is likely to happen at the end of 2005 or beyond the period of analysis of the current study. With fast growth, bond yields will remain lower throughout the two-year period and the housing market may be spared from a collapse. This may look as a good excuse for yet another fiscal package. Unfortunately, with fast growth the benefits to the housing market may be offset by yet another tumble of the equity market.

6 The macroeconomic model employed for the purposes of the book

In pursuing the objectives of the book we make a great deal of use of a macro-econometric model, which is utilised throughout the book. This has been developed by one of us (Elias Karakitsos; the model is referred to in the book as the K-Model) and its essentials are summarised in the book as appropriate. The K-Model is a proprietary model that depicts the interaction of the macro economy with financial markets, in particular, money, bonds, equities and foreign currency for the US.

As just mentioned the K-Model has been developed and perfected by Professor Elias Karakitsos during the last thirty years or so, and, in its various forms, it has been used to provide advice to HM Treasury, the House of Commons, the European Commission, the Brookings Institution and major financial institutions such as, Citibank, Allianz, Oppenheimer, Credit Agricole, Standard Chartered, Abbey National, Kredit Bank, Nestle Pension

Funds and corporations such as, British Airways. Interested readers wishing to obtain more and specific details, in addition to what is explained throughout this book, of the K-Model should contact Elias Karakitsos (e-mail: ekarakitsos@economicresearch.us).

The estimated relationships of the K-Model are well specified with satisfactory statistics/diagnostics. The model structure is stable in that it is capable of explaining with relatively great precision the behaviour of investment in the span of the last 50 years that includes 10 business cycles and over 600 monthly observations. This is remarkable because five of these cycles are demand-led; three of them are supply-led, while the last two are related to serious imbalances in the corporate sector.

2
The Causes and Consequences of the Post-'New Economy' Bubble

1 Introduction

On 26 November 2001 the National Bureau of Economic Research declared that the US economy's recession had begun in March 2001. The expansion had lasted for ten years and it was one of the longest ever recorded by any industrialised country. In the fourth quarter of 1999 the US growth rate reached 7%, the highest in the 1990s. Unemployment fell to a 30-year low (3.9% by April 2000), the rate of inflation was low (averaged 2.5% throughout the whole of 1990s), faster growth in productivity was recorded, and faster growth in real wages. All these factors helped to reduce poverty and stabilise wage inequality (Temple, 2002). More recent data (see Council of Economic Advisors, 2004, table A33), though, reveal that this is true only for the years 1998–2001. The stock market also produced massive gains, so that by the late 1990s the price/earnings ratios reached record levels in the whole of the twentieth century. Every year between 1995 and 1999 the US stock exchange Standard and Poor's Composite Index (S&P 500) produced an annualised total return (including dividends) over 20%. By the end of that period, the performance of the stock market was concentrated in the stocks of large companies and of growth companies (those that had been delivering strong growth in earnings per share and were expected to continue to do so), especially so in the areas of Technology, Media and Telecommunications (TMT). The Nasdaq Composite Index, which was a heavy representative in technology shares, reached the level of 2000 for the first time during 1998 and peaked to 5048 on 10 March 2000.

The years 1998–2000 experienced internet euphoria. Indeed, by 1998 the internet share bubble had become a mania (Lee, 2004, p. 11; see, also, Schiller, 2000, who identifies the internet phenomenon as the main factor of the US stock market mania). The success of the US was the envy of the rest of the world. Politicians around the world were urging their governments and people to follow the US example. But in less than two years after the peak of the business cycle had been reached in 1999, the US economy went into recession and dragged the rest of the world into it. The collapse of the stock market beginning March 2000 caused the optimism that had surrounded the 'new economy' to be followed by pessimism.

The mania to which we have just referred was not confined to the US only. It had spread around the world. By the end of the mania, it was actually more extreme outside the US, and some of the valuations achieved by companies in the stock market were even more far reaching (Lee, 2004). An interesting characteristic of the 1990s financial bubble is that it incorporated not merely the US stock market, but also the global stock market and later on the bond markets. Its impact on wealth (in the form of financial market capitalisation) probably represented the greatest financial mania in monetary history. Its international dimension was far reaching. It was a truly 'global bubble', in as much as it affected all financial markets of the world. The reaction of the monetary authorities to the burst of the bubble, in the US in particular and to a lesser extent in the rest of the world, was unparalleled in world monetary history in that they reacted aggressively and preemptively, slashing interest rates to historically low levels.[1]

The purpose of this chapter is to investigate the causes of the burst of that bubble and its consequences. It is also to examine whether targeting asset prices might avoid bubbles.

2   The 'new economy'

Those developments produced what one might label as the 'new economy' with its own rules, different from what had been conventionally known. In this 'new paradigm' opportunities for growth, particularly in the TMT industry were thought to be limitless. This 'new economy' was based on the premise that its composition comprised services, essentially information which became more important than physical commodities such as steel and copper. Tevlin and Whelan (2002) report that growth in real equipment investment over the period 1992–98 averaged 11.2% a year, due essentially to soaring investment in computers. Indeed, Oliner and Sichel (2000) and Stiroh (2002), amongst others, refer to the business investment in computers and related equipment. The former note that it rose more than fourfold between 1995 and 1999, while the latter suggests that US firms invested more than $2.4 trillion in information technology related assets.

A further important characteristic was that of increasing returns to scale, given that in the knowledge- and information-based economy the cost of producing more units of a given output is very small after the initial investment is undertaken. But above all it was the unexpected acceleration of productivity growth in the mid-1990s that can be construed as the most important characteristic of the 'new economy' (see, also, Temple, 2002). Using growth accounting the contribution of Information and Communication (ICT) capital (it includes computer hardware, software and telecommunications equipment) to productivity growth can be assessed. Temple (2002) provides a summary of studies that have undertaken this exercise. The overall conclusion of this study is that a substantial increase in the contribution of ICT investment to aggregate growth took place, and that 'the production and adoption of ICT can account for most of the acceleration in labour productivity growth between the first and second halves of the 1990s' (p. 248).

Low inflation and falling unemployment are two further characteristics of considerable significance over the period. This, however, appears to be an interesting puzzle about the 'new economy'. How can low and stable inflation be associated with unemployment rates that would normally make rising inflation inevitable? By the beginning of 2000 inflation was at 3.3% and unemployment at 4%. The latter was, in fact, below the 'consensus' estimate of the Non Accelerating Inflation Rate of Unemployment (NAIRU) by about 2 percentage points. Inflation should have been accelerating and monetary policy should have been aggressively tightening. By contrast, the Federal Reserve System (Fed) held interest rates steady. US monetary policy authorities resorted to the 1990s productivity growth to justify a 'loose' rather than a 'tight' policy. Greenspan (2004a) is very explicit on the matter: 'As a consequence of the improving trend in structural productivity growth that was apparent from 1995 forward, we at the Fed were able to be much more accommodative to the rise in economic growth than our past experiences would have deemed prudent. We were motivated, in part, by the view that the evident structural economic changes rendered suspect, at best, the prevailing notion in the early 1990s of an elevated and reasonably stable NAIRU. Those views were reinforced as inflation continued to fall in the context of a declining unemployment rate that by 2000 had dipped below 4 per cent in the United States for the first time in three decades' (p. 3). However important that recognition was for the policy stance of the Fed, productivity growth in itself cannot explain the behaviour of inflation and unemployment at the time. A challenge for the adherents of NAIRU thereby emerged, as Greenspan (2004a) makes clear in the quote just cited. A number of explanations were inevitably put forward. Favourable supply shocks, a decline in the NAIRU, unexpected productivity growth, or a combination of all these factors have been proposed (see e.g., Temple, 2002, for a brief summary, p. 251).

The 'globalised' world economy was another important dimension of the 'new economy'. National economies became interdependent with companies being able to sell into a competitive world economy. In such an economy, the growth potential could be said to be limitless and the 'perfect' nature of competition should not allow inflation to materialise given that 'pricing power' weakened substantially. With inflation being conquered, the possibility of recessions disappeared because no longer would inflation tend to get out of control once economic growth was sustained for some time. The rise in productivity that the TMT supposedly made possible, should have resulted in profit share rising. This, however, could not possibly have materialised in view of the substantially weakened 'price power'. If anything it was higher labour productivity that emerged, which increased real wages rather than the profit share.

In terms of the policy contribution to the 'new economy', Greenspan (2000) distinguishes between the effects of monetary and fiscal policy. In terms of monetary policy he suggests that although it 'did not produce the intellectual insights behind the technological advances that have been responsible for the recent phenomenal reshaping of our economic landscape', it has, nonetheless, 'been instrumental ... in establishing a stable financial and economic environment with low inflation that is conducive to the investments that have exploited these innovative technologies' (p. 3). Fiscal policy also played a crucial role: 'The emergence of surpluses in the unified budget and of the associated increase in government saving over the past few years has been exceptionally important to the balance of the expansion, because the surpluses have been absorbing a portion of the potential excess of demand over sustainable supply associated partly with the wealth effect.[2] Moreover, because the surpluses are augmenting the pool of domestic saving, they have held interest rates below the levels that otherwise would have been needed to achieve financial and economic balance during this period of exceptional economic growth. They have, in effect, helped to finance and sustain the productive private investment that has been key to capturing the benefits of the newer technologies that, in turn, have boosted the long-term growth potential of the U.S. economy' (p. 3). It is implicit in Greenspan's argument that if the surpluses had not reduced demand, the Fed might have raised interest rates to cool the economy down. Indeed, and more recently, Greenspan (2004a) claimed victory in the Fed's battle to limit the damage from the burst of the stock market bubble. The claim focuses on the observation that 'There appears to be enough evidence, at least tentatively, to conclude that our strategy of addressing the bubble's consequences rather than the bubble itself has been successful. Despite the stock market plunge, terrorist attacks, corporate scandals, and wars in Afghanistan and Iraq, we experienced an exceptionally mild recession – even milder than that of a decade earlier ... much of the ability of the U.S. economy to absorb these consequences of shocks resulted from notably improved structural flexibility. But highly aggressive monetary policy ease was doubtless also a significant contributor to stability' (p. 4).

There are strong doubts, however, about the 'new economy' paradigm. Critics claim that there has been no big increase in trend economic growth; this has certainly not been the case globally and perhaps not even in the US. What actually happened was that the financial asset mania suppressed inflation in the US, thereby enabling the business cycle expansion, and the accompanying cyclical upswing in productivity, to be sustained for a longer time period, making what in effect was a cyclical phenomenon look like a secular shift (Lee, 2004). Gordon (2000) expresses similar doubts in his observation that the productivity gains of the 1990s may be temporary. Furthermore, there is no guarantee that inflation will remain low either. Given that there was no productivity acceleration outside the manufacturing sector (although non-manufacturing sector companies were often intensive users of ICT), a great deal of doubt is, in fact, cast on the 'new economy' model. A further blow to the 'new economy' model was the stock market mania, which actually received a great deal of media attention. By 2002, however, the stock market fell substantially so that the 'new economy' optimism disappeared. Indeed, the supporters of the 'new economy' model have been proved wrong!

While it is true that there is some support for the argument that there was no productivity miracle and no increase in potential output growth in the 1990s, in reality the truth may be somewhere in between. TMT produced some productivity gains, especially in the non-manufacturing sector (mainly services), and probably raised potential output growth from 2.2% in the 1980s business cycle to 3%–3.5% in the 1990s cycle. With hindsight potential output growth was 3.1% measured from peak to peak of the cycle (i.e. between 1989 and 2000). The advocates of the new economy paradigm have argued that improved productivity raised potential output growth to 4% or even 6%.

In fact, equity prices fell continuously between March 2000 and the beginning of 2003. That bear market resembles the mid-1970s plunge in equity prices in magnitude. But it differs in terms of the causes, and consequently with respect to the factors that should be monitored to test its progress. In the 1970s, soaring inflation was the reason for the bear market due to the surge in the price of oil. It eroded households' real disposable income and corporate profits. That was a supply-led business cycle. Now, the bear market is caused by asset and debt deflation triggered by the burst of the 'new economy' bubble.

The 2001 recession was very mild, as it was caused by the inventory correction associated with the burst of the 'new economy' bubble. Although with current economic fundamentals based on quarterly data up to the fourth quarter of 2003 the Standard and Poor (S&P) index may be fairly valued (see Table 10.2, Chapter 10) the fair value may fall if the economy moves into a situation, which triggers a property market crash. This may very well happen if interest rates rise. Then poor prospects in the corporate sector may materialise that might affect the real disposable income of the personal sector. The forces that may drive the economy to that situation are related to imbalances in the corporate and personal sectors that they might start infecting the balance sheet of the commercial banks. The final stage of this process involves a spiral between banks and non-bank private sector (personal and corporate). Banks cut lending to the non-bank private sector (credit crunch) that worsens the economic health of the latter, which is reflected subsequently as a further deterioration of the balance sheet of the banks. As the income of the personal sector falls households find it increasingly difficult to service their debt. House repossessions soar as the recession deepens. Similarly, companies cannot service their debt as profits plunge. Banks respond to this adverse development by cutting on new lending (credit crunch) and the liquidity that the central bank injects into the economy fails to reach the ultimate borrowers (what Keynes called the liquidity trap).

3   The bubble and its aftermath

In the course of 1999 fears of a recession following the SE Asian and the Russian crisis in 1997–98 were quickly dispelled and the US economy grew stronger than in the whole of the 1990s. The corporate sector was in a spending spree on IT, in the hope of huge productivity gains that would allow profits to grow even stronger. The personal sector was in an even stronger spending spree, buying houses, cars and other durable goods, as well as services as if there was no tomorrow. The Fed started tightening monetary policy in the middle of 1999 for fear that this huge growth might rekindle inflation. But the Fed move was mainly pre-emptive, as inflation remained tamed, and a soft landing in 2001 had been predicted, meaning a cooling down of the economy to more sustainable rates of growth that would prolong the business cycle and allow prosperity to continue without the threat of inflation. But the economy refused to slow down and the Fed continued to tighten with the Fed Funds rate rising from 4.75% to 6.5%. However, once the economy started responding to the high level of interest rates it decelerated sharply and the pace gathered steam. In the first quarter of 2001 the economy fell into recession. Not only interest rates but also the price of oil contributed to the recession. The price of oil soared from less than $10 per barrel at the end of 1998 to more than $35 in August 2000. The rise in oil price eroded both the income of households and the profits of the corporate sector and accelerated the downswing.

The first signs of strain appeared in manufacturing with a build-up of inventories of unsold goods, in particular durables. The manufacturing sector responded in the second half of 2000 by cutting production, shedding labour and slashing investment expenditure. Services continued to be buoyant and consumer spending remained resilient giving rise to hopes that the soft landing was on target. However, in spite of the huge efforts of the corporate sector to reduce their unwanted stocks the inventories-to-sales ratio continued to rise as sales fell faster than inventories. In the first quarter of 2001 the weakness in manufacturing, instead of having been contained, spread to other sectors of the economy and the NBER officially declared in November the beginning of the recession in March 2001.

What is puzzling in this story is that the economy fell into recession because of excess inventories. This had not been the cause of a recession in the previous fifty years. But the overhang of inventories was only the symptom of the recession, not the cause. The true cause was the burst of the Nasdaq (technology) bubble in March 2000. The technology miracle that promised so many hopes and gave so much prosperity between 1994 and 2000 simply collapsed. The budget surplus of the period 1997–2001 may have caused relevant problems, of course. To the extent that it reduced non-government savings, it may have caused severe problems to the credit structure of the system, thereby promoting the bursting of the bubble.

The problem with the Nasdaq bubble was the ever increasing gap between what is technologically feasible that captures the imagination of the stock market and the harsh reality of the slow adjustment of change in consumer habits. IT companies invested and created the capacity as if all people were to shop from the internet, talk on mobiles with all people around the world all day long and do things that people could not even dream about in less than a decade ago. All of a sudden everything that one could imagine was technologically feasible and companies offered it as if everyone was ready to change their way of lives. Before one generation of telecom was utilised, another was ready to take its place.

It does not mean that the technology would never be used. With time, the economy, the consumer and the society's habits would adapt and the technology would be fully utilised. The dream of the new society where technology would play centre role would become a reality, but it will take a long time. The daydreamers thought that all this change would take place overnight. Internet companies mushroomed and their stock market value soared. Investors adopted the dream and priced such companies as if the dream had become a reality. Unfortunately, most internet companies were making losses, but they held the promise of making profits in the future. For as long as the corporate spending growth on equipment and software carried on increasing the promise of future profitability of internet companies was kept alive. But in March 2000 (after the 2000 computer debug was over) the corporate sector cut drastically its expenditure on equipment and software and with it was lost the dream that the internet companies would ever become profitable. The Nasdaq bubble had been pricked!

The harsh reality is that every bubble is the same. The bubble is always created by an event that changes permanently future profitability. Every discovery that changed permanently future profitability resulted in a bubble. The bubble was always fuelled by credit that allowed the finance of the dream. But in every case the bubble burst because the discovery is not made in a vacuum. For the discovery to be fully exploited the overall economy needs time to adapt and the society's habits need time to change. From this point of view the technology bubble is not different from the railway or canal bubble.

The effects of the burst of a bubble are also qualitatively the same. As asset prices (stock prices, property and land prices) fall the corporate and/or the personal sector are left with huge debts that must be serviced and ultimately repaid. These debts are accumulated when optimism is running high and asset prices are soaring, as in the Nasdaq case, and reflect the perception of the permanent improvement in corporate profitability. Companies are not worried in accumulating debt and banks and investors are not worried in granting the loans or investing in the companies when the corporate expenditure is thought profitable. But because it takes time for the economy and the society habits to adapt to the new environment the expenditure is never profitable in the short run; and if the government budget is in surplus it deteriorates the whole process. The tragic economic consequences of the burst of a bubble are always positively related to the debt level that was accumulated in the rosy years of the expansion. The picture was very different in 1987 when the fiscal deficit helped to prevent similar consequences. The 1987 crash was different in that there was sufficient spending to keep the real economy afloat; indeed, there was enough financial equity to support the credit structure.

There have been three episodes of an asset and debt deflation caused recession in the nineteenth and twentieth centuries.[3] The Great Depression of 1876–90 (associated with the railway bubble), the Depression of 1929–40 (associated with the electricity and automobile bubble) and the deflation of Japan that started in 1989 and has not yet finished (associated with electronics). The current asset and debt deflation is associated with the telecommunications and internet bubble. In all these cases the process of eliminating the serious imbalances associated with the burst of the bubble took a long time, over a decade. As the recent experience of Japan shows, in a secular bear market there are sharp, but short-lived, rallies that give rise to false hopes of an end of the bear market. In an asset and debt deflation environment the non-bank private sector retrenches, as its huge debt, acquired in the rosy years of rising asset prices, is inconsistent with falling asset prices. The process of reducing debt through saving and curtailing spending is long causing a secular bear equity market. This is exactly what happened in the US recently.

The pre-bubble stock market mania produced a huge increase in investment, and a sharp decline in private savings (helped by the government surplus). Historically, the personal and non-financial business sectors in the US (the bulk of the private sector) had not run a deficit until the 1990s (US governments, not all of them, had run deficits; see Arestis et al., 2004); subsequently their financial balance plunged into huge deficit. By 2001, the financial balance of the corporate sector had reached its lowest level over the entire previous fifty years. Thereafter, the corporate sector financial balance turned into a surplus, as a result of corporate restructuring (see Figure 2.1). One important implication of this imbalance was the creation of an enormous build-up of debt within the economy. By 2003, total private debt reached a level equivalent to one-and-a-half times GDP, compared to roughly equal to GDP in the early 1980s (see *Flow of Funds Accounts of the*

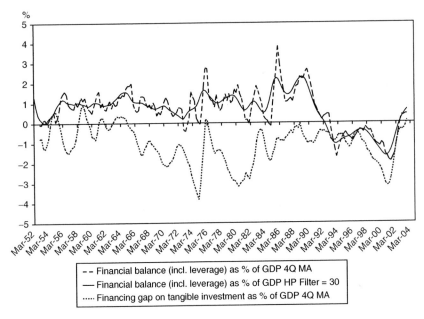

Figure 2.1 Corporate sector financial balance on tangible only and tangible and financial investment

United States, Federal Reserve System, October 2003). Another significant imbalance is the US current account deficit, which has recently reached over 5% of GDP on an annual basis (and by now it is showing little sign of improvement). This has been financed by the huge inflow of capital from overseas, emanating from the desire to save in dollar denominated assets by non-US residents – which resulted in a flood of cheap imports. A staggering $47 billion inflow is needed per month to finance this deficit (although one might suggest that this is how much the overseas sector has to export to meet its savings desire). The relevant monthly average figure for the first eight months in 2003 was $59 billion, actually up from $47.9 billion in 2002. But it slumped in September and October, 2003, to $4.3 billion and $27.8 billion, respectively, thereby falling significantly below the threshold of $47 billion. However, the November and December 2003 figures jumped to $87.5 billion and $75.7 billion, respectively (data from the monthly report of the US Treasury, as reported in *Financial Times*, 18 February 2004).

The US bond market behaviour is relevant to our discussion. The US, and other government, bond markets suffered in 1999 as the internet boom entered its most frenzied phase and the Fed began to raise interest rates. When the equity bubble burst took place, bonds appreciated as investors switched out of equities into bonds. So much so that the argument has been put forward that a complete collapse of the equity market is unlikely so long as the bond market performs strongly (Warburton, 1999). This is possible when central banks keep interest rates low, so that large investors and hedge funds can borrow short term to fund positions in long-term debt.

It may be fruitful to look at the standard income identity as a way of summarising the argument so far:

$$(S - I) + (T - G) = (X - Q)$$

where S is savings, I is investment, T is taxes, G is government expenditure, X is exports and Q is imports. It suggests that the surplus of the private sector, that is the personal sector and the corporate sector combined (S − I), plus the surplus of the government sector (T − G), should always be equal to the foreign sector surplus (X − Q). The equity bear market was accompanied by a sharp fall in investment, so that the corporate sector's deficit was thereby corrected to a significant degree, although it is doubtful whether this correction is yet sufficient. The personal sector deficit has also improved slightly, but it remains a long way from its historic large surpluses. So (S − I) is still in deficit. The government sector (T − G) has turned from surplus to a deeper, so that (X − Q) has also moved into deficit; this, of course, shows the deficiency of savings for the economy as a whole.[4]

In principle, five possible solutions to the problem suggest themselves: (i) a decline in the stock market of sufficient magnitude; (ii) a severe recession in the economy; (iii) a major fall in the dollar exchange rate (in excess of 30 %); (iv) a proactively large government deficit; and (v) a combination of the four factors to which we have just alluded. The first two along with the fourth is the result of insufficient aggregate demand due to a small government deficit that fails to accommodate the savings desires of the domestic and foreign sectors. The third possibility happens when the foreign sector tries to spend rather than save its dollar holdings, which would also tend to increase US aggregate demand.

The inevitable conclusion is then that the US financial bubble exacerbated imbalances in the economy: namely, excessive debt, deficient savings and a growing external imbalance. The financial bubble encourages stronger domestic demand, but it does not encourage necessarily stronger overseas demand. In the ballooning of the bubble the currency may be strengthened by capital inflow attracted by the bubble-boosted returns on domestic assets, but the deterioration in the balance-of-payments trade and current accounts is not sustainable indefinitely, unless, of course, the foreign sector wishes to accumulate US dollar denominated assets indefinitely. Ultimately, though, it is conceivable that the foreign sector may not wish to carry on accumulating US dollar denominated assets. Indeed, 'given the already-substantial accumulation of dollar-denominated debt, foreign investors, both private and official, may become less willing to absorb ever-growing claims on U.S. residents' (Greenspan, 2004b, p. 6). In a general sense, the currency would then fall. Just as the financial bubble was the cause of the (real) dollar exchange rate appreciation, due to investment being higher relative to savings which drew capital into the US, its bursting should be expected to lead to (real) dollar depreciation. But still, there is the question of why the dollar has not depreciated even more than hitherto, as the bubble has been unwinding.[5] Three reasons suggest themselves:

- the global nature of the asset bubble and foreign central bank reaction to its unwinding. The asset bubble was, of course, global in nature. Central banks outside the US also accommodated the financial bubble. However, in the US the monetary authority response was a great deal more aggressive than elsewhere. In the short run, this supports the dollar because of the impression that the European economies are faring no better than the US. In the long run it means that the 'day of reckoning' is merely postponed.
- foreign government and central bank support of the dollar. The bank of Japan has been intervening in the foreign exchange market in an attempt to prevent the yen from appreciating; the other Asian central banks have been accumulating foreign reserves, mostly dollars (the Chinese central bank in particular) and US Treasuries in an attempt to manage their exchange rates against the dollar.
- the exceptionally aggressive easing in US fiscal policy. The federal budget turned from a surplus equivalent to 2.3% of GDP in 2000(1Q), when we had the stock market peak, to a deficit of 4.2% of the GDP by 2003(2Q), a massive swing of 6.5% of GDP. Higher government deficit has been adding to private savings, domestic and overseas; but still government deficit is not enough to meet savings desires. It would appear that the US desired saving rate is short relative to desired investment, and this may be a factor that mitigates the fall in the dollar exchange rate.

The issues raised in this section are dealt with in what follows in the book. More precisely, though, in terms of the three 'reasons' to which we have just alluded a whole chapter is devoted to it, where a different theoretical explanation is put forward (Chapter 9).

4   Should asset prices be controlled?

In this section we examine the possibility of targeting net wealth as a means of avoiding booms and busts of bubbles. This is particularly pertinent in view of the argument advanced in this book (see, Chapter 6 later) that the bubble is still there, with the vestiges of the mania remaining in the stock market, while the force of the bubble has moved to the government bond market, and to the property market in particular.

4.1   Asset price inflation and bubbles

The standard argument in terms of asset price control is that asset price inflation (the percentage yearly change in equity prices, house prices or land prices) is out of the realm of central banks, as it reflects market forces and any control is widely regarded as infringing with the principles of the free market economy, or, indeed, it is the result of 'irrational exuberance'. Bernanke and Gertler (2000) argue that trying to stabilise asset prices is problematic, essentially because it is uncertain whether a given change in asset values results from fundamental or non-fundamental factors or both. In this thesis, proactive monetary policy would require the authorities to outperform market participants. Inflation targeting in this view is what is important, where policy should not respond to changes in asset prices. Clews (2002) argues along similar lines, and concludes that asset price movements 'rarely give simple unequivocal messages for policy on their own' so that they are 'unlikely to be suitable as intermediate targets for a policy whose main aim is to control inflation' (p. 185). Greenspan (2002a) argues that the size of the change in the rate of interest to prick a bubble may be substantial and harmful to the real economy.[6]

Yet the experience of many countries, including of course the US during the period under investigation, shows that successful control of Consumer Price Index-inflation (CPI-inflation) does not guarantee low asset price inflation. When asset price inflation gets out of control bubbles are built and while they grow they generate a lot of euphoria. But bubbles ultimately burst with devastating consequences not only for the investors in the stock markets, but also for the economy as a whole. The experience of the last twenty years shows that the adverse consequences of the burst of a bubble hit not only weak economies, but also strong economies such as the US and Japan. Goodhart's (2001) suggestion, based on Alchian and Klein (1973), that central banks should considerhousing prices and, to a lesser extent, stock market prices in their policy decisions, is very pertinent.

Targeting is possible through interest rates, exactly as in the case of CPI-inflation, by monitoring and targeting the implications of asset prices on the spending patterns of consumers and companies. The variable that lends itself as a primary candidate for monitoring and control of asset price inflation is the net wealth of the private sector. Net wealth is defined as the assets less the liabilities of the personal sector. Assets include both financial and tangible. Financial assets include deposits, bonds and equities. Tangible assets include real estate and consumer durable goods. The liabilities of the personal sector include all forms of debt, mortgage, as well as, consumer credit for all other purposes. Although in the short run the ratio of net wealth to disposable income can fluctuate widely, in the long run it is trendless, as it shows the number of years it takes for households to buy a house and build financial wealth that would finance consumption for the rest of their lives and to leave bequests to their heirs. This ratio can neither be on an upward nor downward trend in the long run, as it would imply intergenerational changes in savings habits. Net wealth as percent of disposable income is mean reverting.[7] It is this mean reverting property of net wealth that allows the detection (or monitoring) of bubbles.

The reason that net wealth is such an ideal variable to monitor (and, perhaps, control) bubbles is that it is at the heart of the transmission mechanism of asset prices and debt to consumption. This is the underlying rationale. In the very long run consumption and real disposable income are growing at the same rate so that the ratio of consumption to income (the *average propensity to consume*) is equal to unity. But in the short run consumption can deviate substantially from income. In the Permanent Income–Life Cycle Hypothesis consumers save in good years and tap on these savings in bad years. Hence, the savings ratio (savings as per cent of disposable income) moves pro-cyclically, it rises in booms and falls in recessions. The validity of this relationship has been questioned (see, e.g. Frowen and Karakitsos, 1996). The argument is that in a leveraged economy the savings ratio moves counter-cyclically (i.e. it falls in a boom and rises in a recession). In boom years asset prices rise faster than usual as consumers borrow against these assets to invest even more (leveraging). Faster than usual rising asset prices make people feel rich inducing them to relax on their effort to save as they believe that they are in a better position to meet their desired levels of savings (e.g. provide for pension, leave to their heirs). Hence, the savings ratio falls in a boom. In a recession asset prices fall and people are left with an overhang of debt. In order to repay their debt people cut on consumption out of current income and intensify on their effort to save in order to rebuild their wealth. Hence, the savings ratio increases in a recession. The counter-cyclical behaviour of the savings ratio, which is a characteristic of leveraged economies, aggravates the adverse consequences on the economy of the boom and bust of bubbles. In the short run, therefore, consumption depends on real disposable income and the savings ratio. The long run forces that determine the savings ratio are net wealth and uncertainty about job security and income growth prospects (see, Chapter 7). For these reasons, a rise in net wealth lowers the savings ratio and vice versa. An increase in uncertainty about job security and income growth prospects makes people more cautious inducing them to refrain from spending out of current income, thereby raising the savings ratio.

During the bubble years in the second half of the 1990s net wealth rose to unprecedented levels and the savings ratio reached rock bottom at the peak of the bubble (see Chapter 6 for the relevant details). As equity prices declined steadily for three years after the burst of the bubble net wealth fell, a whisker from its long-term average of 482% in September 2002, while the savings ratio increased to 4.3% in November 2002. This rise in the savings ratio reflects increased cautiousness on the part of consumers in the face of falling asset prices with undiminished debt. Table 6.1 (Chapter 6) shows the changes in personal sector wealth since the burst of the equity bubble. Net wealth peaked in March 2000 at $43.5 trillion or 625% of disposable income and bottomed at $38.4 trillion or 488% of disposable income in September 2002, as equity prices plunged. The loss in net wealth between the peak and the trough of the equity bubble is $5.1 trillion or 137% of disposable income. The equity market rally since the end of the Iraq war has moderated these losses to $2.2 trillion or 115% of disposable income by the end of the second quarter of 2003 (the latest quarter for which data is available).

These shifts in net wealth obscure the risk of replacing the equity with the property bubble. Table 6.1 (Chapter 6) shows the breakdown of net wealth into its constituent components. By the end of the second quarter of 2003 the losses in total assets (defined as tangible and financial) between the peak and the trough of the bubble had been completely offset. However, this is entirely due to the gains in tangible assets (mainly property), which exactly offset the losses in financial assets. Households, though, have continued to borrow heavily in the last three years of the order of $2.3 trillion or 14% of disposable income. This accounts for the deterioration in net wealth. The rate of debt accumulation in the last three years is unprecedented. There is no other three-year period, since records began in 1952, in which debt increased at such frenetic pace. The second highest rate is 10.2% of disposable income that occurred between April and September 1987, after the peak of the property market in April 1987. The rate of debt accumulation fell rapidly after the equity market crash in October 1987.

Table 6.2 (Chapter 6) shows the role of the property market in supporting consumer expenditure and cushioning the economy in its recent downturn. The boom in the residential property market has resulted in capital gains of the order of $3.4 trillion for households between the peak of the equity bubble and the second quarter of 2003. However, households continuously borrow against their property to finance consumer expenditure. Accordingly, the percentage of owner's equity in household real estate keeps falling. Between the peak of the equity bubble and the second quarter of 2003 the owner's equity in household real estate has fallen from 56.9% of disposable income to 54.3%. This represents $433 billion home equity extraction (i.e. realised capital gains), which accounts for 40% of the consumer expenditure in this period. The fiscal support to the personal sector in the form of tax cuts and other benefits account for an additional $170 billion during this period. Hence, taken together, the fiscal support and the home equity extraction account for 60% of consumer expenditure in the last three years. This explains why the consumer remained resilient throughout the recent downturn. This poses the question of what would happen if property prices were to fall. Would consumers respond by saving more and cutting down on expenditure? In this case the fall in the savings ratio is temporary and will last until the US November 2004 presidential election. It will rise in 2005 and beyond if property prices were to collapse.

4.2 Monetary policy and targeting of net wealth

For the US economy the average net wealth is around five times annual disposable income. Hence, the Fed can have a target of net wealth of five annual disposable incomes, to the extent that it has an implicit target of 2–3% for CPI-inflation. Monetary policy should be tightened as the ratio of net wealth to disposable income raises much above this threshold and vice versa. An admissible range for net wealth may be 400–550% of disposable income. This would allow asset price booms, but it would prevent them from becoming bubbles that will ultimately burst with huge adverse consequences for the economy as a whole. Tightening of monetary policy would certainly prick the bubble, as it did in the case of Japan. Only in that case the Bank of Japan raised interest rates to combat CPI-inflation. Had it done so much earlier, if it had an explicit target on net wealth, it would have prevented the ballooning of the bubble and it would have minimised the consequences of the asset and debt deflation that followed the burst of the bubble. By allowing bubbles to balloon a few people would certainly become much richer, but at the expense of the majority of people becoming poorer. Bubbles are the means through which income is redistributed within the society. Such redistribution is skewed towards the very rich. Hence, bubbles have the unpleasant effect of causing income inequality.

Tightening of monetary policy through interest rates would certainly lower asset prices – equities as well as property – through a number of channels. First, and foremost, an interest rate rise changes market expectations of future corporate profitability. When a central bank avoids stop–go policies (i.e. random swings) and, instead, changes monetary policy in a systematic and persistent way, then it affects market expectations. Investors interpret a rise in interest rates as a step in a series of hikes that would last for a long period of time. Markets, therefore, interpret tightening of monetary policy as a signal of lower growth in the future that will reduce corporate profits. Because markets act as a discounting mechanism of future events they precipitate the fall in equity prices, long before actual profits are affected, thereby helping the task of the central bank.

Second, tightening of monetary policy induces investors to rebalance their portfolios. The expected return on equities falls, while the expected return of the close substitutes rises. A rise in the short-term interest rate by the central bank raises the return on deposits and discourages investors from investing in the equity market. It induces a portfolio rebalancing out of equities into cash. Long-term interest rates also rise as a result of monetary tightening, but by less than short-term ones. Hence, the yield curve flattens or becomes inverted, as a result of monetary tightening. Higher long-term interest rates induce another portfolio rebalancing, this time out of equities into bonds. High or rising interest rates will also prick bubbles in property. Evidence from the K-Model suggests that the long-term interest rate is the single most important variable in the US housing market with a multiplier of two in the first and second years (see Chapter 6). This means that one percentage point hike in the long-term interest rate lowers house prices by more than 2%, both one and two years later.

Asset price inflation always takes place when the economy is overheated – that is, when it grows faster than its potential. It is unthinkable that the economy would be in recession or recovery and asset price inflation would be high. Simply equity prices would be low because corporate profits would be poor. Overheating of the economy may not actually lead to higher CPI-inflation, but to higher asset price inflation. As in the case of the US in the second half of the 1990s or of Japan in the 1980s, the lack of acceleration in CPI-inflation when the economy is overheated leads to the erroneous conclusion that productivity must have risen and this allows the economy to grow at a faster rate without increasing inflation. In other words, it leads to the conclusion that the rate of growth of potential output must have risen. People in the US in the second half of the 1990s frequently spoke of a productivity miracle that raised potential output growth substantially (see, e.g. Greenspan, 2004a). In fact, there was no productivity miracle. In the US there was some productivity improvement in the 1990s, as a result of the widespread use of computers in services. But potential output growth was only raised between 3.00% and 3.50%, hardly substantial.

Since asset inflation is associated with steady or gently rising CPI-inflation when the economy is overheated, there is no real conflict between the two targets. The central bank can pursue simultaneously the targets of asset inflation and CPI-inflation, if it so chooses.[8] If asset inflation were lowered before it becomes a bubble, the economy would have a 'soft landing'. As in the case of the US in 1994, the tightening of monetary policy was regarded as a means of prolonging the business cycle by killing the overheating before CPI-inflation managed to get out of control. Similarly, tightening of monetary policy to kill asset inflation would prolong the business cycle and the economy would enjoy a 'soft landing'. The overall conclusion is that asset inflation targeting is both desirable and feasible and in no way conflicts with the traditional role of the central bank in targeting CPI-inflation. Net wealth as percent of disposable income is the ideal variable for targeting asset price inflation, as it directly affects demand in the economy.

5   Summary and conclusions

Many countries suffered in the last ten years or so from the boom and bust of bubbles and, in some of them, popular demands for action by the authorities have not abated. In this chapter we have dealt with the US experience.

We have examined the 2000 US bubble, the related issue of the 'new economy' paradigm, the aftermath of the bubble, concentrating on its consequences, before dealing with the issue of how we might tackle it. We have suggested that asset price inflation targeting may be both desirable and feasible and in no way conflicts with other policy objectives of the central bank, as for example in the case of inflation targeting.

The process of asset price inflation targeting involves monitoring and targeting the implications of asset prices on the spending patterns of consumers and companies, rather than asset prices themselves. It would simply be unacceptable for a central bank to have a target for one of the main stock market indices. The variable that lends itself as a primary candidate for monitoring and control of asset price inflation is the net wealth of the personal sector as percent of disposable income, as it is at the heart of the transmission mechanism from asset prices and debt to consumption. This variable is trendless (i.e. it is stationary) and reverts back to its mean, which is five times annual disposable income for the US. Monetary policy can be tightened when the ratio of net wealth to disposable income rises above a particular threshold, say 550% for the US.

Critics of asset price inflation targeting claim that monetary tightening kills good growth that generates prosperity. Such arguments are based on the premise that the lack of CPI-inflation when the economy is overheated is evidence of productivity improvement that has raised the growth of potential output. But this is an erroneous conclusion. Simply, the overheating is channelled to asset price inflation rather than CPI-inflation. Clearly, the Fed never contemplated a rate hike to control the bubble, although its chairman tried to influence it with his by now familiar remarks about 'irrational exuberance'. In fact, and more recently, the chairman of the Fed argued that there is tentative evidence to suggest that dealing with the consequences of the bubble is preferable to dealing with the bubble itself (Greenspan, 2004a,b). The case for asset price inflation targeting would become weak if the economy were to remain firmly on a sustained path to recovery. However, as this book would show, in spite of the robust growth of the last nine months or so in 2003, there are still substantial risks to the economy, emanating from the fact that the imbalances that were created by the boom and bust of the bubble have not been corrected. If the economy were to stumble, and these imbalances were reawaken driving the economy down once again, then the case for asset price inflation targeting would become more pertinent.

3
Wages and Prices and the Proper Conduct of Monetary Policy

1 Introduction

Headline consumer price index-inflation (CPI-inflation) peaked at 3.7% in June 2000 and bottomed at 1.1% two years later, in June 2002. It rose steadily to 3% by March 2003 and subsided to 2% by October 2003. Core CPI-inflation, which is preferred by the Fed and taken more seriously than the headline measure in formulating monetary policy, peaked at 2.8% in November 2001 and has declined steadily to 1.3% in October 2003 (see Figure 3.1).[1] Although the Fed, on numerous occasions in the last three years, has expressed fear of deflation the question arises as to what would happen to inflation now that the economy shows signs of robust growth. Is the fear of deflation justified? Or, is the Fed, as the cynics would argue, using the excuse of deflation to keep interest rates unduly low and help the personal, corporate and government sectors get rid of their debt through inflation? Would inflation remain low in the current recovery? When should the Fed tighten monetary policy, if it is to keep up with its hardly won reputation as the guardian of low inflation?

Figure 3.1b shows the dependence of CPI-inflation on producer price inflation (PPI) and imported inflation. Imported inflation has already peaked and is on the way down. This should help ease the pressure on CPI-inflation in the months ahead. However, PPI-inflation is much more important than imported inflation, although it is influenced by the latter. It now stands at a two year high at 3.4%, but it may be near its peak. Figure 3.2 shows the PPI-inflation chain. Producer output prices depend on producer prices paid for intermediate supplies and crude materials. Prices of crude materials peaked six months ago and have fallen precipitously since then. Prices of intermediate supplies have also abated somewhat in the last six months and therefore the outlook for producer output prices has improved. PPI-inflation should be near its peak.

However, even more important than producer prices paid for intermediate supplies and crude materials is the labour cost. Half of the average

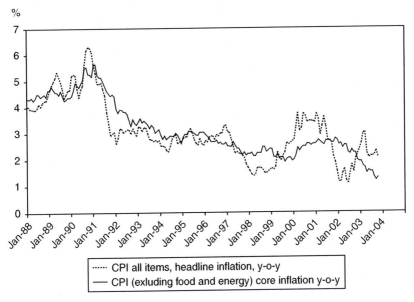

Figure 3.1a CPI, headline and core inflation

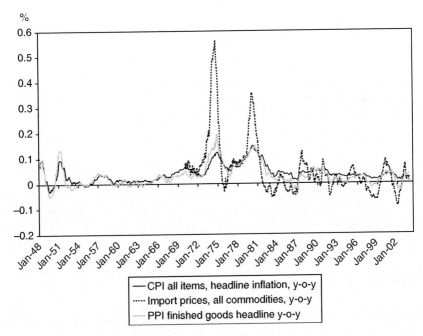

Figure 3.1b CPI, PPI and imported inflation

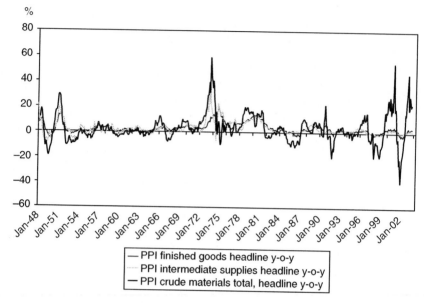

Figure 3.2 The PPI inflation chain

variable cost of production is due to labour costs. Figure 3.3 shows the dependence of PPI-inflation on unit labour cost. The rate of growth of unit labour cost bottomed in September 2002 and started to increase. This triggered a second round of retrenchment in the recent downturn by the corporate sector with the aim of turning unit labour cost decisively down yet again. Companies cut production, laid off workers and slashed investment between July 2002 and April 2003 in an effort to curb unit labour cost and restore profitability. The operation was successful and the rate of growth of unit labour cost has fallen drastically in the last six months and corporate profits have soared. This augurs very well for a fall in PPI-inflation in the months ahead and consequently for a fall in CPI-inflation.

Hence, all factors suggest that inflationary pressures should abate in the near future. But, now that the economy shows signs of robust growth, for how long would this trend last? The success in curbing unit labour cost lies on gains in productivity, as output increases faster than employment. Figure 3.4 shows the dependence of unit labour cost on productivity. It is evident that the large swings in unit labour cost reflect, to a large extent, corresponding fluctuations in productivity. Hence, the extent to which PPI- and consequently CPI-inflation would fall in the course of 2004 depends on the pace of economic growth and the rate of job creation, that is, on the rate of growth of productivity and the entire wage–price nexus.

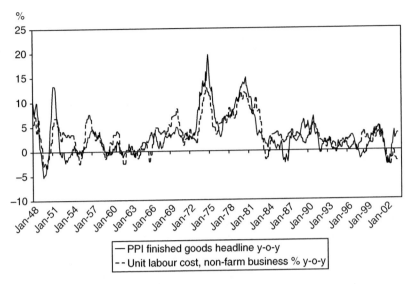

Figure 3.3 Output prices and labour cost

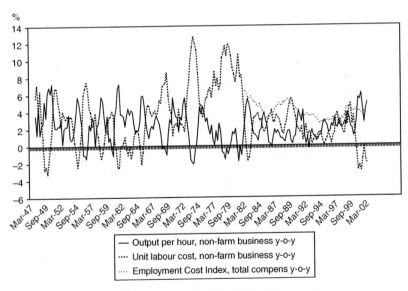

Figure 3.4 ULC, ECI and productivity in non-farm business

This chapter takes the view that since the economy is gathering steam, the risk of deflation over the next two years is almost negligible. Inflation is likely to slow in the near future, as wage inflation is abating, unit labour cost has taken another plunge, the prices of crude materials and intermediate supplies, as well as import prices have subsided in the course of the year. However, how quickly this trend would be reversed depends on how fast the economy grows in the next two years. With slow growth inflation will fall more and will bottom almost a year from now, but will rise sharply in 2005, as productivity falls and unit labour costs rises. With fast growth inflation will not fall as much, but will remain muted in 2005. Fast growth will prevent the drastic drop in crude material prices and will not put a cap on the price of oil and commodity prices resulting in higher CPI-inflation in 2004. However, the slower growth in 2005 will also prevent the revival of inflation in crude material prices thus causing muted CPI-inflation.

In an attempt to throw light on the likely course of inflation in the next two years, and to substantiate the claims just made, we utilise the K-Model to simulate this model under the two scenarios of weak and strong growth in 2004. We are then able to gauge the effects for a two-year period until the end of 2005. The argument becomes clearer once we have highlighted the wage–price sector of the K-Model; this is the task of the section that follows immediately below.

2   The K-Model of the wage–price sector

The K-Model of the wage–price sector consists of ten equations.

1. CPI-inflation (CPI)
2. PPI-inflation (output-prices) (PPI)
3. PPI-inflation of intermediate supplies (PPIS)
4. PPI-inflation of crude materials (PPCM)
5. Wage earnings (W) growth
6. Employment creation (E)
7. Employer's labour cost (ELC)
8. Total hours worked in non-farm business (h)
9. Productivity (PRO)
10. Unit labour Cost (ULC)

Companies price their products in the same way, whether they belong to the retail or producer (wholesale) sector. The structure, therefore, of the first four equations dealing with CPI- and the three categories of PPI-inflation is the same. All companies price their products as a mark-up on average variable cost. The differences arise, first, from the degree of competition they face in their product markets and therefore on the ability to charge supernormal profits; and second, on what variables should be included in the calculation of the average variable cost. Competition is increasing as we move from consumer (or retail) prices to the various categories of producer prices. Companies in the retail sector are the ones that are best shielded from competition. As we move to producer-finished goods, intermediate supplies and crude materials, competition becomes fiercer.

In the long run, consumer prices increase at the same rate as producer output prices, but augmented by a variable-profit margin that depends on the business cycle. When the economy is growing faster than potential output (i.e. when the economy is overheated), the profit margin increases and when the economy is growing at a smaller pace than potential (i.e. when the economy is operating with excess capacity), the profit margin is squeezed, as companies strive to remain in business and maintain market share. In the short run CPI-inflation adjusts to previous disequilibria. If consumer prices were higher than in equilibrium, CPI-inflation would fall; and if consumer prices were lower than in equilibrium CPI-inflation would then increase. It takes five-and-a-half months for the market to move back to equilibrium. CPI-inflation also responds to past and current PPI-inflation and past and current imported inflation. CPI-inflation exhibits strong inertia to past CPI-inflation because of adjustment costs. We may, therefore, have equation (1) as our long-run relationship for CPI:

$$CPI = C(PPI, IP) \tag{1}$$

where the symbols are as above, with the exception of IP which stands for industrial Production.

Producer output prices would increase, in the long run, at the rate of average variable cost that includes normal profits. The average variable cost consists of labour cost and producer prices paid for intermediate supplies and crude materials. In the steady state unit labour cost accounts for 50% of variable cost, intermediate supplies for 40% and crude materials for 10%. It is worth noting that producer output prices are perfectly competitive with only normal profits. This is in contrast to consumer prices. Producer output prices are exposed to fierce foreign competition that results in near perfect competition, which eliminates supernormal profits; whereas consumer prices are somewhat shielded from foreign competition allowing imperfect competition and supernormal profits. Although in the long run producers of finished goods can only earn normal profits, in the short run they can earn supernormal profits in booms, but earn less than normal profits in recessions. In the short run, PPI-inflation responds to previous disequilibria in a self-correcting manner. It takes almost twenty months for the market to move back to equilibrium. PPI-inflation responds to current and past unit labour cost growth, PPI-inflation of intermediate supplies, PPI-inflation of crude materials and the price of oil. PPI-inflation also exhibits strong inertia to past inflation. So that we can formally write the long-run relationship for

PPI as in equation (2)′:

$$PPI = P(ULC, PPIS, PPCM) \tag{2}′$$

Producer prices of intermediate supplies increase at the rate of average variable cost that includes normal profits, in the long run. The average variable cost consists of labour cost and prices paid for crude materials. Labour cost accounts for 70% of average variable cost and crude materials for 30%. In the short run, PPI-inflation of intermediate supplies adjusts to previous disequilibria in a self-correcting manner. It takes four-and-a-half months for the market to move back to equilibrium. PPI-inflation of intermediate supplies responds to current and past labour cost growth and PPI-inflation of crude materials. PPI-inflation of intermediate supplies exhibits inertia to past inflation. As with producers of finished goods, producers of intermediate supplies can earn supernormal profits in booms and earn less than normal profits in recessions in the short run, but in the long run they only earn normal profits. We may, therefore, formally depict PPIS as in equation (3):

$$PPIS = S(ULC, PPCM) \tag{3}$$

Producer prices of crude materials increase at the rate of average variable cost that includes normal profits, in the long run. The average variable cost consists of labour cost, the price of commodities in world perfectly competitive markets and the price of oil. Labour cost accounts for 50% of average variable costs and all commodities, including oil, for the remainder 50%. In the short run, PPI-inflation of crude materials adjusts to previous disequilibria in a self-correcting manner. It takes just less than two months for the market to move back to equilibrium. PPI-inflation of crude materials responds to current and past inflation in world commodity prices and oil. Companies of crude materials are unable to earn supernormal profits neither in the long run, nor in the short run. Equation (4) represents the functional form for PPCM:

$$PPCM = M(ULC, PWC, POIL) \tag{4}$$

where the new symbols are PWC which stands for prices of world commodities (the CRB futures index is utilised for this purposes; see, for example, any issue of the *Financial Times*, under Commodity Prices), and POIL is the price of oil.

Substituting equations (3) and (4) in (2)′ we can arrive at equation (2):

$$PPI = I(ULC, PWC, POIL) \tag{2}$$

In the long run, wage earnings grow at the rate of productivity plus expected CPI-inflation, which is equal to actual, as in the long run expectations are realised. Such an increase in wages is fair because it implies an unchanged distribution of income. However, in the short run wage growth can deviate from its fair value depending on the bargaining power of employees in wage negotiations with employers. In these wage negotiations employees have a target real wage rate and when bargaining they attempt to restore previous deviations from the target real wage rate. The target real wage rate is derived from the worker's perception of the demand for labour (Sargan, 1964; Sawyer, 1982a,b; Arestis, 1986; Rowthorn, 1995). The perceived demand for labour depends negatively on the real wage rate and positively on the demand in the economy for goods and services, CPI-inflation and productivity. In the K-Model the negative slope of the perceived demand for labour implies a trade-off of a drop of 2.7% in the real wage rate for a permanent gain in employment of 100 000. The bargaining power of employees is inversely related to unemployment. A rise in unemployment weakens the bargaining power of employees and they are prepared to accept a smaller than fair increase in wages, and vice versa. Wage growth exhibits very strong inertia to past rates of growth. It takes twelve months for the market to move back to equilibrium. We may write formally the long-run wage earnings relationship as in equation (5):

$$W = W[[(W/P)^a - (W/P)^d], U, CPI, PRO]$$ (5)

where $(W/P)^a$ is actual real wage and $(W/P)^d$ is desired real wage; U stands for unemployment and PRO stands for productivity. We may also have that:

$$(W/P)^d = D(IP, PRO, CPI, E)$$ (5a)

where the symbols are as above.

We also specify an E-relationship as follows:

$$E = E(IP, W)$$ (6)

and treat unemployment as functionally the negative of employment, although this is a weak assumption in view of the fact that the number of discouraged workers are not included in the measure of unemployment. The demand for labour is a positive function of the level of industrial production and a negative function of the real wage rate adjusted for productivity, in the long run. The real wage rate is deflated by producer output prices, rather than consumer prices, because for companies what is essential is the share of labour cost to output price rather than the purchasing power of wages, which is important for employees.[2] In the K-Model 1% increase in industrial production leads in the long run to an increase of 1.1% in the demand for labour, while a 1% increase in the real wage rate leads to 0.7% fall in the demand for labour. In the short run, the rate of growth of employment (job creation) adjusts to previous disequilibria in a self-correcting manner. For example, if actual employment were higher than that implied by the demand for labour, then the current pace of job creation would be lower to bring the market back to equilibrium. In the K-Model it would take four-and-a-half months for the market to go back to equilibrium. Job creation exhibits strong inertia to past rates of job creation, as there are significant costs of adjustment, such as training and compensation for laid-off employees. It is worth noting that although the real wage rate affects the demand for labour in the long run, it plays no role in the short run dynamics of job creation. These are strongly affected, though, by current and past rates of growth of industrial production. The pace of job creation, therefore, in the short run is affected by the demand for output.

Labour cost to employers depends on wage growth and employers contributions for employees' benefits, in the long run. In the short run, labour cost inflation responds to past disequilibria and current as well as past wage inflation and inflation of benefits, with strong inertia. It takes almost forty months for the market to move back to equilibrium, the longest lag in the wage–price sector. In the long run, the total number of hours worked by the labour force depends on the number of employed people, the average weekly hours and the average overtime hours per week. In the short run, the growth rate of hours worked responds with strong inertia to past rates of hours worked because of high costs of adjustment of the labour force. The growth rate of hours worked also responds to current and past rates of growth of employment, weekly hours and overtime. It takes nine months for the market to move back to equilibrium. We may, therefore, have:

$$ELC = L(W, BEN) \tag{7}$$

where BEN stands for employers benefits; we also specify that

$$h = h(E, WH, OH) \tag{8}$$

where WH is weekly working hours, and OH stands for overtime hours.

The level of industrial production, in the long run, influences output of the non-farm business sector, six months ago in one-to-one relationship. In the short run, the rate of growth of output of non-farm business responds to previous disequilibria in a self-correcting manner and to current and past growth rates of industrial production. By definition, the rate of growth of productivity is determined by the output growth of non-farm business less the rate of growth of hours worked. In the long run, unit labour cost is a positive function of the labour cost to employers and a negative function of the level of productivity. In the short run, the rate of growth of unit labour cost adjusts to correct any previous disequilibrium. It also responds positively to past and current labour cost inflation, but negatively to current and past productivity growth. Equation (9) depicts productivity as:

$$PRO = O(h, E) \tag{9}$$

and equation (10) depicts unit labour cost as:

$$ULC = U(ELC, PRO) \tag{10}$$

The rationale of the K-Model is summarised in Figure 3.5. The wage–price spiral is depicted with the medium grey boxes. The light grey boxes illustrate the exogenous variables that introduce shocks in the wage–price spiral, while the dark grey boxes denote other important variables that provide an extra loop. The rationale of the K-Model is as follows. Consider a shock in fiscal or monetary policy or a shock in world trade that lifts growth. Faster economic growth leads to higher labour productivity in the short run, as employment is fixed. However, over time employment will increase, which, in turn, will lower productivity. The increased demand for labour will raise wages, which will be further boosted by the higher productivity. The higher wages will raise unit labour cost that will be offset in the short run by increases in productivity. However, the increase in unit labour cost will accelerate through time, as the higher level of employment will gradually erode the initial gains in productivity. The higher unit labour cost will feed through into higher producer prices of finished goods (i.e. higher PPI-inflation of finished goods) that will then affect consumer paid prices or retail prices (i.e. CPI-inflation). The latter will lead to expectations of higher inflation, which will then affect the new round of wage negotiations setting in motion the wage–price spiral.

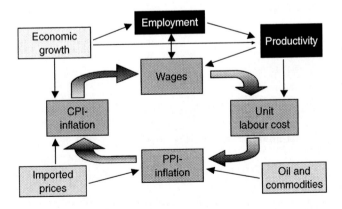

Figure 3.5 Wage–price spiral

The wage–price spiral is usually stable. This means that once a shock sets it in motion it does not become explosive. After a large number of rounds that may take over three years, in which the marginal increase in wages and prices diminishes in every round, the wage–price spiral converges to a new steady state in which wages, unit labour cost, PPI-inflation and CPI-inflation are all higher than the initial steady state. The stability of the wage–price spiral is ensured by rising unemployment that caps wage growth and falling profitability, through lower profit margins, that curbs the ability of companies to pass on to their prices the higher cost of production. If the wage–price spiral is unstable, it leads to hyperinflation, which has been experienced by many countries. In this case expectations of inflation are rising faster than the curb of inflation through higher unemployment and falling profitability. Since expectations of inflation are the problem of hyperinflation, what is needed for the system to become stable again is appropriate and credible economic policies.

Imported inflation feeds through to consumer (retail) prices both indirectly and directly. Imported final goods and services and certain commodities, like oil, affect directly consumer prices. Imported crude materials and intermediate supplies affect consumer prices indirectly through the chain link of producer prices. These factors are reflected as the two bottom yellow boxes in Figure 3.5.

3   The likely path of wage and price inflation

This section concerns itself with an attempt to throw more light on the likely course of the entire wage–price spiral over the next two years. We employ the K-Model to simulate two alternative scenarios.

Scenario I (weak recovery in 2004): What would happen to the wage–price sector if the current recovery were to falter in 2004 and become once again anaemic?

Scenario II (strong recovery in 2004): What would happen to the wage–price sector if the recovery that started after the Iraq war continues to be strong throughout 2004?

3.1   Scenario I (weak recovery in 2004)

The essence of this scenario lies on the assumption that the strength of the second and third quarters of 2003 was due to one-off factors related to the fiscal package of the Bush Administration and rising confidence because of lower geopolitical risks after the end of the Iraq war. The stance of fiscal policy turned 1.6% of GDP easier with the 'Jobs and Growth Tax Relief Reconciliation Act of 2003'. The act provided for an additional first-year bonus depreciation write-off, increasing the immediate depreciation write-off from 30% (provided for in the 'Job Creation and Worker Assistance Act of 2002') to 50% for property acquired after 5 May 2003, and placed in service before 1 January 2005. The additional depreciation provided for by the 2003 act is estimated to have increased depreciation expenses in the second quarter by $75.2 billion. In addition, the 2003 act provided for a reduction of $100.9 billion in July in personal tax and non-tax payments. The act reduced withheld federal taxes in the order of $45.8 billion as a result of new marginal tax rates, the expansion of the 10% income tax bracket, and acceleration in 'marriage-penalty' relief. Federal non-withheld taxes (payments of estimated taxes plus final settlements less refunds) were reduced by $55.5 billion because of advance payments of the child tax credit that began being mailed out 25 July 2003. The fiscal stimulus provided through the depreciation incentives and tax relief, ignoring the additional measures on dividend income, as they are controversial with respect to their effect on the demand in the economy, is estimated to be 1.6% of nominal GDP.

In addition, monetary policy was eased once more at the end of June 2003 with the Fed funds rate cut to 1%. The accommodative stance of fiscal and monetary policy will keep the economy going, but the imbalances in all sectors will weigh down on the economy and the recovery will begin to falter during the course of 2004 from the torrid pace of 8% in the third quarter of 2003. Nonetheless, the economy will grow at the rate of potential output in 2004 and 2005 with industrial production growth averaging 3%. Average weekly hours will remain largely unchanged from their current level at 33.9, while overtime hours will average 4.2 in the two-year period. Employers' benefit costs will abate somewhat from their current rate of 6.5% to 5% throughout the two-year period. The price of oil (Brent) will stabilise at $29 per barrel, while commodity price inflation will dissipate from 17% down to 11% until the end of 2005. Import prices will accelerate from 0.9% to 2%, as a result of the weaker dollar. Unemployment will fall to 5.6% of the labour force. Table 3.1 summarises all the assumptions underlying Scenario I, along with their current values as of October 2003.

With these assumptions CPI inflation is on a downward trend and will fall to 1.2% by the end of 2004 from 2% in October 2003, but will rise to 2.6% by the end of 2005 (see Table 3.1 for a summary of the results and Figure 3.6a for the projected trajectories under the two scenarios). Part of the drive for lower inflation in the next twelve months is due to the higher than equilibrium prices in the past, which stood at 6.9% in October 2003 (see Table 3.1 under the current long run equilibrium row). As the market moves back to equilibrium inflation will fall. CPI-inflation will bottom twelve months from now in October 2004. The forecast error in the K-Model of CPI-inflation is only 0.35%. This means that with an error of 0.7% the model can explain 95% of the history of inflation in the last 35 years. Indeed, in the last 405 months there have been only four instances where the CPI-inflation error has exceeded 0.7% (see Figure 3.6a). On that basis the forecasting

Table 3.1 US wage–price sector

	Current values Oct. 03	CPI-inflation % y-o-y	PPI-inflation finished goods, % y-o-y	PPI-inflation intermediate supplies % y-o-y	PPI-inflation crude materials % y-o-y	Average hourly earnings, total private, % y-o-y	Labour cost, ECI, total compensation, % y-o-y	Monthly job creation 6M MA	Productivity, % y-o-y	Unit labour cost, % y-o-y
				Scenario I (weak recovery)			Scenario II (strong recovery)			
Assumptions										
Industrial production (%)										
1st year	0.6			3			4.6			
2nd year				3			1.4			
Average weekly hours (level)										
1st year	33.8			33.9			34			
2nd year				33.9			33.8			
Weekly overtime hours (hours)										
1st year	4.2			4.2			4.5			
2nd year				4.2			3.9			
ECI benefits costs (%)										
1st year	6.5			5			5			
2nd year				5			5			
Price of oil (Brent) $ per barrel										
1st year	28.2			29			35			
2nd year				29			23			

CRB Index (%)									
1st year	17		11				20		
2nd year			11				2		
Unemployment (% of labour force)									
1st year	6.0		5.6			5.4			
2nd year			5.6			5.7			
Import prices, all commod (% y-o-y)									
1st year	0.9		2		6				
2nd year			2		-2				
Current level	2.0	3.4	1.6	20.5	2.4	3.9	12	4.1	-1.1
Deviation from long-run Equilibrium (LRE)	6.9	2.7	-3.9	14.1	-0.5	-1.0	-5.2	4.1	-2.7
Scenario I (weak recovery)									
12-M SRE (future short-run equilibrium)	1.2	-0.1	1.9	-14.8	0.0	3.2	171	1.1	3.6
24-SRE (future short-run equilibrium)	2.6	3.9	5.1	17.0	1.9	3.2	222	1.0	3.8
12-M SRE and current level (difference)	-0.8	-3.5	0.3	-35.3	-2.4	-0.7	160	-3.0	4.7
24-M SRE and current level (difference)	0.5	0.5	3.5	-3.5	-0.5	-0.8	210	-3.1	4.9
Scenario II (strong recovery)									
12-M SRE (future short-run equilibrium)	2.1	1.4	3.7	-7.8	1.0	3.5	225	1.1	3.9
24-SRE (future short-run equilibrium)	1.6	1.5	3.1	0.7	0.7	3.1	180	0.7	3.9
12-M SRE and current level (difference)	0.1	-1.9	2.0	-28.3	-1.3	-0.4	213	-3.0	5.0
24-M SRE and current level (difference)	-0.4	-1.9	1.4	-19.8	-1.6	-0.8	168	-3.4	4.9

48

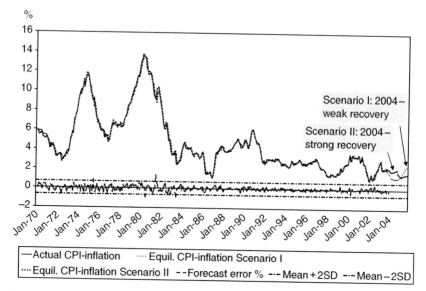

Figure 3.6a CPI-inflation – short-run equilibrium

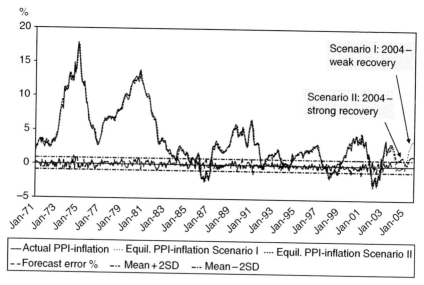

Figure 3.6b PPI-inflation (finished goods): short-run equilibrium

ability of the model is such as to claim that with 95% probability CPI-inflation in the future will lie within the interval of the central projection plus or minus 0.7%. This assumes that the assumptions are valid and that the behaviour of CPI-inflation will continue to be governed by the same structure that is encapsulated in the K-Model. The assurance here rests with the fact that the model can explain CPI-inflation equally well both during the supply-led business cycles of the 1970 to the 1980s as well as the demand-led business cycles since the late 1980s. Hence, there is no reason to assume that the structure of the K-Model will be invalidated in the short-term future.

The fall and rise in CPI-inflation in the next twenty-four months is largely due to a similar pattern in PPI-inflation. In the next twelve-months PPI-inflation of finished goods will drop from 3.4% to −0.1% (see Table 3.1 and Figure 3.6b). However, PPI-inflation will surge to 3.9% in the following twelve months. PPI-inflation will bottom six months earlier than CPI-inflation, in April 2004, but will remain subdued for some time before it begins to rise again. The forecast error of the K-Model for PPI-inflation is 0.45% and the model can explain both demand and supply-led business cycles. The PPI-inflation chain can trace the fall and rise in CPI-inflation. The fall in PPI-inflation of intermediate supplies is expected to be moderate compared to PPI-inflation of finished goods, although both will bottom in April 2004. Intermediate supplies will rise even faster than finished goods to 5.1% twenty-four months from now (see Table 3.1 and Figure 3.7). The forecast

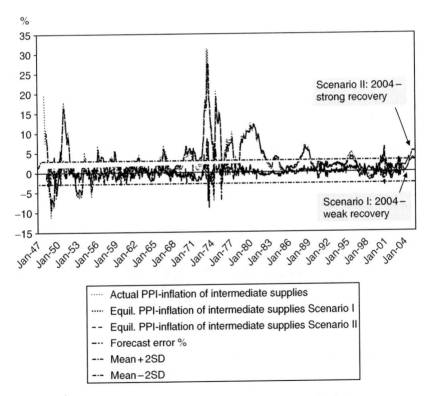

Figure 3.7 PPI-inflation of intermediate supplies – short-run equilibrium

50

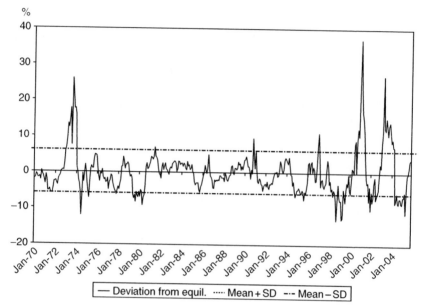

| — Deviation from equil. ····· Mean + SD --- Mean − SD |

Figure 3.8a   Deviation from equilibrium crude materials prices

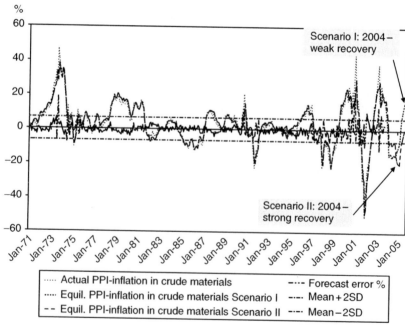

Scenario I: 2004 –
weak recovery

Scenario II: 2004 –
strong recovery

····· Actual PPI-inflation in crude materials	---- Forecast error %
····· Equil. PPI-inflation in crude materials Scenario I	--- Mean + 2SD
-- Equil. PPI-inflation in crude materials Scenario II	---- Mean − 2SD

Figure 3.8b   PPI-inflation of crude materials – short-run equilibrium

error of the K-Model for intermediate supplies is 1.4% and the model can explain all nine business cycles in the last fifty-five years.

The driving force behind abating inflationary pressures in the next twelve months is due to a sharp fall in the prices of crude materials with inflation falling to −15% from 20.5% in October 2003 (see Figure 3.8a). The expected fall in crude materials prices is partly due to higher than equilibrium prices in the course of 2003 triggered by the rapid growth of China, which by October 2003 amounted to 14%. Crude materials inflation will bottom in March 2004, but will remain at these levels for another six months before it begins to rise very fast, climbing to 17% by the end of 2005 (see Table 3.1 and Figure 3.8b). The forecast error of the K-Model for crude materials 3.3% and the model can explain the demand and supply-led business cycles of the last thirty-five years. Hence, the one factor that accounts for the fall and rise of CPI-inflation is the pattern of crude materials prices that will continue to fall for another six months, will then stabilise for another six months and then will surge up again until the end of 2005. These fluctuations in the prices of crude materials will feed to the prices of intermediate supplies, finished goods and ultimately to consumer prices. The other factor that accounts for the fall and rise of CPI-inflation is the pattern of unit labour cost. But this is a composite variable that depends on wage inflation and labour productivity.

Wage inflation will fall to zero in the next twelve months, partly because of easing inflationary pressures that will dampen expected inflation, and partly because the real wage rate has been higher than equilibrium in the last two years. At the end of 2001 the real wage rate was 3.9% higher than its long run equilibrium (see Figure 3.9a). Its adjustment back to equilibrium will help ease wage inflation in the near future. However, wage inflation will bottom in September 2004 and will begin to rise again to 1.9% by the end of 2005 (see Figure 3.9b for the expected trajectory of wage inflation). Higher expected inflation and falling unemployment will combine to push wage inflation up again in 2005. The forecast error of the K-Model for wage inflation is 0.65% and the model can explain the history of wage inflation in demand and supply-led business cycles in the last thirty years. Despite the rise and fall in wage inflation, the labour cost to employers, measured by the Employment Cost Index (ECI), will abate in the next two years, mainly because of the assumption of lower benefits costs (see Figure 3.10). However, labour costs would only abate marginally from 3.5% to 3% in the next two years. The forecast error of the K-Model for ECI is just 0.1%. However, the validity of the projection depends to a large extent on the assumption that benefit costs would dissipate.

Job creation will be strong throughout the two-year period. With growth in the economy around potential output and industrial production averaging 3% in the next two years, there would be little impediment to job creation. Moreover, the level of employment has been smaller than equilibrium

52

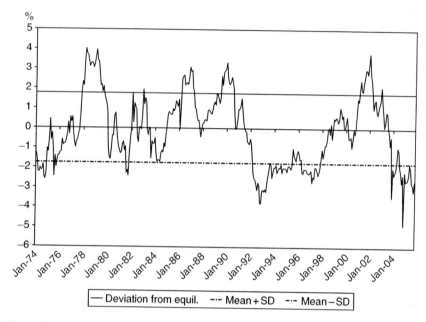

Figure 3.9a   Deviation from equilibrium real wage rate

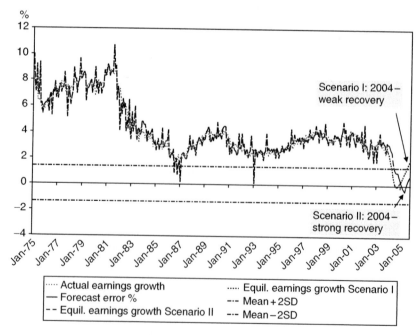

Figure 3.9b   Wage earnings growth – short-run equilibrium

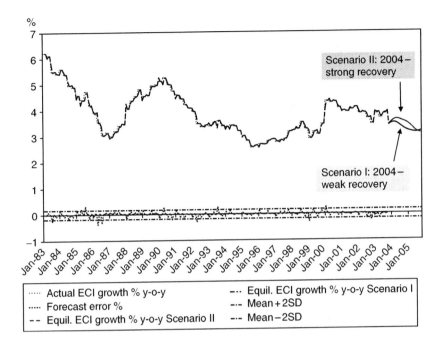

Figure 3.10 Employment Cost Index – short-run equilibrium

in the last two years and this should boost job creation in the next two years (see Figure 3.11a for the deviation from equilibrium employment). Job creation, as a six month moving average, will jump from 12 thousand in October 2003 to 171 thousand in the next twelve months and 222 thousand during the course of 2005 (see Figure 3.11b). The forecast error of the K-Model for job creation is 44 thousand and the model can explain nearly forty years of job creation in demand and supply-led business cycles. The rate of growth of productivity is near its peak because output would dissipate from its torrid pace of the last six months, while job creation would gather steam in the next two years. Productivity will decline from 4.1% (year-on-year) in the third quarter of 2003 to just 1% for most part of the next two years (see Figure 3.12). The forecast error of the K-Model for productivity is 0.7%. With ECI growth expected to decline only marginally in the next two years and productivity falling drastically, unit labour cost will surge to 3.9% by the end of 2005 (see Figure 3.13). The forecast error of the K-Model for unit labour cost is only 0.4%.

Overall, the scenario of weak recovery implies rising unit labour cost for the next two years because of lower output growth and strong job creation that would result in lower productivity. Despite rising unit labour cost,

54

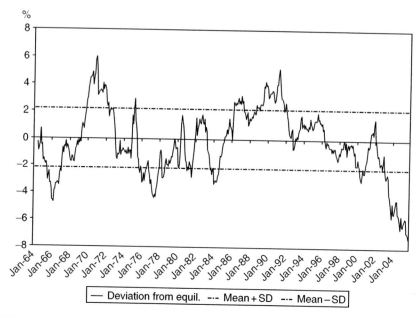

Figure 3.11a Deviation from equilibrium employment

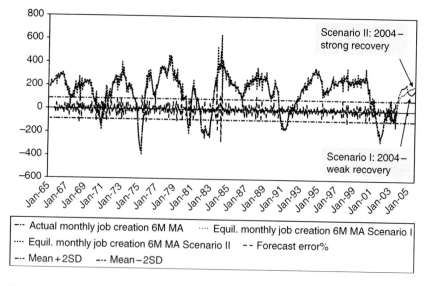

Figure 3.11b Monthly job creation – short-run equilibrium

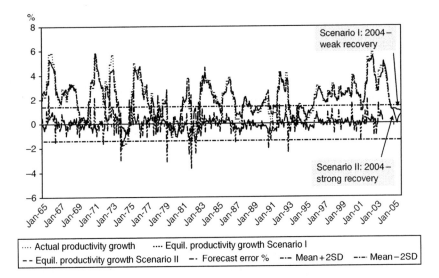

Figure 3.12 Productivity growth

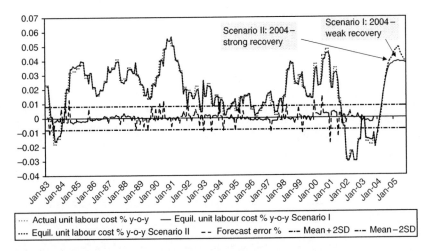

Figure 3.13 Unit labour cost: short-run equilibrium

falling crude material prices will exert downward pressure in the next twelve months on the prices of intermediate supplies that would then feed through to finished goods and ultimately to consumer prices. The decline in CPI-inflation will be moderate compared to PPI because of rising import prices, due to the lower value of the dollar and higher profit margins, as demand in the economy will grow at potential output. However, in the course of 2005 all inflation indices will accelerate, as the effect of falling crude material prices tapers off and unit labour cost continues to surge.

3.2 Scenario II (strong recovery in 2004)

The essence of scenario II lies on the premise, which is largely true, that a combined fiscal and monetary stimulus will last for at least a year, and probably eighteen months, before it tapers off. Given that the fiscal stimulus was introduced between May and July 2003, the economy should remain strong until the end of 2004. The role of the accommodative stance of monetary policy is to prevent long-term interest rates from rising and, therefore, in addition to the stimulus of low interest rates, prolong the effects of the fiscal stimulus. However, despite forty years of low short-term interest rates introduced by the Fed in the last three years, long-term interest rates have risen sharply since June 2003 and the yield curve is extremely steep. If interest rates stay at this high level, or even rise further, which is very likely, the stimulus from monetary and fiscal policy will ultimately peter out. This means that growth will diminish in 2005 and beyond, other things being equal. Given that the average growth for the four quarters just before the fiscal stimulus was introduced, was 2.6%, that the fiscal stimulus was 1.6% of GDP and that the first year multiplier is about unity, the central projection for average growth until the second half, or the end, of 2004 should be 4.2%. Since the depreciation incentives on new structures will only count if premises are ready for service at the beginning of 2005, companies that would like to take advantage of the scheme should already have started spending. This explains the buoyant recovery of investment in the second quarter of 2003 that was responsible, to some extent, for the unexpectedly strong growth in that quarter. The other major factor that contributed to the unexpectedly strong second quarter was the explosion of defence spending because of the Iraq war.

The stunning 8.2% growth in the third quarter of 2003 was caused by the combination of strong consumption, due to the income tax cuts that were introduced in that quarter, the last wagon effect for those companies that wanted to take advantage of the depreciation incentives on new structures; and worldwide improving confidence because of lower geopolitical risks after the end of the Iraq war that boosted US exports in the third quarter. To a large extent the current worldwide-improved confidence is caused by the US. But US exports are unlikely to remain as robust as in the third quarter of 2003. This implies that the stunning third quarter growth was due to one-off factors that are likely to dissipate in the first half of 2004. Nonetheless, the US economy should still grow at 4.2% – central projection until the second half of 2004. Industrial production will average 4.6% growth in 2004, but will fall to 1.4% in the course of 2005. The average rate of growth of industrial production over the two-year period will be 3%, the same as in

Scenario I of weak recovery. However, in Scenario II growth would be stronger in 2004 and weaker in 2005 than in Scenario I, but with the same average growth for the two-year period. The assumption that the average for the two-year period is the same under Scenarios I and II pertains to all variables that form the maintained hypothesis (see Table 3.1 for the detailed assumptions of Scenario II).

Average weekly hours will increase to 34 in 2004, but will decline to 33.8 in 2005. Over the two-year period the average will be the same as in Scenario I at 33.9. Similarly, overtime will increase in 2004 to 4.5 hours per week, but will fall to 3.9 hours in 2005 with an average of 4.2 hours for the two-year period. The employers' benefit costs will maintain the same values as in Scenario I, because they are not influenced by economic factors, but by legislation. The price of oil will shoot up to $35 per barrel in 2004, but will fall to $23 in the course of 2005, as growth falters. Commodity prices will accelerate even more in the course of 2004 to 20% because of strong growth, but will abate to 2% in 2005. Unemployment will fall to 5.4% of the labour force in 2004, but will climb back to 5.7% in 2005 because of sub-par growth. Import prices will accelerate to 6% in 2004, but will abate in 2005 to −2%. With these assumptions the prices of crude materials will fall in 2004 half the rate in Scenario I, mainly because of stronger growth that will prevent their drastic drop. Crude material prices will bottom much later than in Scenario I, in March 2005, before they begin to rise again. But by October 2005 they will only have recovered to zero growth compared with 17% in Scenario I (see Figure 3.8b for a comparison of the trajectory of crude materials inflation under the two scenarios). Most likely, crude material prices will continue to rise beyond the forecast period. The relative higher inflation of crude materials in Scenario II implies that the prices of intermediate supplies will not abate as in Scenario I. PPI-inflation of intermediate supplies will not subside under Scenario II in 2004, and will rise in 2005, but less than in Scenario I (see Figure 3.7). This means that PPI-inflation of finished goods will not fall as much as in Scenario I in 2004, but will rise less in 2005 (see Figure 3.6b). This pattern of PPI-inflation will feed through to CPI-inflation. During 2004 consumer price inflation will be higher than in Scenario I, but will remain muted during 2005 (see Figure 3.6a).

The fall in wage inflation will be less rapid in Scenario II compared with Scenario I because of stronger growth. Wage inflation will bottom much later and its increase after a while will be more muted than in Scenario I (see Figure 3.9b). This implies that the ECI will be marginally higher than in Scenario I (see Figure 3.10). Despite the stronger growth the pace of job creation in 2004 under Scenario II will be slower than Scenario I because of relatively higher wages. However, in the course of 2005 job creation under Scenario II not only will catch up with Scenario I, but will also exceed it (see Figure 3.11b). Productivity will fall at the same rate in 2004 under the two Scenarios, but will fall even more in 2005 under Scenario II (see Figure 3.12).

As a result, unit labour cost will fall at the same rate in both Scenarios in the course of 2004, but will catch up in 2005.

Overall, in Scenario II the stronger growth in 2004 will prevent the drastic drop in crude material prices and will not put a cap on the price of oil and commodity prices resulting in higher CPI-inflation. However, the slower growth in 2005 will also prevent the revival of inflation in crude material prices thus causing muted CPI-inflation. The stronger growth in 2004, but weaker in 2005, will cause a more rapid job creation in 2004, but slower in 2005. But because of lagged effects, these fluctuations in employment and output will trigger greater fall in productivity in 2005 under Scenario II, which will be reflected in unit labour cost. But the worse outlook for unit labour cost under Scenario II will not have enough time to feed through to prices in 2005, although this will probably happen beyond the forecast period – in 2006. Nonetheless, over the next two years CPI-inflation will be less volatile and more muted under Scenario II than in Scenario I.

3.3   Sensitivity of Scenario II (strong recovery in 2004)

The plausibility of this scenario depends on how sensitive the projections for the wage–price sector are to their determinants. It is convenient in comparing the impact of the various determinants in the wage–price sector to look at multipliers. The multiplier measures the ratio of the percentage change of, say, CPI-inflation to a given percentage change in one determinant, say, industrial production growth. For meaningful comparison multipliers are calculated in two different ways. First, every determinant has been perturbed by one standard deviation of its historical volatility. This allows a comparison of the effects on the wage–price sector by standardising the multipliers with respect to their historical volatility. For example, industrial production has fluctuated in the last fifty years by 6%, while the price of oil by 35%, which amounts to $10 per barrel. Hence, in calculating volatility adjusted multipliers industrial production has been perturbed by 6%, while the price of oil by $10 per barrel. This allows for a comparison of the various effects on the basis of plausible magnitudes. Second, every determinant has been perturbed by 1% of its value in *Scenario II*. This allows for a ranking of the multipliers in terms of importance and enables scale comparisons. For example, if 1% change in industrial production raises CPI-inflation by 0.1667% in two years, then 5% change in industrial production will raise CPI-inflation by five times 0.1667, or 0.8%.

Tables 3.2 and 3.3 provide the first and second year multipliers of the wage–price sector with respect to each of the four determinants. All multipliers are expressed as percentages, except job creation, which is expressed as thousand of jobs created in a month. Looking first at the volatility-adjusted multipliers, Table 3.2 shows that if industrial production growth was 6% higher than assumed in Scenario II, then, other things being equal, CPI-inflation will be higher by 0.4% after 12 months, and 1% after 24 months.

Table 3.2 Sensitivity of Scenario II – 1st and 2nd year multipliers %

	CPL-inflation		PPI-finished goods		PPI-inter goods		PPI-crude materials	
	1-year	2-year	1-year	2-year	1-year	2-year	1-year	2-year
Volatility adjusted multipliers (1-standard deviation)								
Industrial production (+6%)	0.4	1.0	0.2	1.1	1.2	0.9	0.1	0.5
Price of oil (+$10)	0.6	0.6	1.3	0.8	0.7	1.1	4.2	1.7
Commodity prices CRB (+13%)	0.4	0.4	0.8	0.6	1.1	1.2	6.1	0.8
Import prices (+9%)	0.5	0.6	0.1	0.1	0	0.2	0	0.1
Size adjusted multiplier (1% change)								
Industrial production	0.0667	0.1667	0.0333	0.1833	0.2000	0.1500	0.0167	0.0833
Price of oil	0.0174	0.0174	0.0377	0.0232	0.0203	0.0319	0.1218	0.0493
Commodity prices	0.0308	0.0308	0.0615	0.0462	0.0846	0.0923	0.4692	0.0615
Import prices	0.0556	0.0667	0.0111	0.0111	0	0.0222	0	0.0111

Table 3.3 Sensitivity of Scenario II – 1st and 2nd year multipliers % (except job creation)

	Wage inflation		Labour costs		Job creation		Productivity		Unit labour cost	
	1-year	2-year	1-year	2-year	1-year	2-year	1-year	2-year	1-year	2-year
Volatility adjusted multipliers (1-standard deviation)										
Industrial production (+6%)	0.5	1.0	0.3	0.4	198	235	0.1	−0.3	0.4	0.6
Price of oil (+$10)	0.5	0.6	0.1	0.2	0	0	0	0	0.2	0.2
Commodity prices CRB (+13%)	0.3	0.4	0.1	0.1	0	0	0	0	0.1	0.1
Import prices (+9%)	0.5	0.7	0.1	0.2	0	0	0	0	0.2	0.2
Size adjusted multipliers (1% change)										
Industrial production	0.0833	0.1667	0.0500	0.0667	33	39	0.0167	−0.05	0.0667	0.1
Price of oil	0.0145	0.0174	0.0029	0.0058	0	0	0	0	0.0058	0.0058
Commodity prices	0.0231	0.0308	0.0077	0.0077	0	0	0	0	0.0077	0.0077
Import prices	0.0556	0.0778	0.0111	0.0222	0	0	0	0	0.0222	0.0222

With this perturbation in industrial production growth all inflation indices and wages will increase by approximately 1% after two years, while labour costs by 0.5% and there will be almost 240 thousand new jobs per month. The effect of industrial production on inflation builds up through time, as the second year multipliers are higher than in the first year. The effect of industrial production on productivity is almost zero after two years, as the higher output is offset, in the long run, by an equivalent increase in hours worked. The effect of industrial production on employment is very rapid, as 200 thousand new jobs per month are created in the first year compared with 235 in the second year. This shows that the jobless (or better job-loss) recovery of the last two years is due to falling industrial production. If the recovery was to accelerate at, or above, potential output growth, then there will be sufficient job creation. With 6% higher growth in industrial production, there will be 5.6 million new jobs after two years. The size-adjusted multiplier shows that for each 1% increase in industrial production 40 thousand new jobs per month will be created.

An increase in the price of oil by $10 per barrel will raise CPI-inflation by 0.6% after 12 and 24 months. Hence, the pass-on to consumer prices of a hike in the price of oil is very fast. The effect on PPI, though, is more dramatic as finished goods will increase by 0.8%, intermediate supplies by 1.1% and crude materials by 1.7%, after two years. In the case of finished goods and crude materials the first-year multipliers are higher than those in the second year. This means that the effect of a hike in the oil price is passed on very rapidly to producer prices. In the first year there is overshooting of the long-run equilibrium, with the effect tapering off in the second year. The effect on wage inflation also builds up very quickly, as the first-year, and second-year, multiplier is around 0.5%. Unit labour cost will increase by only 0.2%. The effect on productivity and employment is zero by definition. Output and employment will be affected through lower household income (real disposable income) and lower profits. As these variables are outside the current model, the effect of the price of oil on employment, output and productivity is zero.

An increase in commodity prices (CRB-Index) of the order of 13%, equivalent to one standard deviation of historical volatility, raises CPI-inflation by 0.4% after 12 and 24 months. But the effect on PPI is more dramatic as finished goods increase 0.6%, intermediate supplies 1.2% and crude materials 0.8% after two years, other things being equal. There is overshooting of the long-run equilibrium in the case of finished goods and crude materials. An increase in import prices of the order of 9% raises CPI-inflation by 0.5% with the effect passed on very quickly. The effect on PPI is lower because all commodity prices, including oil, are unchanged. Hence, the effect of import prices on PPI is small because it is only indirect through the effect of CPI-inflation on wage inflation and unit labour cost.

The conclusions of this sensitivity analysis are as follows. First, industrial production is the most important determinant of CPI-inflation judged either on volatility- or size-adjusted multipliers. Import prices, commodity prices and oil occupy the first, second and third positions, respectively. Second, industrial production is also the most important factor affecting wage inflation, labour costs and unit labour costs. Third, commodity prices and the price of oil are more important than industrial production as far as PPI-inflation is concerned.

4   Summary and conclusions

Inflationary pressures are likely to abate in the near future. The real wage rate is coming down adjusting back to equilibrium, which is likely to lead to lower wage inflation in the near future. Unit labour cost has taken another plunge in the last six months as a result of a big improvement in productivity, caused by the second round of retrenchment by the corporate sector between July 2002 and April 2003. This is also likely to filter through producer prices later on and ultimately to consumer prices. Moreover, the prices of crude materials and, to a lesser extent, the prices of intermediate supplies have abated in the course of the year. These declines will feed through to producer prices and therefore PPI-inflation is near its peak. Import prices have also abated in the last six months thereby also helping to ease CPI-inflation in the near future.

However, now that the economy is gathering steam the question arises as to whether the fear of deflation is justified, as well as whether, and for how long, this downward trend in inflation would last before it is reversed. We have used the K-Model to throw light on these issues. The risk of deflation depends on whether the economy would continue to operate with slack in capacity. If the economy continued to grow at a smaller pace than potential output for a long time, then the risk of deflation would have been justified. Even then, it would have taken a long time for prices to begin to fall, as the upward pressure on inflation from the price of oil, commodity prices and import prices, due to the lower value of the dollar, would have taken a long time to unwind. Now that the economy is likely to grow at, or above, potential output growth (i.e. in excess of 3.0–3.25%) the risk of deflation over the next two years is almost negligible. Hence, the key question that remains is how long would it take before the downward trend in inflation is reversed?

To answer this question we have simulated the K-Model for a two-year period under two alternative scenarios: Scenario I – weak growth in both 2004 and 2005. The economy is assumed to grow near potential output with industrial production growth at 3%, throughout the two-year period. In

Scenario II – the economy is assumed to grow much faster than potential output in 2004, but to weaken substantially in 2005. Average industrial production growth is assumed to be the same under the two scenarios, but whereas in Scenario I it is flat at 3%, in Scenario II it is as high as 4.6% in 2004 but only 1.4% in 2005.

In Scenario I weak growth would allow CPI-inflation to continue falling for another twelve months before it begins to rise. Weak growth would put a lid on the price of oil and commodity prices and would enable the disinflation process, already in progress, to work its way through. However, the scenario of weak recovery in 2004 implies rising unit labour cost for the next two years because of lower output growth and strong job creation that would result in lower productivity. Despite rising unit labour cost, falling crude material prices will exert downward pressure in the next twelve months on the prices of intermediate supplies that would then feed through to finished goods and ultimately to consumer prices. The decline in CPI-inflation will be moderate compared to PPI because of rising import prices, due to the lower value of the dollar and higher profit margins, as demand in the economy will grow at potential output. However in the course of 2005 all inflation indices will accelerate, as the effect of falling crude material prices tapers off and unit labour cost continues to surge.

In Scenario II stronger growth in 2004 will prevent the drastic drop in crude material prices and will not put a cap on the price of oil and commodity prices resulting in higher CPI-inflation. However, the slower growth in 2005 will also prevent the revival of inflation in crude material prices thus causing muted CPI-inflation. The stronger growth in 2004, but weaker in 2005, will cause a more rapid job creation in 2004, but slower in 2005. But because of lagged effects, these fluctuations in employment and output will trigger greater fall in productivity in 2005 under Scenario II, which will be reflected in unit labour cost. But the worse outlook for unit labour cost under Scenario II will not have enough time to feed through to prices in 2005, although this will probably happen beyond the forecast period – in 2006. Nonetheless, over the next two years CPI-inflation will be less volatile and more muted in Scenario II than in Scenario I.

The sensitivity analysis shows that industrial production is the most important determinant of CPI-inflation, wage inflation, labour costs and unit labour costs. Commodity prices and the price of oil are more important than industrial production as far as PPI-inflation is concerned. There is one more implication of the two simulations of slow and fast growth, which relates to job creation. The job-loss recovery of the last two years is due to falling industrial production. If the recovery was to accelerate at, or above, potential output growth, then there will be sufficient job creation. With 6% higher growth in industrial production, there will be 5.6 million new jobs after two years. The size adjusted multiplier shows that for each 1%

increase in industrial production 40 thousand new jobs per month will be created.

What are the implications for the conduct of monetary policy over the next two years under the two alternative scenarios? Paradoxically, the Fed should tighten sooner under Scenario I (weak growth) than under Scenario II (strong growth). We assume that the Fed would not jeopardise its hardly won reputation as the guardian of low inflation and will not use the excuse of deflation to keep interest rates unduly low to help the personal, corporate and government sectors get rid of their debt. Instead, we assume that the Fed will act promptly and strike pre-emptively to curb inflation pressures. With Scenario I inflation will fall more and will, probably, bottom a year from now, that is, in October 2004, assuming that the assumptions made turn out to be correct. Yet, inflation will rise sharply in 2005. If the Fed is to strike pre-emptively, then interest rates should begin to rise when PPI-inflation hits bottom. PPI-inflation of intermediate supplies will begin to rise in May 2004 and PPI-inflation of crude materials and finished goods in November 2004. Hence, under Scenario I the Fed should tighten anytime between May and November 2004. However, given the long time lags of monetary policy on CPI-inflation, approximately two years, the Fed should tighten in May rather than in November. Early tightening is also advisable because of the presidential election in November 2004. The Fed would abstain from any action once the pre-election campaign develops in earnest. Hence, with Scenario I the Fed should tighten once PPI-inflation hits bottom, probably as early as April or May 2004. For once, markets may be right, but for the wrong reasons. The futures market is discounting that interest rates will begin to climb in April or May 2004, as they extrapolate that growth will remain at the torrid pace of 8.2% of the third quarter of 2003. It would be interesting to see if the futures markets revises its view of the tightening of monetary policy for later on if growth decelerates in the next one or two quarters.

With Scenario II (strong growth) inflation will not fall as much in 2004 as with Scenario I and will remain muted in 2005 compared to a surge with the alternative scenario. Hence, the Fed can afford to wait for much longer. Inflation will ultimately rise because of falling productivity, but this will probably happen beyond the two-year period, in 2006. Given the long lags of monetary policy on inflation the Fed may tighten after the US presidential election.

The seemingly paradox that monetary policy should be tightened sooner under slow rather than fast growth reflects the thesis that, although there is no trade-off between growth and inflation, there is a trade off between the volatility of growth and the volatility of inflation. In Scenario I the volatility of growth is zero, as growth is the same in the two years. However, this leads to high volatility in inflation, which given the lags of monetary policy requires early monetary tightening. In Scenario II, the volatility of growth is high, whereas the volatility of inflation is low. This allows monetary policy to be tightened later rather than sooner. Surely, the argument of the chapter would support the thesis taken by Greenspan (2004a,b) for a great deal of discretion in the conduct of monetary policy, especially so in the uncertain world of economics, rather than the monolithic rules of other central banks, an example of which is the ECB (see, e.g. Duisenberg, 2002).

4
Corporate Profits and Relationship to Investment[1]

1 Introduction

Reported earnings in the second half of the 1990s showed a dramatic improvement in profitability, which was interpreted as the reversal of the long-term decline in US profitability. However, National Income Accounts did not confirm this argument at that time, which financial markets ignored entirely. The 'governance crisis' that ensued confirmed that creative accounting was mainly responsible for that interpretation. Consequently, the question of whether the US economy is still characterised by long term declining profitability is pertinent. A further question is whether this decline might reverse itself with the current recovery. The alternative interpretation would be that any improvement might be temporary in view of the US long-term trend of shifting production overseas. We address these issues in this chapter.

US profitability soared in the second and third quarters of 2003, as growth accelerated. The pricing power of companies showed a partial recovery and profits margins surged. The single most important factor that contributed to the spectacular recovery of total profits was actually profit margins. The surge in profit margins is due to the first phase of the adjustment to higher growth, which lifts productivity and lowers unit labour cost, because the increase in growth is not matched by job creation. The second half of 2003 saw the first phase of this adjustment process. However, in the second phase companies would need to hire new employees. Greenspan (2004b) puts it even more optimistically: 'In all likelihood, employment will begin to grow more quickly before long as output continues to expand. Productivity over the past few years has probably received a boost from the efforts of businesses to work off the stock of inefficiencies that had accumulated in the boom years. As those opportunities to enhance efficiency become scarcer and as managers become more confident in the durability of the expansion, firms will surely once again add to their payrolls' (p. 3). This erodes the initial gains in productivity, and unit labour cost begins to rise. This second phase of the adjustment process is most likely to be experienced in 2004.

This will erode profit margins and will slow the rate of profitability. Fast growth in 2004 may moderate the fall in profits, but it is likely to cause much slower growth than potential output in 2005, which will trigger a collapse of profits. Hence, large volatility in growth is undesirable, as it implies large volatility in profits.

How much profits would fall in the next two years depends on the pace of job creation. If confidence were to evaporate and companies became once more very cautious in hiring new employees, then the gains in productivity will be eroded more gradually than otherwise, and unit labour cost will not rise as steeply. In this case the fall in profit margins would be slower, so that unit-profit and total profits will fall by less than otherwise. The recent profit recovery is not a mirage, in spite of its expected decline in the projection period. Rather it is mid-cycle profit crisis, which is typical in business cycles. A mid-cycle profit crisis has on some occasions led to a correction in the equity market. But when it did not, this was because growth of industrial production was extremely robust – usually double digit. In the current environment growth is strong, but industrial production is very weak, although it would improve in the next two years. Therefore, the risk of correction in equity markets is non-negligible.

In order to highlight these issues we have simulated the K-Model for a two-year period under the alternative scenarios of strong and weak growth in 2004. In Section 2 we examine the factors that affect corporate profitability. In Section 3 we present a schematic form of the K-Model of corporate profits. In Section 4 we discuss the simulation results. In Section 5 we review the evidence from previous cycles and attempt to ascertain the extent to which disappointment with corporate earnings at an advanced stage of the business cycle can lead to market corrections. In Section 6 the mid-cycle profits crisis and its impact on the equity market are discussed. The final Section 7 summarises and offers some conclusions.

2   Factors affecting corporate profitability

In the second and third quarters of 2003 corporate profits soared, from very low levels, and the economy showed signs of robust recovery. Financial markets have rallied relentlessly since the end of the Iraq war in response to this news; indeed, they may have been oversold before that. Consensus estimates for growth in 2004 have been upgraded to 4.4% from an expected 3.1% in 2003, while for corporate profits they have been raised to 15.9%, only marginally lower than the 17.6% expected for 2003. However, the question arises as to whether profits would be as strong as expected by the consensus and whether the equity market would price in these consensus forecasts for 2004. Disappointment with corporate earnings may cap the upside of equity markets around the world and may even lead to a correction. In the third quarter of 2003 total corporate profits with inventory valuation (IVA) and

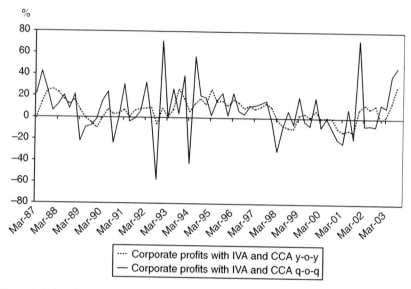

Figure 4.1   Total corporate profits with IVA and CCA

capital consumption adjustment (CCA) soared $105.5 billion or 47% compared to the second quarter and 30% year-on-year (y-o-y) (see Figure 4.1). The quarter-on-quarter (q-o-q) improvement in profits came predominantly from the domestic industries that surged 52.8%, while profits from the rest of the world showed a meagre 5.2% recovery, in spite of the dollar plunge. Within the domestic industries the improvement was widespread with profits from non-financial enterprises surging 60.2%, while profits of financial corporations improved at half the rate.[2]

Although in the second quarter of 2003 corporate profits had a similar spectacular increase that was entirely due to the provisions of the Jobs and Growth Tax Reconciliation Act of 2003, the increase in the third quarter was caused by improved economic fundamentals. The Act provided for an additional first year bonus depreciation write-off, increasing the immediate depreciation write-off from 30% (provided for in the Job Creation and Worker Assistance Act of 2002) to 50% for property acquired after 5 May 2003, and placed in service before 1 January 2005. As a result of these depreciation incentives the capital consumption adjustment increased by $83.7 billion in the second quarter (from $115.3 billion to $199 billion), compared with an increase of $5.6 billion in the first quarter of 2003. The inventory valuation adjustment increased by $24.7 billion (from −$26.9 billion to −$1.2 billion), in contrast to a decrease of $18.4 billion. Stripping down the influence of both capital consumption and inventory valuation adjustment, profits in the second quarter of 2003 decreased by $19.8 billion or −15.3% (q-o-q). However, in contrast

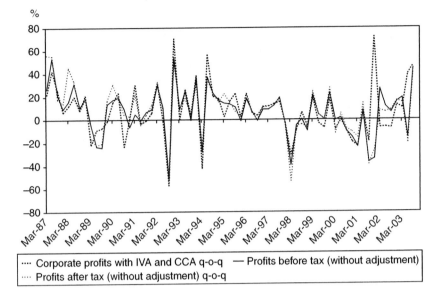

Figure 4.2 Corporate profits, before and after tax (q-o-q)

to the second quarter in the third quarter the capital consumption adjustment increased only $30.9 billion, while the inventory valuation adjustment decreased by $3.4 billion from −$5.6 to −$2.2 billion. Figure 4.2 shows total profits with IVA and CCA, profits before tax (that excludes these adjustments) and after tax profits (that excludes in addition the tax liability). Hence, the spectacular recovery of profits in the third quarter is to a large extent due to improved economic fundamentals.

Further insight into the outlook for corporate profits can be obtained by analysing the constituent components of the profits of non-financial corporations (the highest level of aggregation for which data is available).[3] In the third quarter of 2003 total profits of non-financial corporations with IVA and CCA increased by 43.2% (y-o-y). The profit per unit of output increased 36.9% (y-o-y) and 51% (q-o-q), while the volume of sales (the real gross product of non-financial business) increased 4.2% (y-o-y) and 8.6% (q-o-q), (see Figures 4.3 and 4.4). Hence, in spite of the spectacular increase of the volume of sales, the tremendous improvement in profits is, to a large extent, due to unit-profits. All factors contributed to the improvement in unit-profit in the third quarter. After a temporary plunge of pricing power in the second quarter of 2003, companies continued to increase prices. The price per unit of output increased by 0.8% in the third quarter, after a similar drop in the second quarter. In the corresponding 2002 quarter, unit price continued to recover from its bottom in September 2002 to 0.4% in the third quarter of 2002 (see Figure 4.5).

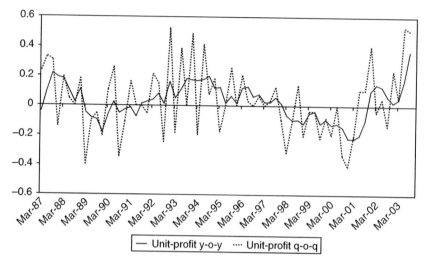

Figure 4.3 Unit-profit (corporate profits of non-financial corporations with IVA and CCA; unit-profit from current production)

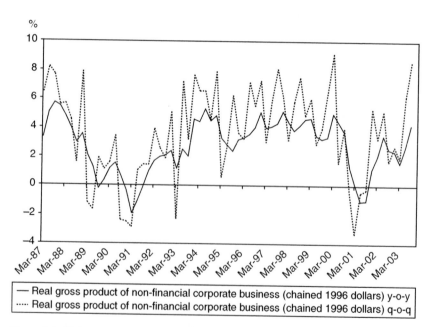

Figure 4.4 Volume of sales of non-financial corporations

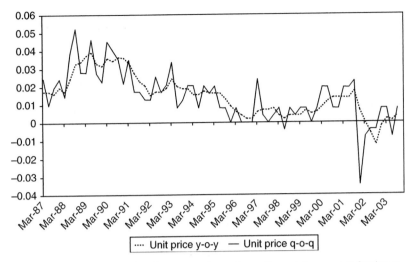

Figure 4.5 Price per unit of real gross product of non-financial corporate business

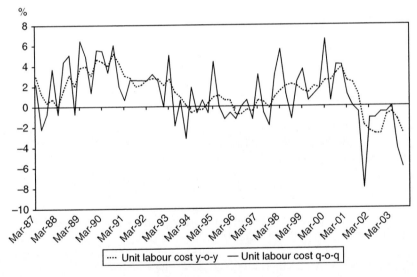

Figure 4.6 Unit labour cost (compensation of employees)

Cost cutting was very successful in the last two quarters of 2002, reducing both labour and non-labour unit cost thereby contributing to the improvement of unit-profit. Unit labour cost fell 6% (q-o-q) in the third quarter of 2002, after a 4.1% in the second. The drop of unit labour cost in the last two quarters of 2002 reversed the trend of the previous five quarters (see Figure 4.6).

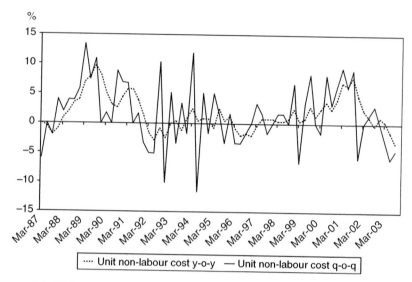

Figure 4.7   Unit non-labour cost

The rate of growth of unit labour cost bottomed in September 2002 and started to increase. This triggered a second round of retrenchment in the recent downturn by the corporate sector with the aim of turning unit labour cost decisively down yet again. Companies cut production, laid off workers and slashed investment between July 2002 and April 2003 in an effort to curb unit labour cost and restore profitability, in an effort to scale down operations to lower output levels. This retrenchment is tantamount to a double-dip recession for the tradable part of the economy. The operation was successful and the rate of growth of unit labour cost fell drastically in the second half of 2003, thereby enabling corporate profits to soar.[4] Moreover, unit non-labour cost fell by 4.5% (q-o-q) in the third quarter of 2003, after an increase by 5.9% in the second quarter (see Figure 4.7). Unit non-labour cost has fallen at the time of writing (February 2004) for three consecutive quarters.

The success of cost cutting is evident in the phenomenal recovery of profit margins, which in the third quarter of 2003 soared to 50.1% (q-o-q), after increasing by 54.2% in the second quarter (see Figure 4.8). The profit margin bottomed in December 2000 and, with the exception of two quarters, has improved since then. In the early 1990s recession profit margins did not improve for a long time after the trough of the recession. In the early 2000 recession company restructuring was much more effective. Labour cost is the single most important factor accounting for more than two-thirds of total cost. Capital consumption and net interest account for 17% of total cost. Hence, successful restructuring requires curbing of labour cost. Figure 4.9 shows the inverse relationship between the rate of growth of profit margin

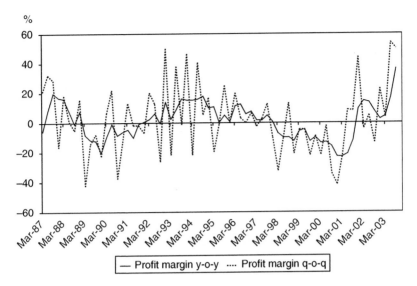

Figure 4.8 Profit margin

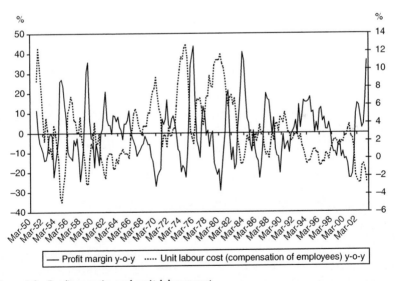

Figure 4.9 Profit margin and unit labour cost

and unit labour inflation cost. This supports the hypothesis that successful restructuring depends on curbing labour cost. The double-dip recession in the tradable part of the economy between July 2002 and April 2003 coincided with a drive to improve the profit margin that peaked in March 2002 and was in decline until December 2002. The restructuring was successful because unit labour cost fell once again and as a result profit margins increased in the last six months.

In order to appreciate the likely course of corporate profits over the next two years we first highlight the essentials of the theoretical framework that captures the essentials of profit behaviour, all embedded in the K-Model of profits. We turn our attention to this aspect next.

3   The K-Model of corporate profits

Our approach to profits in this chapter is tightly linked to the chapter that follows on investment. This is crucial to our explanation of corporate profits and their relationship to investment. In fact, the dependence of profits on investment emanates from the theory of income distribution, and from Kaldor's (1955) contribution in particular. More precisely, and in its simplest form, the relationship can be couched as in the following expression:

$$P = (I - s_w Y)/(s_p - s_w)$$

where P is profits, I is investment, Y is the level of income, and s_w, s_p are the marginal propensities to save out of wages and profits respectively (Kalecki, 1971; see, also, Sawyer, 1985). Profits would be negative unless investment is greater than $s_w Y$. The direction of causation runs from investment to profits, so that a larger volume of investment produces a higher level of profits. However, the drive for higher profits and the search for profitable opportunities, in which to invest, lead to increased production. Clearly, the pursuit of profits and the availability of past profits lead to higher investment. Indeed, if there were no higher investment, there would be no requirement for profits to finance investment. Consequently, a higher level of profits provides the finance for investment in the form of retained profits. Profits are a major source of finance and the ability to raise further finance is affected by the level of profits (Eichner, 1987). This argument along with the above expression for profits, clearly implies that there is a double-sided relationship in all this: profits finance future investment, but investment (actual) augments capital stock, which helps to create more profits in the future, if of course there is sufficient aggregate demand (see also, Robinson, 1964). Minsky (1986) has also emphasised this double-sided relationship: just as profits determine investment so investment determines profits.

A number of other studies focus on the crucial role of profits to investment. These contributions build on ideas of Kalecki (1943), Minsky (1986) and on Keynes's (1936) 'animal spirits'. Kalecki (1943) argues for the importance of financing constraints, and suggests that this may affect decision on net investment (capital accumulation) via profits, which determine the ability of the firm to invest in the future (see also, Baddeley, 2003). Stegman (1982) tests for the impact of corporate profitability on investment within an accelerator type of model. The results of this study support the contention that profitability is best viewed as a constraint to investment, rather than as a conventional explanatory variable. It is shown that using 'switching regression' analysis, profitability as a constraint outperforms conventional accelerator type specification. However, the presence of what Keynes (1936) labelled volatile 'animal spirits' can render these relationships unstable. Our approach in this book builds on the insights of the contributions to which we have just referred.

The K-Model of corporate profits and of investment determination (see Chapter 5), for non-financial companies (the highest level of aggregation for which data exist), is based on the theoretical propositions just summarised. It consists of the following six equations.

1. The output of non-financial corporations (QNFC)
2. The unit labour cost of non-financial corporations (ULCNFC)
3. The price per unit of output charged by non-financial corporations (PQNFC)
4. The profit margin of non-financial corporations (PMNFC)
5. The unit-profit of non-financial corporations (UPNFC)
6. Total profits of non-financial corporations (TPNFC)

In the long run, the output of NFC grows at the same rate as real GDP thereby connecting the outlook for profits to the rest of the real sector of the economy and hence to fiscal and monetary policy. It also connects developments in the rest of the world, which are best reflected in changes in world trade and currency movements. In the short run, output growth adjusts to correct any previous deviation from equilibrium in output. Thus, when output is higher than in equilibrium, then growth slows down; similarly, growth accelerates if output is less than in equilibrium. It takes just over a year for output to come back to equilibrium. Output growth adjusts to current real GDP growth and exhibits strong inertia to past output growth. This enables us to write formally the long-run relationship for QNFC as in equation (1):

$$QNFC = Q(GDP, WT, ER) \tag{1}$$

where GDP is Gross Domestic Product, WT stands for World Trade and ER for the Exchange Rate.

In the long run the unit labour cost of NFC grows at the same rate as the unit labour cost of non-farm business, thus connecting the outlook of profits to the whole wage–price sector of the economy. In the short run the unit labour cost of NFC adjusts to correct any previous disequilibria. Thus, when the unit labour cost is higher than in equilibrium, unit labour cost growth slows down; when unit labour cost growth is lower than in equilibrium, it accelerates. It takes almost twenty months for the labour cost to adjust back to equilibrium. Unit labour cost inflation exhibits strong inertia to past inflation. The unit labour cost inflation of NFC also adjusts to current and past unit labour cost inflation of non-farm business. We may, thus, write:

$$ULCNFC = U(ULCNFB) \tag{2}$$

where ULCNFB stands for the ULC of the Non-Farm Business.

In the long run the unit price of NFC grows at the same rate as PPI-inflation of finished goods, thus again linking the outlook for corporate profits to the wage–price sector. In the short run price inflation in NFC adjusts to correct any previous disequilibria. Thus, when the unit price of NFC is lower than in equilibrium, then the price inflation of NFC accelerates, and decelerates when it is higher than in equilibrium. Price inflation adjusts to current and past PPI-inflation and exhibits strong inertia to past price inflation of NFC. Equation (3) depicts the long-run relationship for PQNFC:

$$PQNFC = P(PPI) \tag{3}$$

In the long run, the profit margin (the ratio of unit-profit to unit price, i.e. UPNFC/PQNFC) depends negatively on unit labour cost and positively on output. In the short run the growth of profit margin adjusts to correct any previous deviation from equilibrium. Thus, if the profit margin is lower than in equilibrium, then its rate of growth will increase in the future, and decrease if it is greater than in equilibrium. It takes about sixteen months for the profit margin to come back to equilibrium. The growth of profit margin adjusts to current and past unit labour cost inflation, current and past output growth and exhibits strong inertia to past growth rates of profit margin. Unit-profit growth is, by definition, equal to profit margin growth plus unit price inflation. Total profits are the product of unit-profit by output. Hence, profits growth is equal to the sum of unit-profit growth and output growth. We may now write:

$$PMNFC = M(ULCNFC, QNFC) \tag{4}$$

We may also have for completeness sake:

$$UPNFC = PM \times PQ \tag{5}$$

and

$$TPNFC = UPNFC \times QNFC \tag{6}$$

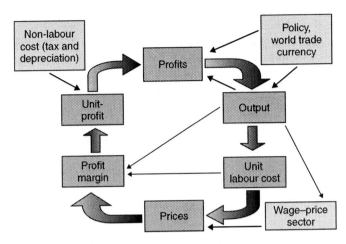

Figure 4.10 Profit model

The rationale of the K-profits model is summarised in Figure 4.10. The medium grey boxes illustrate the variables that belong to the profits loop. The light grey boxes illustrate the variables that cause a shock to the profit spiral. Shocks to the profit spiral are introduced by fiscal and monetary policy, developments in the rest of the world that affect world trade or the external value of the currency. Shocks are also introduced by all the variables that affect the wage–price spiral. Finally, corporate taxes, depreciation incentives and interest rates affect non-labour cost and set in motion the profit spiral.

Consider, for example, a shock in policy (domestic or foreign) that stimulates the real sector of the economy and leads to higher real GDP growth. This increases the output of NFC thereby raising productivity, which lowers unit labour cost in the short run. However, this sets in motion the entire wage–price spiral, which will ultimately affect the unit price of NFC. In the short run, the lower unit labour cost will reduce the pricing power of NFC. In the long run the gains in productivity will be eroded by increases in employment and therefore the unit labour cost will rise and therefore the price of NFC. In the short run, the lower prices will lift profit margins, other things being equal, which will then increase unit-profit and ultimately total profits. The higher profits will stimulate real GDP and a new cycle will be set in motion. In every round the marginal increase in profits will be smaller than the one before and after approximately sixteen months the system would reach a new long-run equilibrium in which the profit margin, unit-profit and total profits would be higher than the initial equilibrium.

There are some further direct effects in the profit spiral. First, the stimulus to output will raise directly the profit margin, as companies will incorporate expectations of higher growth very quickly into their profit margins. The stimulus to output will also boost directly total profits, as the volume of sales increases. This effect is in addition to the indirect effect of output on profit margin through unit labour cost and prices. Second, the lower unit labour cost will directly raise profit margins, in addition to the indirect effect through prices.

Any shock in the wage–price sector, such as commodity prices or oil prices, will raise prices and will set in motion a profit spiral too, that would interact with the wage–price spiral. Moreover, changes in corporate taxation or interest rates or incentives on depreciation will affect unit-profit directly and set in motion the profit spiral. The increase in profits from any shock is not explosive. This means that the profit spiral is stable. The stability is ensured because of corresponding increases in employment that erode the initial gains in productivity.

The recent behaviour of corporate profits can easily be accounted for in terms of the K-Model. Thus, the recent recession set in motion a downward profit spiral through lower output that reached bottom in March 2001 (see Figure 4.1). The diminishing pricing power of companies until December 2001 was due to the fall in output (see Figure 4.5). The depreciation incentives in May 2003 set in motion the profit spiral accounting, to some extent, for the profit recovery of the last six months. The acceleration of economic growth in the last six months explains the impact effect on productivity and unit labour cost and accounts for the second source of improved corporate profitability during this time. Any lingering fears that the improvement in profitability may prove to be a mirage are due to the differences between the short- and long-run effects of output on productivity, unit labour cost and profit margins. The impact or short-run effect of the increase in output is to spur productivity and lower unit labour cost. In the last two quarters productivity surged and unit labour cost fell, as employment was cut or remained stagnant. This part of the process was felt in the second half of 2003. However, the long-run effect of lower productivity, higher unit labour cost, is lower profit margins and hence lower unit-profit. If growth in 2004 turned out to be strong, as the consensus expects, then there would be sufficient job creation that would erode the initial gains in productivity and raise unit labour cost. This will reduce profit margins and hence unit-profit. But even if output growth remained robust, total profits growth will still be reduced, as the largest part of the improved profitability (80% in the last six months) is due to profit margins, while output growth accounts for a small part (only 20%). Hence, a fall in unit-profit would more than offset the effect of output and total profits growth would fall. The first part of the process has already been felt, now is the turn of the second part that lowers productivity, raises unit labour cost, profit margins and unit-profit.

4 The likely course of future corporate profits

To throw more light on the likely course of the entire profit spiral over the next two years we have used the K-Model to simulate two alternative scenarios.

Scenario I (weak recovery in 2004): What would happen to corporate profits if the current recovery were to falter in 2004 and became once again anaemic?

Scenario II (strong recovery in 2004): What would happen to corporate profits if the recovery that started after the Iraq war continued to be strong throughout 2004?

4.1   Scenario I (weak recovery in 2004)

The essence of this scenario lies on the assumption that the strength of the second and third quarters of 2003 was due to one-off factors related to the fiscal package of the current US Administration and rising confidence because of lower geopolitical risks after the end of the Iraq war. The stance of fiscal policy turned 1.6% of GDP easier with the 'Jobs and Growth Tax Relief Reconciliation Act of 2003'. The act provided for an additional first-year bonus depreciation write-off, increasing the immediate depreciation write-off from 30% (provided for in the 'Job Creation and Worker Assistance Act of 2002') to 50% for property acquired after 5 May 2003, and placed in service before 1 January 2005. The additional depreciation provided by the 2003 act increased depreciation expenses in the second quarter by $83.7 billion and in the third quarter by $30.9 billion. In addition, the 2003 act provided for a reduction of $100.9 billion in July in personal tax and non-tax payments. The act reduced withheld federal taxes $45.8 billion as a result of new marginal tax rates, the expansion of the 10% income tax bracket, and acceleration in 'marriage-penalty' relief. Federal non-withheld taxes (payments of estimated taxes plus final settlements less refunds) were reduced by $55.5 billion because of advance payments of the child tax credit that began being mailed out 25 July 2003. The fiscal stimulus provided through the depreciation incentives and tax relief, ignoring the additional measures on dividend income, as they are controversial with respect to their effect on demand in the economy, is estimated to be 1.6% of nominal GDP.

In addition, monetary policy was eased once more at the end of June 2003 with the Fed funds rate cut to 1%. The accommodative stance of fiscal and monetary policy keeps the economy going, but the imbalances in all sectors will weigh down on the economy and the recovery will begin to falter during the course of 2004 from the torrid pace of 8% in the third quarter of 2003. Nonetheless, the economy will grow at the rate of potential output in 2004 and 2005 with industrial production growth averaging 3%. Average weekly hours will remain largely unchanged from their current level at 33.9, while overtime hours will average 4.2 in the two-year period. Employers' benefit costs will abate somewhat from their current rate of 6.5% to 5% throughout the two-year period. The price of oil (Brent) will stabilise at $29 per barrel, while commodity price inflation will dissipate from 17% down to 11% until the end of 2005. Import prices will accelerate from 0.9% to 2%, as a result of the weaker dollar. Unemployment will fall to 5.6% of the labour force. Table 4.1 summarises all the assumptions underlying Scenario I, along with their current values as of October 2003.

With these assumptions the output of NFC will grow 2.8% in the next twelve months (from November 2003 to October 2004) and 3.2% in the following twelve months (from November 2004 to October 2005). However, under Scenario I this represents slower growth until the end of 2004 from 5.4% in the third quarter of 2003. One more factor will contribute to slower growth until the end of 2004. The output of NFC is, currently, higher than in equilibrium by 1.8%. Hence, in the next twelve months growth will slow to move output closer to equilibrium. Output growth will decelerate in the next twelve months and will reach bottom in December 2004 (see Table 4.1 and Figure 4.11 for the full trajectory of output growth). During the course of 2005 output growth will accelerate rising gently to 3.2% by October. The forecast error of the K-Model for output is 0.5%.

The projection of lower output growth by the end of 2004 means that unit labour cost is near its bottom and will rise over the two-year projection period. As we have already stressed in the context of the theoretical model, the impact or short run effect of higher output is to raise productivity, as employment is fixed and output rises. Indeed, this is exactly what happened in the second half of 2003; output increased, while employment fell. Hence,

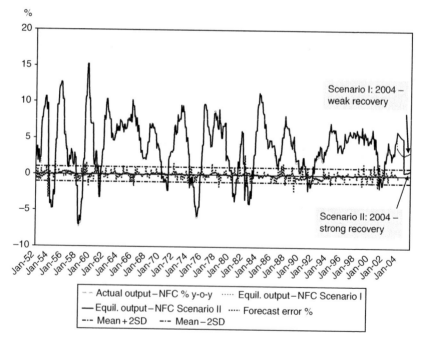

Figure 4.11   Output in non-financial corporations

Table 4.1 US corporate profits – (non-financial corporations NFC)

		Current values Oct. 03	Total profits y-o-y	Unit profit y-o-y	Profit margin y-o-y	Price per unit of output NFC y-o-y	Unit labour cost NFC y-o-y	Output NFC y-o-y
				Scenario I (weak recovery)			Scenario II (strong recovery)	
Assumptions								
Industrial production %	1st year	0.6		3.0			4.6	
	2nd year			3.0			1.4	
Average weekly hours level	1st year	33.8		33.9			34	
	2nd year			33.9			33.8	
Weekly overtime hours hours	1st year	4.2		4.2			4.5	
	2nd year			4.2			3.9	
ECI benefit costs %	1st year	6.5		5.0			5	
	2nd year			5.0			4	
Price of oil (Brent) $ per barrel	1st year	28.2		29.0			35	
	2nd year			29.0			23	
CRB index %	1st year	16.9		11.0			20	
	2nd year			11.0			2	
Unemployment % of labour force	1st year	6.0		5.6			5.4	
	2nd year			5.6			5.7	
Import prices, all commod % y-o-y	1st year	0.9		2.0			6	
	2nd year			2.0			-2	
Current Level			33.1	27.7	27.7	0.6	-1.8	5.4
Deviation from long-run equilibrium (LRE)			22.0	15.2	20.3	-5.0	-4.6	1.8

Table 4.1 Continued

	Current values Oct. 03	Total profits y-o-y (%)	Unit profit y-o-y (%)	Profit margin y-o-y (%)	Price per unit of output NFC y-o-y (%)	Unit labour cost NFC y-o-y (%)	Output NFC y-o-y (%)
		Scenario I (weak recovery)			Scenario II (strong recovery)		
Assumptions							
Scenario I (weak recovery)							
12-M SRE (future short-run equilibrium)		−4.0	−6.9	−7.5	0.7	4.2	2.8
24-M SRE (future short-run equilibrium)		−6.2	−9.5	−11.7	2.2	5.3	3.2
12-M SRE and current level (difference)		−37.1	−34.6	−35.2	0.1	6.0	−2.6
24-M SRE and current level (difference)		−39.3	−37.2	−39.4	1.6	7.1	−2.2
Scenario II (strong recovery)							
12-M SRE (future short-run equilibrium)		0.5	−4.7	−6.0	1.4	4.4	5.1
24-M SRE (future short-run equilibrium)		−13.2	−13.9	−15.4	1.5	5.4	0.7
12-M SRE and current level (difference)		−32.6	−32.4	−33.7	0.7	6.3	−0.3
24-M SRE and current level (difference)		−46.3	−41.6	−43.1	0.9	7.2	−4.7

productivity soared and unit labour cost fell. However, the long-run effects of higher output are gradual reversal of these trends. With time higher output induces firms to hire more employees and this erodes the initial gains in productivity and increases unit labour cost. This is exactly what should happen in the projection period if growth were to be maintained at the pace of potential output, as it is assumed in Scenario I. We assume that job creation would be strong throughout the two-year period of the order of 171 thousand in 2004 rising to 222 in 2005. The combination of strong job creation with lower output (deceleration from 5.2% in the third quarter to 2.8% until the end of 2004) will lower productivity and increase unit labour cost. Unit labour cost is 4.6% lower than in equilibrium and therefore over the next 20 months its growth rate will accelerate to bring it back to equilibrium. The unit labour cost of NFC will rise from −1.8% in the third quarter of 2003 to 4.2% (y-o-y) in twelve months and 5.3% in twenty four months (see Table 4.1 and Figure 4.12). The forecast error of the K-Model for unit labour cost is 0.5%.

The higher labour cost over the two-year projection period should push the unit price charged by NFC up. Moreover, the unit price is 5% lower than in equilibrium and therefore price inflation should increase to bring the unit price back to equilibrium. However, PPI-inflation of finished goods will fall precipitously over the next six months from 3.2% in October 2003 to −0.2% by April 2004, according to this Scenario. This will inevitably restrain the

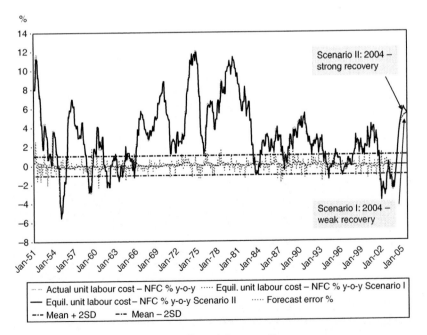

Figure 4.12   Unit labour cost in non-financial corporations

increase in price inflation of NFC until January 2005. However, in the course of 2005 the pricing power of NFC will accelerate to 2.2% by October (see, Table 4.1 and Figure 4.13), as PPI-inflation turns around, unit labour cost increases and the forces that bring the system back to equilibrium finally exert their power. The forecast error of the K-Model for unit price is only 0.35%.

The combination of lower output growth and higher unit labour cost over the next twelve months implies that profit margin is near its peak. Moreover, the profit margin is 20.3% higher than in equilibrium and this should also exert downward pressure on its rate of growth over the next sixteen months. This is the third time in more than fifty years of history that the profit margin has deviated so much from its equilibrium (see Figure 4.14 for the extent to which the profit margin has deviated from equilibrium since 1950). The highest deviation was 33.7% in August 1997. The profit margin is expected to fall under Scenario I from 27.7% in the third quarter of 2003 to −7.5% in the next twelve months and to −11.7% in twenty-four months (see Table 4.1 and Figure 4.15). The forecast error of the K-Model for the profit margin is 2.55%. This means that with an error of 5.1% the model can explain 95% of the history of profit margin in the last fifty years. Indeed, in the last 622 months there have been only twelve instances where the profit margin error has exceeded 5.1% (see Figure 4.15). On that basis the forecasting ability of the model is such as to claim that with 95% probability the profit margin growth in the future will lie within the interval of the central projection plus

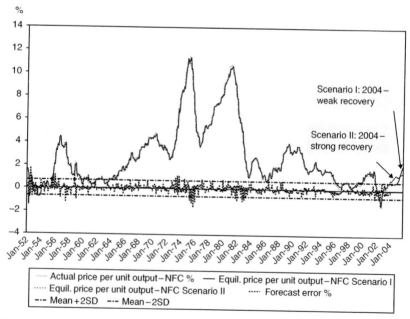

Figure 4.13   Price per unit of output in non-financial corporations

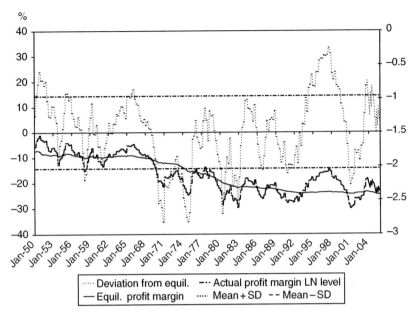

Figure 4.14 Profit margin (level) long-run equilibrium

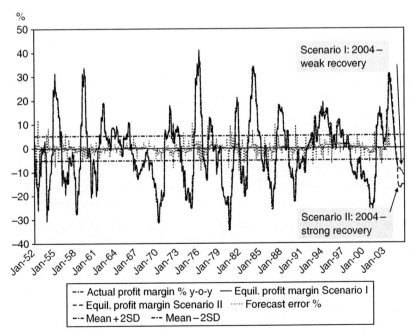

Figure 4.15 Profit margin in non-financial corporations

or minus 5.1%. This assumes that the assumptions are valid and that the behaviour of the profit margin will continue to be governed by the same structure that is encapsulated in the K-Model. The assurance here rests with the fact that the model can explain profit margin growth equally well in the last nine business cycles, which were demand-led in the 1950s and 1960s, supply-led in the 1970s and 1980s and again demand-led ever since. Hence, there is no reason to assume that the structure of the K-Model will be invalidated in the short-term future. As stated earlier, the forecast error of the profit margin is 2.55%, which is rather small when account is taken of the large volatility of the profit margin. The standard deviation of the profit margin is 13.6% and this implies that with 95% probability the profit margin growth lies within plus or minus 27.2%.

Since in terms of growth rates unit-profit is the sum of profit margin and unit price, and since the former is expected to fall, while the latter is expected to rise mildly, it follows that unit-profit is expected to fall but not by as much as profit margin. Hence, unit-profit is expected to fall by 6.9% in twelve months and 9.5% in twenty-four months (see Table 4.1 and Figure 4.16). The forecast error of the K-Model for unit-profit is 2.6%.

Since in terms of rates of growth total profit is the sum of unit-profit and output, and since the former is expected to fall, while the latter is expected to grow, but at a smaller pace, it follows that total profits should fall, according

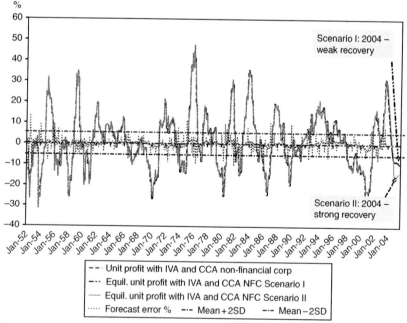

Figure 4.16   Unit-profit in non financial corporations

to Scenario I, by 4% and 6.2% at the end of 2004 and 2005, respectively (see Table 4.1 and Figure 4.17). The forecast error of the K-Model for total profits is 2.7%.

Overall, in Scenario I the output of NFC will decelerate in the next twelve months adjusting down from the torrid pace of 8% in the third quarter of 2003 to 3%. However, in spite of this deceleration, growth in the economy would remain strong at the rate of potential output. This would lead to robust job creation over the next two years, which would erode the initial gains in productivity and gradually reverse the fall in unit labour cost. The higher labour cost would increase the pricing power of NFC, but its impact would be offset in the course of 2004 by abating PPI-inflation of finished goods. However, in the course of 2005 the pricing power of NFC will accelerate as PPI-inflation turns around and unit labour cost increases. The combination of lower output growth and rising unit labour cost will lower profit margin growth throughout the two-year period. The gradual return of pricing power will moderate the impact of falling profit margins on unit-profit, while the robust growth will restrain the impact on total profits.

The essence of Scenario I is that profit margin is near its peak and will fall in the next two years, as productivity falls and unit labour cost rises. The validity of this scenario depends on the assumption that there will be strong job creation in the next two years. If confidence were to evaporate and

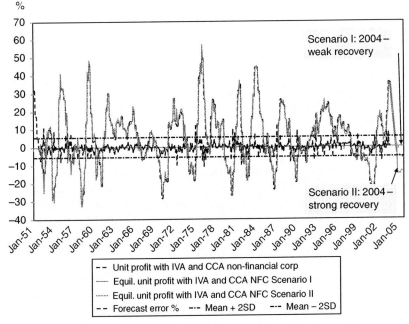

Figure 4.17 Profits in non-financial corporations

companies became once more very cautious in hiring new employees, then the gains in productivity will be eroded more gradually than assumed in Scenario I and unit labour cost will not rise as steeply. In this case the fall in profit margins would be slower and profits will fall by less than assumed in Scenario I.

4.2   Scenario II (strong recovery in 2004)

The essence of scenario II lies on the premise, which is largely true, that a combined fiscal and monetary stimulus will last for at least a year, and probably eighteen months, before it tapers off. Given that the fiscal stimulus was introduced between May and July 2003, the economy should remain strong until the end of 2004. The role of the accommodative stance of monetary policy is to prevent long-term interest rates from rising and therefore prolong the effects of the fiscal stimulus. However, despite low short-term interest rates introduced by the Fed in the 2000–03 period, long-term interest rates have risen sharply since June 2003 and the yield curve is extremely steep. If interest rates stay at this high level, or even rise further, which is very likely, the stimulus from fiscal policy will ultimately peter out. This means that growth will diminish in 2005 and beyond, other things being equal.

Given that the average growth for the preceding four quarters before the fiscal stimulus was introduced was 2.6%, that the fiscal stimulus was 1.6% of GDP and that the first year multiplier is about unity, the central projection for average growth until the second half, or the end, of 2004 should be 4.2%. This is very close to the consensus projection for 4.4% growth in 2004. Since the depreciation incentives on new structures will only count if premises are ready for service at the beginning of 2005, companies that would like to take advantage of the scheme should already have started spending. This explains the buoyant recovery of investment in the second quarter of 2003 that was responsible, to some extent, for the unexpectedly strong growth in that quarter. The other major factor that contributed to the unexpectedly strong second quarter in 2003 was the explosion of defence spending because of the Iraq war.

The stunning 8% growth in the third quarter of 2003 was caused by the combination of strong consumption, due to the income tax cuts that were introduced in that quarter, the last wagon effect for those companies that wanted to take advantage of the depreciation incentives on new structures, which accounted for $30 billion. It was also due to the worldwide improving confidence because of lower geopolitical risks after the end of the Iraq war that boosted US exports in the third quarter. To a large extent the worldwide-improved confidence is caused by the US. Hence, US exports are unlikely to remain as robust as in the third quarter of 2003. This implies that the stunning third quarter growth was due to one-off factors that are likely to dissipate in the first half of 2004. Nonetheless, the economy should still grow at 4.2% – central projection until the second half of 2004. Industrial production will average 4.6% growth in 2004, but will fall to 1.4% in the course of 2005. The average rate of growth of industrial production over the two-year period will be 3%, the same as in Scenario I of weak recovery. However, in Scenario II growth would be stronger in 2004 and weaker in 2005 than in Scenario I, but with the same average growth for the two-year period. The assumption that the average for the two-year period is the same under Scenarios I and II pertains to all variables that form the maintained hypothesis (see Table 4.1 for the detailed assumptions of Scenario II).

Average weekly hours will increase to 34 in 2004, but will decline to 33.8 in 2005. Over the two-year period the average will be the same as in Scenario I at 33.9. Similarly, overtime will increase in 2004 to 4.5 hours per week, but will fall to 3.9 hours in 2005 with an average of 4.2 hours for the two-year period. The employers' benefits costs will maintain the same values as in Scenario I, as they are not influenced by economic factors, but by legislation. The price of oil will shoot up to $35 per barrel in 2004, but will fall to $23 in the course of 2005, as growth falters. Commodity prices will accelerate even more in the course of 2004 to 20% because of strong growth, but will abate to 2% in 2005. Unemployment will fall to 5.4% of the labour force in 2004, but will climb back to 5.7% in 2005 because of sub-par growth. Import prices will accelerate to 6% in 2004, but will abate in 2005 to −2%.

With these assumptions output growth would continue accelerating for a little longer than Scenario I (see Figure 4.11 for a comparison of the output trajectory under the two scenarios). Growth would peak in early 2004 and the economy would decelerate gradually until the end of 2004. However, the assumption that growth would slow in 2005 implies a collapse for the output of NFC at the beginning of 2005. Since productivity is near its peak and unit labour cost is near its bottom, it makes little difference whether growth would be stronger or weaker in 2004. Although it sounds counterintuitive, the stronger the growth in 2004 is, the greater the increase in unit labour cost, because the first phase of the adjustment to higher output, which leads to higher productivity and lower unit labour cost, has already taken place. From now on, the stronger the growth is, the faster the pace of job creation and therefore the greater the increase in unit labour cost. This is typical of the second phase of the adjustment process to higher output, which is bound to begin as the economy moves in earnest in 2004. Strong growth (Scenario II) leads to 225 thousand new jobs per month in 2004 compared to 171 with weak growth (Scenario I). The weaker growth in 2005 under Scenario II compared with Scenario I, means that job creation would fall to 182 thousand under the former, but will increase under the latter. This fully explains the results that unit labour cost would increase to 4.2% in Scenario I and 4.4% in Scenario II after twelve months and 5.3% and 5.4%, respectively after twenty-four months (see Table 4.1 and Figure 4.12).

The higher unit labour cost under Scenario II implies that the unit price charged by NFC will be higher than Scenario I in 2004 (see Figure 4.13). One more reason explains why price inflation is higher with strong than weak growth in 2004 and this is the different behaviour of PPI-inflation under the two scenarios. Weak growth leads to a fall in PPI-inflation of finished goods from 3.4% in October 2003 to −0.1% in twelve months, whereas strong growth limits that fall to 1.4%. However, under Scenario II PPI-inflation in 2005 remains flat at 1.4%, whereas it rises to 3.9% under Scenario I. The pricing power of NFC in 2004 will increase 1.4% in Scenario II compared to 0.7% in Scenario I. In 2005, the pricing power will rise by another 1.5% in Scenario II, but will soar to 2.2% in Scenario I (see Table 4.1).

The effect on profit margin depends on output and unit labour cost. Since the difference between the two scenarios is small relative to unit labour cost in 2004, but large relative to output, the fall in profit margin is smaller in Scenario II than in I. The weaker growth in 2005 under Scenario II relative to Scenario I, in combination with the same increase in unit labour cost, implies a larger fall in profit margin (see Figure 4.15). Thus, the profit margin would fall 7.5% in 2004 under Scenario I, but the higher growth under Scenario II would limit that fall to 6.0%. In 2005, the reverse is true. The fall in profit margin is 15.4% under Scenario II, but 11.7% in Scenario I, because growth is weaker in the former compared to the latter. The behaviour of unit-profit and total profits is, qualitatively, the same with the profit margin. In 2004, unit-profit and total profits fall less in Scenario II than in Scenario I, but more in 2005 (see Table 4.1 and Figures 4.16 and 4.17).

Overall, in Scenario II, profit margins, unit-profit and total profits would fall both in 2004 and 2005. However, the fall would be limited in 2004, but it would be much larger in 2005. The stronger output in 2004 compared to Scenario I would not deter the fall in profits because we are about to enter the second phase of the adjustment to higher output. This implies lower productivity and higher unit labour cost because the stronger growth is channelled towards creating jobs rather than increasing productivity. The large volatility of output under Scenario II implies a similar large volatility in profits. In contrast the small volatility of output in Scenario I implies small volatility in profits. Hence, large volatility in output is undesirable, as it implies large volatility in profits.

5   Sensitivity of Scenario II (strong recovery in 2004)

The plausibility of this scenario depends on how sensitive the projections for the profit spiral are to their determinants. The profit model is linked with the wage–price sector and, therefore, the sensitivity analysis requires perturbation of the exogenous variables of the wage–price sector. It is convenient in comparing the impact of the various determinants in the wage–price–profit sector to look at multipliers. The multiplier measures the ratio of the percentage change of, say, the profit margin to a given percentage change in one determinant, say, industrial production growth. For meaningful comparisons multipliers are calculated in two different ways. First, every determinant has been perturbed by one standard deviation of its historical volatility. This allows for a comparison of the effects on the profit sector by standardising the multipliers with respect to their historical volatility. For example, industrial production has fluctuated in the last fifty years by 6%, while the price of oil by 35%, which amounts to $10 per barrel. Hence, in calculating volatility-adjusted multipliers industrial production has been perturbed by 6%, while the price of oil by $10 per barrel. This allows for a comparison of the various effects on the basis of plausible magnitudes. Second, every determinant has been perturbed by 1% of its value in Scenario II. This allows for a ranking of the multipliers in terms of importance and enables scale comparisons. For example, if one per cent change in industrial production raises profit margins by 1.2833% in two years, then 5% change in industrial production will raise profit margins by five times 1.2833, or 6.4%.

Table 4.2 provides the first and second year multipliers of the wage–price–profit model with respect to each of the four determinants. All multipliers are expressed as percentages. Looking first at volatility adjusted multipliers Table 4.2 shows that if industrial production growth was 6% higher than that assumed in Scenario II, then, other things being equal, the output of NFC will be higher by 8.7% after twelve months and 7.9% after twenty-four months. The increase in industrial production will set in motion the wage–price spiral, which will have an indirect effect on the unit labour cost of NFC. However, the increase in output of NFC will have a direct impact on the unit labour cost of NFC, which will rise 0.3% in twelve months and 0.7% in twenty-four months. The higher unit labour cost will have no effect on the unit price of NFC after twelve months, but will raise it 0.5% in twenty-four months. The higher output will boost profit margins, but the higher unit labour cost will moderate it. After twelve months profit margins will increase 7.7%, but the effect will dissipate very rapidly and after twenty-four months profit margins will be only 0.4% higher. Unit-profit will rise more than the profit margin because of higher prices. Total profits will increase even more than unit-profit because the increase in output exceeds the increase in unit price.

An increase in the price of oil by $10 per barrel will have no effect on the output of NFC, because the wage–price–profit sub-model has no feedback from the real sector of the economy. Higher CPI (Consumer Price Index) inflation will lower the real disposable income of households that would decrease consumption, while lower profits would have an effect on investment. Hence, in the full model an oil price rise would lower demand in the economy that would diminish the output of NFC. Since the wage–price–profit model is not linked with the real sector, the effect of the oil price rise on output is, by assumption, zero.

The higher oil price would increase unit labour cost by 0.1% after twelve months and 0.3% after twenty-four months. The unit price will increase

Table 4.2 Sensitivity of Scenario II – 1st and 2nd year multipliers (%)

	Total profits		Unit-profit		Profit margin		Unit price		Unit labour cost		Output	
	1 year	2 year	1 year	2 year	1 year	2 year	1 year	2 year	1 year	2 year	1 year	2 year
Volatility-adjusted multipliers (1– SD)												
Industrial production (+6%)	16.4	8.8	7.7	0.9	7.7	0.4	0	0.5	0.3	0.7	8.7	7.9
Price of oil (+$10)	0.3	0.1	0.3	0.1	−0.3	−0.6	0.6	0.7	0.1	0.3	0	0
Commodity prices CRB (+13%)	0.2	0.1	0.2	0.1	−0.2	−0.4	0.4	0.5	0.1	0.2	0	0
Import prices (+9%)	−0.3	−0.4	−0.3	−0.4	−0.3	−0.5	0	0.1	0.1	0.3	0	0
Size-adjusted multipliers (1% change)												
Industrial production	2.7333	1.4667	1.2833	0.1500	1.2833	0.0667	0.0000	0.0833	0.0500	0.1167	1.4500	1.3167
Price of oil	0.0087	0.0029	0.0087	0.0029	−0.0087	−0.0174	0.0174	0.0203	0.0029	0.0087	0	0
Commodity prices	0.0154	0.0077	0.0154	0.0077	−0.0154	−0.0308	0.0308	0.0385	0.0077	0.0154	0	0
Import prices	−0.0333	−0.0444	−0.0333	−0.0444	−0.033333	−0.0556	0	0.0111	0.011111	0.0333	0	0

even more 0.6% and 0.7%, respectively. Since output is, by assumption, unchanged, while unit labour cost rises, profit margins are squeezed. After twelve and twenty-four months respectively, profit margins will be −0.3% and −0.6% lower. But the sufficiently higher prices will offset the squeeze in profit margins and unit-profit will rise slightly. Total profits will increase at the same rate as unit-profit, since output is fixed.

An increase in commodity prices (CRB-index) of the order of 13%, equivalent to one-standard deviation, would have no effect on output, for the same reasons as in the price of oil, but will raise unit labour cost and prices. Profit margins will be squeezed, but unit-profit and total profits will be slightly up because of higher prices.

An increase in import prices of the order of 9% would have similar effects the price of oil and commodities. However, the increase in prices would be smaller than either the oil or commodities shock, because the effect of import prices on the unit price of NFC is indirect through its impact of CPI-inflation on PPI-inflation. Since the effect of import prices on the unit price of NFC is small, total profits and unit-profit would fall.

The conclusions of this sensitivity analysis show that industrial production is the most important determinant of profitability, judged either on volatility- or size-adjusted multipliers. Import prices, commodity prices and oil occupy the second, third and fourth positions respectively. The first year profit multiplier is greater than unity, but it dissipates very rapidly in the second year falling almost to zero.

6 Mid-cycle profits crisis and its impact on the equity market

A mid-cycle crisis in profits, like the one that is envisaged over the next two years is not uncommon in business cycles. Figure 4.18 shows the behaviour of unit-profit for eight quarters before and sixteen quarters after the trough of the recession, as per cent of the year earlier period. To simplify comparisons only four lines are shown, the average of the five demand-led recessions in 1947–72, the average of the three supply-led business cycles in 1973–84, the early 1990s recession and the recent one. In all cyclical downturns unit-profit is a coincident or leading indicator of the trough of the business cycle. In the demand-led business cycles the unit-profit bottomed at the trough of the business cycles. In the supply-led business cycles the unit-profit bottomed one quarter earlier than the trough. However, in both cases the rebound in unit-profit was very buoyant in the first year of the recovery, although it declined in the second year. In the early 1990s recession unit-profit did not recover for a long time. It had a double bottom and it remained throughout the recovery phase at the worst subdued rate in the post-Second World War era. Nonetheless, it recovered in mid-cycle. In the recent downturn unit-profit fell very sharply in the downswing, yet it bottomed three quarters

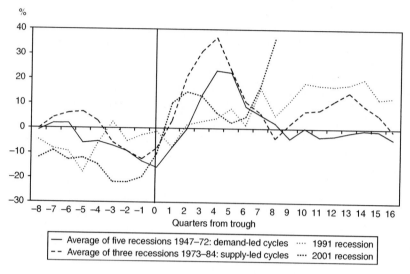

%

— Average of five recessions 1947–72: demand-led cycles	···· 1991 recession
– – Average of three recessions 1973–84: supply-led cycles	···· 2001 recession

Figure 4.18   Corporate unit-profit y-o-y (for eight quarters before and sixteen after the trough)

before the trough and recovered but only for two quarters after the trough. It slowed for another year and in the last two quarters it staged a remarkable recovery. Over the next two years it is expected to slow substantially.

The mid-cycle crisis in profits occurred both in the average demand and supply cycle. In the average demand-led business cycle of 1947–72 unit-profit slowed after the first year of the recovery from 23.3% to −4.0% in the following five quarters. In the average supply-led business cycle unit-profit peaked after a year from the trough of the business cycle at 36.7% and fell for twelve months to −3.9%. In the early 1990s recession unit-profit took quite some time to recover from the recession, but did not fall in mid-cycle. Hence, it does not provide any clues. We may look at Figure 4.19 that shows the behaviour of unit labour cost for eight quarters before and twelve quarters after the trough of the recession. In the average demand cycle unit labour cost bottomed after a year from the trough of the recession and rose for the next five quarters, thereby fully accounting for the slowdown of unit-profit throughout that period. Similarly, in the average supply cycle unit labour cost bottomed after a year from the trough of the recession and rose for the next four quarters, again fully accounting for the decline in unit-profit. In the early 1990s recession unit labour did not increase throughout the recovery, but simply oscillated around 1.7%, fully accounting for the strong profitability in the third and fourth years from the trough of the business cycle.

Figures 4.20 and 4.21 show the behaviour of industrial production and employment for twenty-four months before and after the trough. In the average

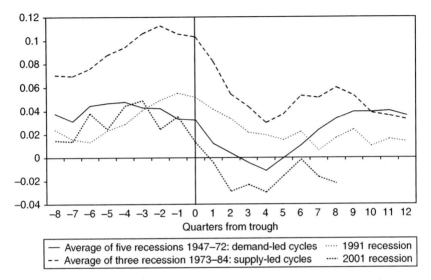

Figure 4.19 Unit labour cost % y-o-y (for eight quarters before and after the trough)

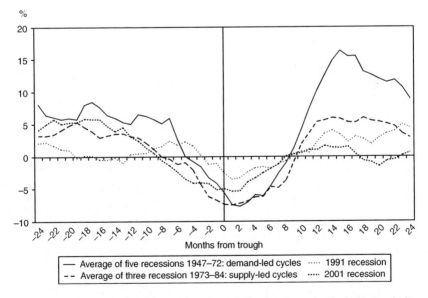

Figure 4.20 Total industrial production % y-o-y (twenty-four months before and after the trough)

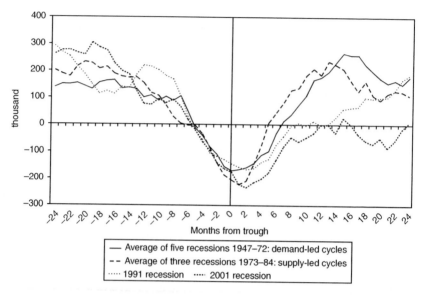

Figure 4.21 Monthly job creation/losses in non-farm payroll, 6M MA, thousands (twenty-four months before and after the trough)

demand cycle industrial production slowed in the second year of the recovery, but was very robust. It slowed from 16.3% fifteen months after the trough to 8.9% after twenty-four months. In contrast, in the average supply side industrial production peaked at 5.3% after twelve months from the trough and slowed to 2.9% after twenty-four months. In the same period, job creation was very strong in the average demand cycle. After twelve months from the trough job creation was 177 thousand, it peaked at 267 thousand, fifteen months from the trough and slowed for the remainder of the second year of the recovery to 178 thousand. In contrast in the average supply cycle job creation peaked thirteen months from the trough at 236 thousand and slowed to 109 thousand after twenty-four months. In the early 1990s recession industrial production oscillated around 3% in the second year of the recovery, while job creation steadily increased from zero to 185 thousand.

Figure 4.22 shows the S&P 500 level re-based at 100 at the trough of the recession. In the average demand-led business cycle of 1947–72 the equity market continued to advance during the five quarters in which unit-profit fell. The S&P advanced from 127.5 at the end of the first year of the recovery to 144.3 or 13.2% at the end of the following five quarters. However, during that period growth remained very robust and this deterred any correction in the equity market. In the average supply-led business cycle the equity market fell during the four quarters in which unit-profit fell. The S&P fell from 126.2 to 118.7 or −6%. However, growth was only a third of what it was in the demand

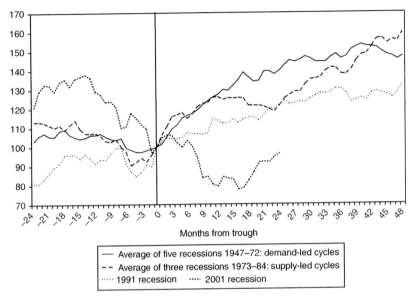

Months from trough

— Average of five recessions 1947–72: demand-led cycles
-- Average of three recessions 1973–84: supply-led cycles
····· 1991 recession   ····· 2001 recession

Figure 4.22   S&P 500 (rebased at trough = 100)

cycle. In the early 1990s recession the equity market continued to advance throughout the recovery, but there was no mid-cycle profit crisis. This is not very helpful in that it does not provide any further insights into the problem.

Overall, the evidence is mixed on the impact of mid-cycle profit crisis on equities. In the past, the equity market has moved up in demand-led cycles, but it has fallen in supply-side cycles. However, in the demand cycle, when the equity market moved up, growth was three times higher than the supply cycle and this has, no doubt, contributed to the different behaviour of the equity market. In the current recovery growth is very strong, but industrial production is very weak, although it would improve in the next two years. Therefore, the risk of correction in the equity market from a mid-cycle profit crisis is non-negligible.

7   Summary and conclusions

The spectacular increase in profitability in the second and third quarters of 2003 is largely due to a huge improvement in unit-profit and, to a lesser extent, to higher sales. For example, unit-profit contributed 87% of the improvement in profits in the third quarter, while the volume of sales only 13%. Although the contribution of sales sounds very little, it should be borne in mind that the economy registered one of the fastest growth rates in the third quarter of 2003, 8%. It is therefore always the case that whenever profits increase disproportionately to the economy this is due to unit-profit.

In turn, the tremendous increase in unit-profit is largely due to a huge recovery in profit margins and, to a lesser extent, in the recovery of the pricing power of companies. For example, profit margins contributed almost 98% of the improvement in unit-profit, while the pricing power contributed only 2%. This is, perhaps, excessively low, but nonetheless underlines the premise that any spectacular increase in unit-profit is largely due to profit margins.

The increase in the profit margin of non-financial corporations was 31% in the third quarter of 2003, the fourth largest in the last fifty years (see Figure 4.15). This recovery of profit margins in the second half of 2003 is due to the first phase of adjustment to higher output growth that started with the end of the Iraq war. The impact, or short-run effect of higher output is to increase productivity that leads to lower unit labour cost. The combination of higher growth and lower unit labour cost pushes profit margins up. In the second half of 2003, productivity soared to 4.7% (y-o-y) at the end of September from 2.6% in the first quarter. In the same period unit labour cost fell 6% from 0% in the first quarter. The surge in productivity is due to faster growth, while employment continued to fall. This differential adjustment of growth and job creation is typical of the first phase of adjustment to higher output growth. Companies are reluctant to hire more employees in the first phase of the adjustment, because they are uncertain as to whether the recovery of demand is permanent or temporary. Given the high costs of adjusting employment, due to large training costs, as well as to high costs of hiring and firing, companies are cautious in hiring new people until they are sure that the recovery of demand is permanent. However, in the second phase of the adjustment process, the continuation of strong growth, the recovery of profitability and continued optimism induces companies to hire more people. This gradually erodes the initial gains in productivity and unit labour cost begins to rise. The period March–December 2003 marked the first period of adjustment and the second phase will gather steam in the course of 2004. Hence, the spectacular increase in profit margins in the second half of 2003 is unsustainable, and they are bound to increase at a much smaller pace in the course of 2004. If profit margins are near their peak in terms of rate of growth, so are unit-profit and total profits.

To answer the question of how much profitability would decline in the next two years we have simulated the K-Model under two alternative scenarios: Scenario I – weak growth in both 2004 and 2005. The economy is assumed to grow near potential output with industrial production growth at 3%, throughout the two-year period. In Scenario II – the economy is assumed to grow much faster than potential output in 2004, but to weaken substantially in 2005. Average industrial production growth is assumed to be the same under the two scenarios, but whereas in Scenario I it is flat at 3%, in Scenario II it is as high as 4.6% in 2004 but only 1.4% in 2005.

In Scenario I the output of NFC will decelerate in the next twelve months adjusting down from the torrid pace of 8% in the third quarter of 2003 to 3%.

However, in spite of this deceleration, growth in the economy would remain strong at the rate of potential output. This would lead to robust job creation over the next two-years, which would erode the initial gains in productivity and gradually reverse the fall in unit labour cost. The higher labour cost would increase the pricing power of NFC, but its impact would be offset in the course of 2004 by abating PPI-inflation of finished goods. However, in the course of 2005 the pricing power of NFC will accelerate as PPI-inflation turns around and unit labour cost increases. The combination of lower output growth and rising unit labour cost inflation will lower profit margin growth throughout the two-year period. The gradual return of pricing power will moderate the impact of falling profit margins on unit-profit, while the robust growth will restrain the impact on total profits.

In Scenario II the stronger growth would lead to an even faster pace of job creation. Accordingly, the reversal in the trends of productivity and unit labour cost would be slightly more pronounced than in Scenario I. The combination of stronger growth and higher unit labour cost will accelerate the return of pricing power of companies and will moderate the fall in profit margin, unit-profit and total profits growth in 2004 compared to Scenario I. However, the assumption of slower growth in 2005 under Scenario II will accelerate the process of falling profit margin, unit-profit and total profits compared to Scenario I.

The recent profit recovery is not a mirage, in spite of its expected decline in the projection period. Rather it is mid-cycle profit crisis, which is typical in business cycles. There are two more implications for profitability from these simulations. First, the average growth in both scenarios is the same, but in Scenario I the volatility is zero, while in Scenario II the volatility of growth is high. The high volatility of growth under Scenario II implies a similar high volatility in profits. In contrast, the low volatility of growth in Scenario I implies low volatility in profits. Hence, high volatility in growth is undesirable, as it implies high volatility in profits.

The conclusions of the sensitivity analysis show that industrial production is the most important determinant of profitability, judged either on volatility- or size-adjusted multipliers. Import prices, commodity prices and oil occupy the second, third and fourth positions respectively. The first year profit multiplier is greater than unity, but it dissipates very rapidly in the second year falling almost to zero. Irrespective of which scenario materialises the crux of the matter is that profit margin is near its peak and will fall in the next two years, as productivity falls and unit labour cost rises. The validity of this conclusion depends on the assumption that there will be strong job creation in the next two years. If confidence were to evaporate and companies became once more very cautious in hiring new employees, then the gains in productivity will be eroded more gradually than assumed in the two scenarios and unit labour cost will not rise as steeply. In this case the fall in profit margins would be slower and unit-profit and total profits will fall by less than assumed in either scenario.

The evidence on the impact of mid-cycle profit crisis on the equity market is mixed. In the past, in demand-led cycles the equity market moved up when profits were falling, but in supply-led cycles the equity market fell when profits fell. However, in the demand cycle, when the equity market moved up, growth was three times higher than the supply cycle and this has, no doubt, contributed to the different behaviour of the equity market. In the current recovery growth is very strong, but industrial production is very weak, although it would improve in the next two years. Therefore, the risk of correction in the equity market from a mid-cycle profit crisis is non-negligible.

5

Long-term Risks to Investment Recovery

1 Introduction

In the first year of the current recovery investment grew at the worst-ever anaemic pace. Both short- and long-run factors contributed to it. However, in the second half of 2003, following the end of the Iraq war, both the short-run and long-run factors that affect investment have improved. The current accommodating stance of fiscal and monetary policy is probably sufficient for the economy to be booming at the time of the presidential election in November 2004, as there is sufficient momentum already built in. The long-term risk to investment stems from the fact that the current US Administration is not willing to take the risk that the economy would only be growing at the rate of potential output in 2004 as investment growth may be very subdued by then. It is, therefore, considering yet another fiscal package to stimulate the economy in the run up to the presidential election. Although such package would ensure that the economy is booming at the time of the election, it will raise long-term interest rates even more and will foster the forces that would ultimately weaken investment in 2005 and beyond. Hence, the long-term risk to investment would not dissipate by the introduction of yet another fiscal package. Instead, it would increase such risk.

We argue the case in this chapter by examining the recent behaviour of investment in section 2. We then study the short- and long-run factors that affect investment in sections 3 and 4, respectively. The theoretical aspects of the investment relationship are brought together in section 5. The long-run risks to investment are then examined through two scenarios, where we conduct relevant sensitivity analysis in section 6. We summarise and conclude in section 7.

2 Recent behaviour of investment

Real gross private domestic investment in fixed capital (both residential and non-residential, which includes plant, equipment and inventories) is the most volatile component of aggregate demand that invariably leads the economy into recession, but is a coincident or lagging indicator in recoveries. It is, in fact, 'the pace and pattern of business investment in fixed capital' that 'are central to our understanding of economic activity' (Chirinko, 1993, p. 1875).

In the recent downturn, investment fell 11% in the three quarters leading up to the trough compared with 15% average fall in the last ten recessions (see Table 5.1). Investment peaked in the second quarter of 2000, doubly bottomed in 2001, recovered strongly in the first quarter of 2002, but lost steam for another year until March 2003 (see Figure 5.1). To a large extent the spectacular recovery of investment in just one quarter (2002: Q1) reflected the end of de-stocking and increased depreciation incentives on investment in equipment and software following September 11. Replacement investment also played a role as the cycle of computers is two to three years and there was a rush of buying just before 2000 that had to be replaced by 2003. Investment in structures bottomed in September 2002 and recovered since then, although it lost some steam in 2003:Q3. Residential investment has been the strongest component of investment in the recent downturn because of the buoyancy of the housing market. Investment in equipment and software took another plunge in 2003:Q1, but recovered strongly in the next two quarters. How does the hitherto recovery in investment compare with previous business cycles?

Figures 5.2 and 5.3 show the behaviour of investment for eight quarters before and after the trough of the recession, as per cent of GDP and as per cent of the earlier year. To simplify comparisons only four lines are shown, the average of the five demand-led recessions in 1947–72, the average of the three supply-led business cycles in 1973–84, the early 1990s recession and the current one. In all cyclical downturns investment bottoms either at the trough of the business cycle or with one quarter lag. Hence, investment is either a coincident or lagging indicator of the trough of the business cycle.

The fall in investment in the recent downturn was the steepest of all recessions, 3.4% of GDP. In the average demand-led cycle, investment fell by 2% of GDP, while in the average supply-led cycle it fell by 2.8% and in the 1991 downturn it fell by 2.4%. In the recovery of 1991 investment grew at the smallest pace of all nine previous business cycles, dubbing the recovery anaemic. In the first year of the recovery investment grew by 0.3% of GDP, compared with 1.8% in the average demand- and supply-led cycle. By the end of the second year of the recovery, investment had grown by 1.7% of GDP in the early 1990s downturn, 0.5% less than the average demand- and supply-led cycle, thereby somewhat catching up with previous business cycles. In the recent downturn investment grew by just 1% of GDP in the first two years since the trough, thereby becoming the worst-ever anaemic recovery.

The anaemic nature of the current recovery is also confirmed in Figure 5.3 that shows investment growth on the year earlier period. On this measure,

Table 5.1 Business cycles

	Percentage change over three quarters leading up to trough										
Trough	1949-II	1954-I	1958-I	1960-IV	1970-IV	1975-I	1980-III	1982-III	1991-I	2001-III	Average
GDP (%)	-1.5	-2.7	-2.8	-1.6	0.0	-2.9	-1.9	-1.7	-1.5	-0.6	-1.7
Consumption (%)	2.5	-0.5	-0.5	1.0	1.0	-0.5	-1.4	1.5	-0.9	1.3	0.4
Gross domestic fixed capital formation (%)	-30.4	-11.0	-13.3	-21.6	-3.9	-21.9	-16.4	-12.0	-12.6	-11.0	-15.4
Exports (%)	7.1	-3.9	-15.3	6.6	4.6	-2.6	4.7	-7.8	1.2	-9.2	-1.5
Government consumption (%)	11.9	-4.4	1.5	3.7	-0.7	1.4	0.5	1.2	1.4	2.5	1.9
Job creation/losses	-32	-38	-64	51	-28	-27	18	-157	-9	-40	-33

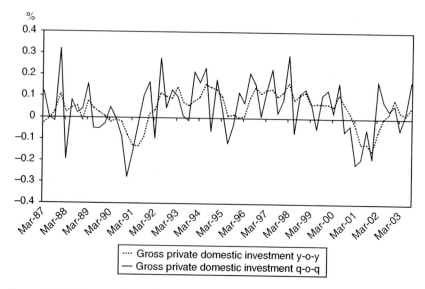

Figure 5.1 Real gross private domestic investment (including inventories) in the last business cycle

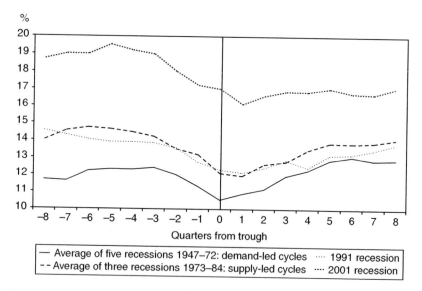

Figure 5.2 Investment as a % of GDP (for eight quarters before and after the trough)

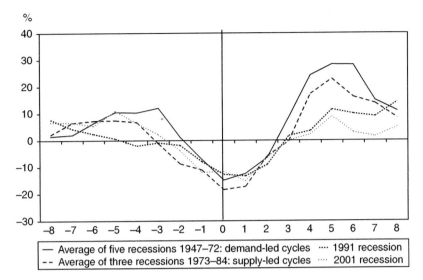

Figure 5.3 Real investment y-o-y (eight quarters before and after the trough)

in the first year of the current recovery the investment growth differential from the bottom was 24.8%, almost the same as in the early 1990s recovery (24%), which is, however, 40% less than the average demand or supply cycle. The causes of the current anaemic recovery are the balance sheet problems (or imbalances) not only of the business sector, as was the case in 1991, but of the personal sector, too, essentially because of prior budget surpluses. In the last two quarters of 2003, investment growth accelerated thereby raising hopes that the recovery would, finally, become sustainable. There are, though, downside risks to this scenario, which we explore below in this chapter.

3 Short-run factors affecting investment

Investment must turn around if the recovery is to become sustainable. This, in turn, implies that profitability, must begin to recover and capacity utilisation must also bottom. Figure 5.4 shows that capacity utilisation kept falling in the first eighteen months of the recovery. This implies that the excess capacity that was installed in the euphoria years of the bubble in the second half of the 1990s had not been dented, in spite of the resilient consumption. The low capacity utilisation (or excess capacity) shows the extent to which demand was overestimated in the second half of the 1990s that, until recently, has acted as a hindrance to the recovery of investment, due to some extent to overtly tight fiscal balance. However, capacity utilisation

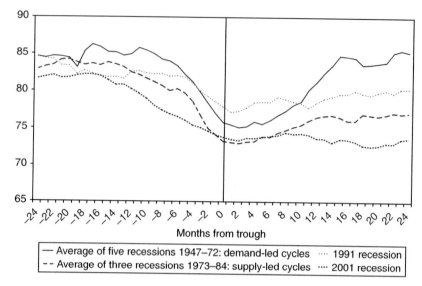

Figure 5.4 Capacity utilisation in manufacturing (twenty-four months before and after the trough)

turned around in the last seven months rising to 74.5 in December from 72.6 in May 2003, thereby raising hopes that if demand is kept at a high rate then the excess capacity might be absorbed.

Figure 5.5a shows the growth rate of non-farm, non-financial corporate profit per unit of output on the year earlier period. It is clearly a coincident or leading indicator of the trough of the business cycle. In the demand- and supply-led business cycles the rebound in unit-profit was very buoyant in the first year of the recovery, although it declined in the second year. In the early 1990s recession unit-profit did not recover for a long time. Throughout the recovery phase it even remained at the worst subdued rate in the post Second World War era. In the recent downturn unit-profit bottomed three quarters before the trough. It then recovered sharply, but only for a brief period thanks to the one-off incentives on depreciation following September 11. Unit-profit peaked in just two quarters after the trough and decelerated for a year after, as the effect of these one-off measures faded away. However, it has rebounded strongly in the last two quarters raising hopes that the worst is over, although part of the boost is due again to one-off factors (i.e. the depreciation incentives of the 2003 fiscal package).

Stripping down the effect of these one-off factors, which are captured in the inventory and capital consumption adjustment, the improvement in profitability is very modest. Figure 5.5b shows corporate sector pre-tax profits (which exclude the influence of all adjustments) as a per cent of GDP.

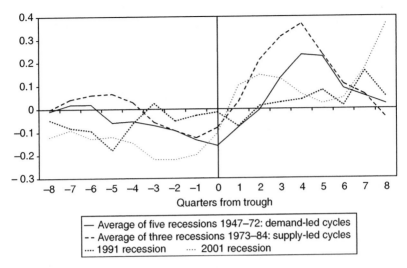

Figure 5.5a Corporate unit profit y-o-y (for eight quarters before and after the trough)

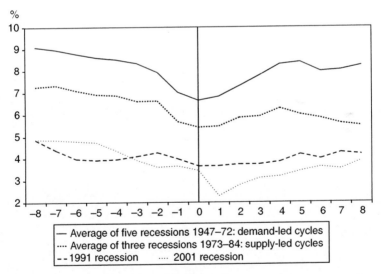

Figure 5.5b Corporate sector pre-tax profits as % of GDP (for eight quarters before and after the trough)

Pre-tax profits have deteriorated in every downswing, although they have bottomed at the trough of the business cycle. In the demand-led business cycles corporate profits bottomed at 6.6% of GDP, whereas in the supply-led business cycles they bottomed at 5.4%. In the early 1990s recession profits deteriorated even more. They bottomed at only 3.7% of GDP. In the recent recession they bottomed at 2.3% of GDP. The much talked dramatic improvement in profitability in the second half of the 1990s did not prove to be sustainable. All gains were lost in the last year leading to the trough. Thus, the popular perception of a revival in corporate profitability in the second half of the 1990s simply proved to be a mirage based on creative accounting. Pre-tax profits improved a mere 0.3% of GDP in the last six months of the year, just slightly above the trough level and nowhere near the 21% growth of profits with inventory and capital consumption adjustment.

However, profit margins depend on unit labour cost in relation to price power. For profit margins to turn around unit labour cost must peak and begin to decline, as it accounts for more than two-thirds of total cost. Figure 5.6 shows that the year-on-year (y-o-y) rate of growth of unit labour cost is a leading indicator of the trough of the business cycle by one to four quarters. In the recent downturn unit labour cost peaked three quarters before the trough. However, it bottomed a year after the trough and increased for the following two quarters. This deterioration in unit labour cost triggered a new round of retrenchment in the corporate sector with cuts

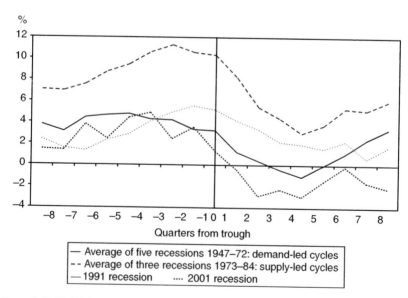

Figure 5.6   Unit labour cost % y-o-y (for eight quarters before and after the trough)

in production, laying-off labour and slashing once more investment. The retrenchment was successful and unit labour cost receded in the last two quarters. Hence, the outlook for profit margins and therefore for unit-profit has improved. Now that the war is over and uncertainty has dissipated, the dollar continues to fall, while fiscal and monetary policy remain accommodative, the chances for faster growth and therefore the outlook for profitability have improved. This bodes well for a sustained recovery of investment.

The other factor that restrains earnings and must be corrected for the recovery to take place is that companies must first liquidate their inventories of unsold goods. Thus, the inventory-to-sales ratio in manufacturing is a leading indicator of the trough of the business cycle by one or two months (see Figure 5.7). In the worst case it is a coincident indicator. In the current downturn it already peaked four months before the trough, but bottomed nine months after the trough and increased slightly in the following seven months. However, during the second round of retrenchment inventories became very lean thus paving the way for an increase in industrial production.

In a typical cycle production is resumed after excess inventories are liquidated. Hence, industrial production is a lagging indicator of the trough of the business cycle by one or two months (see Figure 5.8). In the 1991 recession it bottomed with one-month lag and at a higher rate than the average demand- or supply-led business cycle. However, it grew at a smaller pace during the recovery, thus underlining the anaemic nature of the recovery.

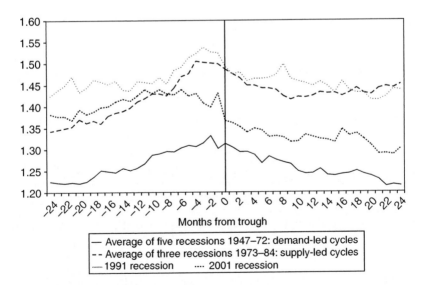

Months from trough

| — Average of five recessions 1947–72: demand-led cycles |
| - - Average of three recessions 1973–84: supply-led cycles |
| ⋯ 1991 recession   ⋯⋯ 2001 recession |

Figure 5.7 Inventory to sales ratio in manufacturing (for twenty-four months before and after the trough)

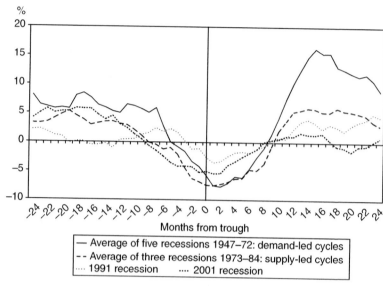

Figure 5.8 Total industrial production % y-o-y (twenty-four months before and after the trough)

In the recent downturn it bottomed two months after the trough and the recovery fizzled out after the first year. During the second round of retrenchment production cuts led to double-dip recession in manufacturing, but the reduction of unit labour cost, the restoration of profitability and the lean inventories have paved the way for increased production growth. Hence, the last nine months' upturn record is not an aberration, but confirmation of a new up-trend.

Overall, investment had a lacklustre performance in the last two years and played a significant role in making the recovery anaemic. However, it has improved in the last two quarters and the short-run analysis suggests that this is not transient, but a change of trend. Higher growth in the economy is taking care of the excess capacity that was installed in the euphoria years of the bubble and consequently capacity utilisation has started to improve. Profitability has also recovered, but not as much as the headline figures suggest, because they are influenced by one-off factors. Nonetheless, even the small improvement in profitability is supportive of a new trend, as it is due to the reduction in unit labour cost and the corresponding increase in profit margins. Hence, the double-dip recession in manufacturing has paid off its fruits by bending labour cost yet again, improving profit margins, creating lean inventories and paving the way for increased industrial production. Therefore, all the short-run factors that affect investment have changed for the better. The short-term (over the next twelve months) outlook for investment has therefore improved.

4 Long-run factors affecting investment: corporate sector imbalances

The anaemic recovery of corporate profitability in the early 1990s downturn was due to the poor financial health of the corporate sector. The net worth of the corporate sector, measured as assets less liabilities at current prices, deteriorated even during the recovery phase of the 1991 downturn. By contrast, it improved around the trough in the demand- and supply-led business cycles and fluctuated within a small range throughout the cyclical downturn (see Figure 5.9). Moreover, throughout the early 1990s downturn (two years before and after the trough) the net worth of the corporate sector was on a downtrend. This is due to the high debt gearing, characteristic of modern corporate finance. In every business cycle debt levels have increased.[1] In the demand-led business cycles debt as per cent of GDP peaked at the trough at 28% (see Figure 5.10). In the supply-led business cycles it increased to 33% of GDP at the trough, but in the 1991 recession it soared to 43%. In the current downturn debt as per cent of GDP soared to 47% at the trough. However, debt was reduced in the second half of 2003, showing that the balance sheet restructuring is working, and government deficit spending returning as well.

The high debt levels require not only more expensive servicing, as interest rates are usually high during the downswing phase of the business cycle, but

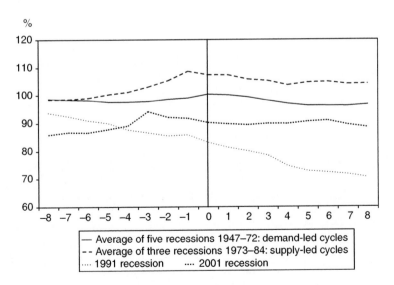

Figure 5.9 Corporate sector net worth as % of GDP (for eight quarters before and after the trough)

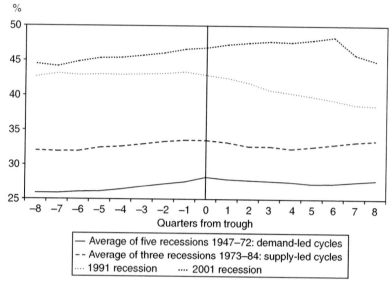

Figure 5.10   Corporate sector debt as % of GDP (for eight quarters before and after the trough)

also large volumes of new issues to replenish maturing debt. In the down-swing phase access to capital markets and the terms of issuing new debt deteriorate. Companies are, therefore, forced to cut drastically on new credit poised to finance investment and restrict themselves into refinancing existing obligations, even at worse terms. This makes the recovery anaemic, as companies attempt to pay back debts and refrain from spending on new investment; and all this on top of low demand for company products. This is exactly what happened in the recovery of the 1991 recession. Thus, although the 1991 downturn was demand-led, it differed substantially from the previous recessions of 1947–72 because the corporate sector was involved in the long process of curbing its high debt levels and restoring a healthy balance sheet. By the end of the second year of the 1991 recovery companies had repaid 5% of their debt as per cent of GDP. By contrast, in the average demand- and supply-led cycle companies repaid debt only in the first year of the recovery and only by 1% of GDP, while debt was again on the increase in the second year.

In the current downturn, although debt levels have continued to rise for most part of the recovery there has been a dramatic drop of 3.5% of GDP in just the last two quarters. This has taken place as the rate of growth of the economy by far exceeded the rate of debt accumulation (see Figure 5.10). This bodes well for a recovery of investment in the future. However, despite this buoyant growth the net worth of the corporate sector has fallen 2.4%

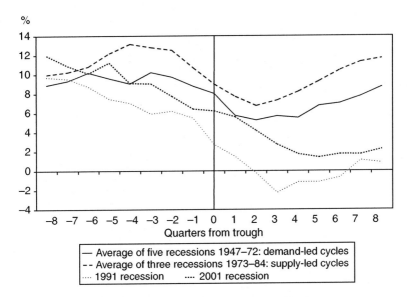

Figure 5.11 Corporate debt % y-o-y (for eight quarters before and after the trough)

of GDP in the last two quarters (see Figure 5.9). The conclusion is that although restructuring has been taking place successfully, it has not been completed yet.

The rate of growth of corporate debt peaks between one or two years before the trough, as companies cut back on new investment (see Figure 5.11). In the average demand- and supply-led business cycle the rate of growth of debt bottomed two quarters after the trough, but at a positive rate. Hence, debt never stopped growing. Its rate of growth simply slowed. By contrast, in the early 1990s downturn the growth of debt bottomed in three rather than two quarters, but at negative rate, too. So, for the first time firms reduced debt levels to restore financial health in their balance sheet. Debt began to increase again nearly two years after the trough. In the recent downturn, demand for credit was reduced from 11.2% at the peak to 1.4% five quarters after the trough. Debt has increased since then but only slightly (see Figure 5.11). Hence, companies are very cautious in borrowing despite the buoyant recovery in the second half of 2003.

The ways debt levels affect other company decisions can be judged by examining the degree of debt leverage, measured by the stock of debt as per cent of internal funds. The latter is defined as after-tax corporate profits, less dividends plus depreciation (net cash flow). Figure 5.12 shows this measure of debt leverage. Although companies are usually cutting on debt growth in the downswing of the cycle, internal funds decline even faster and debt leverage is increasing. In the recovery internal funds improve faster and debt leverage

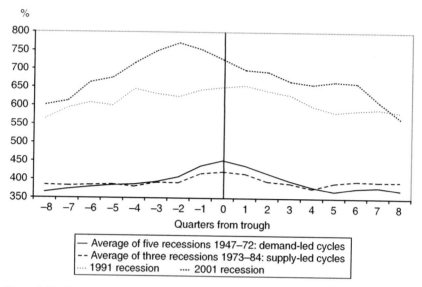

%
800
750
700
650
600
550
500
450
400
350

−8 −7 −6 −5 −4 −3 −2 −1 0 1 2 3 4 5 6 7 8
Quarters from trough

— Average of five recessions 1947–72: demand-led cycles
-- Average of three recessions 1973–84: supply-led cycles
···· 1991 recession   ···· 2001 recession

Figure 5.12 Degree of debt leverage: corporate sector debt as % of internal funds (for eight quarters before and after the trough)

is decreasing. In the average demand-led cycle debt leverage increased 87% in the downswing, but fell 80% in the recovery. In the average supply-led cycle debt leverage increased 37% in the downswing, but fell 26% in the recovery. In the 1991 downturn debt leverage increased 90% in the downswing, but fell 72% in the recovery. In the current downturn debt leverage soared 170% in the downswing, but fell 204% in the recovery. Hence, companies have managed to restructure their balance sheet faster than any other business cycle, although part of this success is due to the one-off measures that boosted profitability; increased government deficit helps, too.

The extent of any retrenchment depends on the ease of refinancing the stock of debt and the burden of servicing it on profits and net cash flow. The ability to refinance debt depends on its composition as well as on the Fed funds rate. The more companies rely on long-term debt as opposed to short-term, the easier it becomes to sustain a high level of debt in a cyclical downturn, other things being equal. Figure 5.13 shows the long-term debt relative to the total. Long-term debt is defined as corporate bonds, municipal securities, which are issued by the local authorities to provide finance to local businesses, and mortgages. Short-term debt is defined as commercial paper, bank loans and other loans and advances, mainly from finance companies. In the average demand- and supply-led business cycle the ability of firms to switch from short- to long-term debt was limited. It only started one or two quarters before the trough and was maintained for one year into the recovery. In the average demand-led cycle the switch to long-term debt was

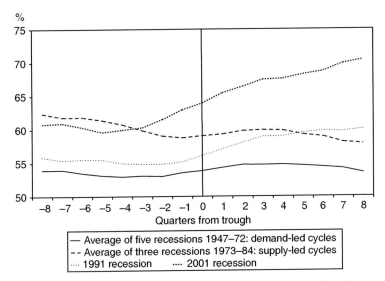

%

Figure 5.13 Long-term debt (securities and mortgages) to total debt (for eight quarters before and after the trough)

only 1.7% of the total. In the average supply-led cycle the switch was only 1% of the total. By contrast, in the 1991 downturn companies found it easier to switch into long-term debt by over 5%. Thus, despite the fact that the level of debt was much higher in the 1991 downturn than in previous recessions, companies found it easier to switch into long-term debt. In the more recent downturn companies started switching into long-term debt much earlier than ever before, five quarters compared to one or two; indeed companies switched almost 11% of total debt into long-term debt. But whether such switch is beneficial to the net cash flow depends on the relative cost of finance between capital markets and banks. In this context it is worth mentioning that the Fed dropped interest rates much faster and more aggressively during the recent downturn than the 1991 one.

Figure 5.14 shows the spread between Moody's AAA bond yield and the bank prime-lending rate. In the average demand-led cycle this spread was almost zero in the downswing and around 50 basis points in the recovery. So, the switch from short- to long-term debt was not very important. In the average supply-led cycle the switch into long-term debt would have been beneficial to the net cash flow, as it would have been much cheaper to borrow from capital markets than from banks. However, high-grade companies were unable to do so. In the 1991 downturn high-grade companies switched much more than ever before into long-term debt. In the downswing it was beneficial, as it was cheaper to borrow from the capital markets than the banks, but the benefit was lost in the recovery, as the relative cost of borrowing was

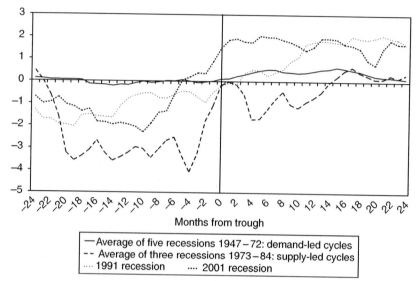

Figure 5.14 Spread between AAA yield and Prime Lending Rate (for twenty-four months before and after the trough)

reversed. This adversely affected the net cash flow of the high-grade companies in the recovery phase and provides another cause for the anaemic recovery. In the current downturn the switch into long-term debt has been even more pronounced and took place much earlier. However, the benefit also disappeared sooner. In the first year of the recovery it was more expensive for high-grade companies to borrow from the capital markets than the banks. Hence, the switch into long-term debt became a hindrance in the recovery. The situation may not improve in the future if yields on sovereign debt were to increase further putting upward pressure on corporate bond yields.

For low-grade companies the situation was even worse. Figure 5.15 shows the spread between Moody's BAA bond yield and the bank prime-lending rate. Very soon in the 1991 cycle it became more expensive than ever before to borrow from capital markets than from banks. This was another reason for the anaemic recovery. In the current downturn the situation was by far worse in the first year of the recovery. The large switch into long-term debt was misconceived, as the rate spread increased by nearly 5% making borrowing from capital markets totally unattractive in the first year of the recovery, thereby explaining the worst ever anaemic recovery. The situation has only marginally improved in the second year of the recovery, as the spread declined 0.5%. The risk of rising spreads because of burgeoning budget deficits does not bode well for investment.

So, in the current downturn companies are more indebted than ever before, but they have managed to switch from short- into long-term debt.

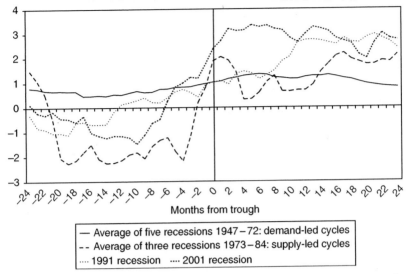

Figure 5.15 Spread between BAA yield and Prime Lending Rate (for twenty-four months before and after the trough)

This represents a reversal of a long-term trend. In the early 1950s the dependence on long-term debt was around 70%. In the following thirty years companies reduced their dependence on long-term debt and increased that on short-term debt. Indeed, the ratio of long-term to total debt had been reduced to 53% by 1985, some 17% less than in the early 1950s. From then onwards companies increased their dependence on long-term debt again and reduced that on short-term. The latest figures show that the proportion of long-term debt to total stands at 71%. Hence, the trend has been completely reversed. Although the dependence on long-term debt is beneficial in the long-run, it can be a drawback in the recovery phase. This is so since, although the cost of borrowing from banks is reduced, that on capital markets is increased, thereby making the recovery anaemic. This adversely affected the recovery both in the early 1990s and in the current recovery. Although the situation has somewhat improved, as the cost of borrowing from the capital markets for high- and low-grade companies has narrowed by 0.5% relative to the cost of borrowing from banks, there is a serious risk of even higher spreads as soaring budget deficits threaten to raise bond yields even higher.

The extent of the damage from the dependence on long-term debt depends on the burden that the servicing of debt imposes on profits and net cash flow. Figure 5.16 shows corporate interest payments relative to net cash flow. Debt service is only 14.6% of net cash flow down from 19.3% at its

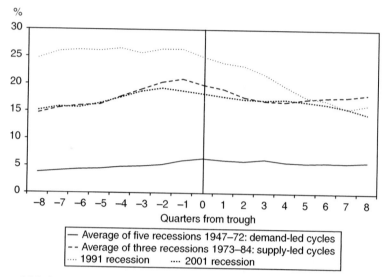

Figure 5.16   Interest payments as % of net cash flow (for eight quarters before and after the trough)

peak two quarters before the trough. This is less than the average supply-led cycle, when debt service peaked at 21% of net cash flow one quarter before the trough. In those days companies were not so much indebted, but interest rates were very high. In the 1991 downturn the combination of high interest rates with high indebtedness made debt service even more difficult, as it reached a peak of more than 26% of net cash flow. However, in the course of the recovery the burden of debt service was reduced drastically to 15% over the following two years. In spite of this drop in the burden of debt service the recovery was anaemic. The situation in the current downturn is much better as debt service is only 14.6% of net cash flow. It may very well be the case that debt service may not be the key variable in the recovery.

Overall, the long-run analysis suggests that in the current downturn debt levels and the degree of leverage are higher than ever before. The switch into long-term debt has helped in the downswing, but it became a hindrance in the recovery, as companies did not benefit from the low interest rates that the Fed had introduced. Credit risk soared after the burst of the bubble, and the interest differential between capital markets and banks widened. These problems contributed to the anaemic recovery of investment in the one-and-a-half-year of the new cycle. However, the long-run factors affecting investment improved dramatically in the last six months. The net worth of the corporate sector has deteriorated only slightly compared to the early 1990s downturn, as companies were very quick in restructuring their balance sheet. Debt levels as per cent of GDP have been reduced, as growth in the economy was very brisk. Moreover, interest rates are lower than in any other cycle and debt service is lower than the last thirty years. Credit risk has now somewhat abated. Moreover, interest rates remain low relative to previous downturns. This improvement in the long-run factors has paved the way for a sustained investment recovery.

5 The K-Model of investment

The K-Model of investment encapsulates the above short-run and long-run factors affecting investment. The rationale of the K-Model is summarised in Figure 5.17. The medium grey boxes illustrate the variables that belong to the investment loop. The light grey box illustrates the variables that cause a shock to the investment spiral. Shocks to the investment spiral are introduced by monetary policy through changes in the interest rate and fiscal policy, directly through depreciation incentives on investment, as in the last two years, and indirectly through influencing demand in the economy via changes in tax rates and government expenditure. Assume that the economy is in long-run equilibrium so that the investment spiral is idle. Consider now a shock in policy (fiscal or monetary) that stimulates demand in the economy and leads to higher GDP growth. If the shock stems from a change in monetary policy, the lower interest rates will affect both demand in the economy and the cost of capital that directly stimulates investment. The increase in investment will further increase demand in the economy. If the shock stems from personal sector tax cuts or increases in government expenditure the effect is to stimulate demand in the economy, which can

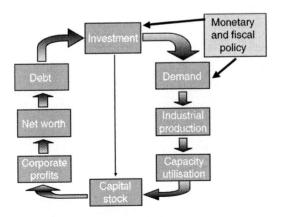

Figure 5.17 Investment model

permanently increase aggregate demand if the deficit spending is sustained. If the shock consists of depreciation incentives, like those that were implemented in 2001 and 2003, the effect on investment is direct and timely.

The higher level of growth in the economy will boost production, either immediately if inventories are lean, or after a fashion, if there is an overhang of unwanted stocks. The higher level of output would lift capacity utilisation and corporate profits. The latter would raise the net worth of the corporate sector that may induce companies to increase borrowing. All these factors, with the exception of borrowing, would boost investment. The increase in investment would boost again demand and a second round would be set in motion. In every round the additional increase in investment would become smaller and after an infinite number of times, the loop will converge to a new long-run equilibrium. Given the size of the government deficit and the net desire to save in financial assets, investment, industrial production, capacity utilisation and profits are higher than the original equilibrium. The increase in investment from any shock (e.g. depreciation incentives) is not explosive. This means that the investment spiral is stable. The stability is ensured by the fact that in every round the increase in investment raises the capital stock nearer to its desired level, for a given level of demand. Moreover, the extra stimulus to demand is also becoming smaller and therefore the desired level of capital stock converges to a new higher, but not infinite, level. Finally, the increase in profits is also finite (see Chapter 3) and the higher level of debt also dampens the increase in investment.

It is clear from the above analysis that investment depends on six variables. We may assemble together the relevant variables and group them into two categories, just as our analysis above suggests. This implies four short-run variables: Capacity Utilisation (CU), Industrial Production (IP), Corporate Profits (CP), and the Prime-Lending Rate (PLR). It also implies two long-run variables: Debt-to-Investment ratio (DI) and Corporate Sector Net Worth to GDP ratio (NW).

We may, thus, have as our fundamental equation:

$$(GI) = GI(CU, IP, CP, PLR, DI, NW) \qquad (1)$$

where GI stands for gross investment.

Clearly, our approach to the determinants of investment begins with the general proposition that a number of variables can affect it. We may distinguish economic activity variables (such as CU and IP), essentially based on the accelerator investment model, interest rate/cost-of-capital variables (such as the PLR)[2] and quantity of finance variables. The distinction between cost-of-finance and quantity-of-finance effects relies heavily on the more realistic assumption of imperfect capital markets. The imperfection of capital markets is explained by resorting to a number of factors, but asymmetric information between lenders and borrowers, which might lead to credit rationing, is the most predominant one (Stiglitz and Weiss, 1981; Bernanke and Gertler, 1989). Financial variables and constraints are explicitly included in investment models through the usage of cash flow variables in the menu of explanatory variables for investment (see, e.g. Fazzari, 1993; Fazzari and Peterson, 1993; the ideas behind this formulation, however, are embedded in Keynes, 1936). Full recognition of the importance of financial variables in the determination of investment was neglected for a long time in view of the influence of the Modigliani-Miller theorem that corporation leverage and personal leverage of investors were perfect substitutes. As has just been suggested, it is now recognised that this is no longer the case.

Financial factors as crucial determinants of investment have attracted a great deal of interest. External funds are no longer thought as perfect substitutes for internal funds, in view of the recognition that capital markets are imperfect. Finance matters again and significantly, just as it did in Keynes (1936) work (see, also Mayer, 1994).[3] The quantity-of-finance variables can be internal finance variables (such as CP which can be viewed as a critical variable in terms of internal finance; high CP indicates greater capacity by the corporate sector to generate internal funds) and external finance variables (such as DI, an external cash/flow component, on the assumption that a high-debt environment is less likely to provide a stable financial base necessary for investment to materialise). Internal funds and net worth variables are thought to be particularly significant variables in the study by Hubbard (1998) when reviewing capital-market imperfections and investment. He concludes that '(1) all else being equal, investment is significantly correlated with proxies for changes in net worth or internal funds; and (2) that correlation is most important for firms likely to face information related capital-market imperfections' (p. 193). The importance of the external funds and cash flow variables is central to, and particularly emphasised, in the 'new consensus' macroeconomics (see, e.g. Bernanke and Blinder, 1988; Bernanke and Gertler, 1989, 1999). It has also been vetted more recently by Greenspan (2002b), who argues that 'capital investment will be most dependent on the outlook of profits and the resolution of the uncertainties surrounding the business outlook and the geopolitical situation. These considerations at present impose a rather formidable barrier to new investment.... A more rigorous and broad-based pickup in capital spending will almost surely require further gains in corporate profits and cash flows' (p. 7).

Next, we turn our attention to capacity utilisation, and propose that it is mostly affected by industrial production. A higher volume of industrial production is expected to engineer a higher degree of capacity utilisation. This association is thought to be strongly positive. This is due to the role of capital stock, which is thought to be fixed in the short run. This relies on the theory of irreversibility of investment under conditions of uncertainty (see, e.g. Dixit and Pindyck (1994). We may, thus, write:

$$(CU) = CU(IP) \tag{2}$$

We also endogenise industrial production as in equation (3):

$$(IP) = IP(PMI) \tag{3}$$

where PMI proxies for existing and expected business conditions. PMI is an index of these conditions and it is based on surveys conducted by the Institute for Supply Management (ISM). It is clear that equation (3) is based crucially on Keynes's 'animal spirits' hypothesis and the uncertainty that characterises expectation in the work of Keynes (1936). It is, thus, the case that in our modelling strategy ultimately 'animal spirits' and uncertainty of expectations critically influence investment, but the relationship works basically through industrial production and profitability, variables that play a critical role in determining gross investment and capacity utilisation. This approach also attempts to account for the suggestion made by Eisner (1974), some time ago, that 'Major progress in discerning reliable and stable investment functions will require facing up to and illuminating the fundamental relations between past, present and future' (p. 102).

Industrial production and capacity utilisation were the main determinants of investment in the demand-led business cycles of 1947–72. But a model that relied on only those factors would have missed the behaviour of investment in the supply-led business cycles of 1973–84. Corporate profitability and real interest rates were additional variables, desperately required to explain investment in the supply-led business cycles. But a model that relied on these four factors would have been incapable of explaining investment in the last two business cycles. The long-run factors are needed, in addition to the short-term ones, to explain investment in the last two cycles. This does not imply that some of the variables are needed in some cycles, but not in others. If that were the case then one and the same model (i.e. one structure) would not have been sufficient to explain investment in all business cycles. Instead, three different models would have been required to explain investment in all ten cycles; the structure would not have been unique. In our model the structure is unique and that implies that the importance of each variable in explaining investment has remained stable in all business cycles. However, the variability of each variable in every cycle has been different. In this sense, the long-run factors did not vary significantly to contribute to the explanation of the volatility of investment in the first eight cycles, but they were extremely important in explaining why investment fell to the extent that it did in the last two cycles. Had these variables assumed different values to those that they actually did in any of the last fifty years then the model would have still been able to explain investment.

The forecast error in the K-Model of investment is only 1.55%. This means that with an error of 3.1% the model can explain 95% of all past investment volatility. Indeed, in the last 600 months there have been only nineteen instances where the investment error has exceeded 3.1% (see Figure 5.18a). On that basis the forecasting ability of the model is such as to claim that with 95% probability investment in the future will lie within the interval of the central projection plus or minus 3.1%. This assumes that the behaviour of investment will continue to be governed by the same structure that is encapsulated in the K-Model. The assurance here rests with the fact that even from a theoretical point of view there are no other cycles except demand, supply and debt deflation, associated with imbalances in the corporate sector. Hence, there is no reason to assume that that the structure of the investment model will be invalidated in the short-term future.

Clearly, in forecasting investment three more relationships are in order. One is for predicting industrial production, the other capacity utilisation and the third corporate profits. The forecast error of the industrial production relationship is only 1.15% in the last 10 business cycles that cover more than half a century of monthly data. Figure 5.18b shows that there have been only twenty instances in more than 600 of monthly observations in the last fifty years where the forecast error of industrial production has exceeded 2.3%. The forecast error of the capacity utilisation relationship is only 0.25%. Figure 5.18c shows that there have been only 18 instances in the last fifty

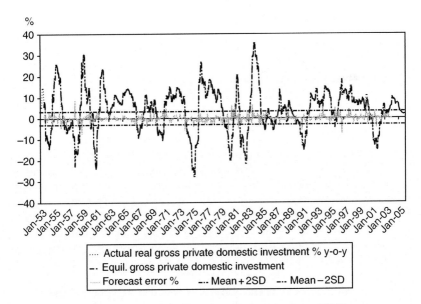

Figure 5.18a Real gross investment (based on the momentum of PMI)

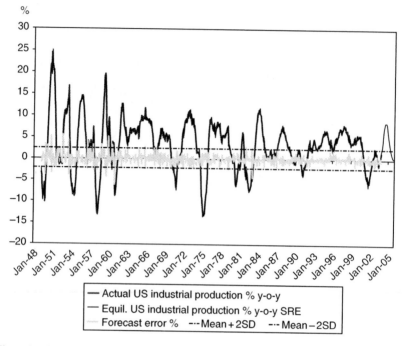

Figure 5.18b   US industrial production (based on the momentum of PMI)

years where the forecast error of capacity utilisation has exceeded 0.5%. The properties of the profits model are discussed in Chapter 3.

6   The long-term risks to investment

In an attempt to assess the long-term risks of the entire investment spiral over the next two years we have conducted a number of simulations using the K-Model. In the first set of simulations we have used (1) the investment model outlined above; (2) the profits model; (3) the wage–price model; and (4) the expectations model of PMI. The PMI is based on a survey of business intentions. These expectations are affected by economic developments, but in the absence of news on economic fundamentals such expectations would follow their own momentum with optimism building up first, then fading away and followed by a similar cycle of pessimism. In the long run such expectations would peter out and the PMI would reach long-run equilibrium. Figure 5.18d provides support for the hypothesis that the momentum of business expectations can explain the PMI.

These four models have been used simultaneously to simulate the effects on investment under the following assumptions. First, corporate debt and

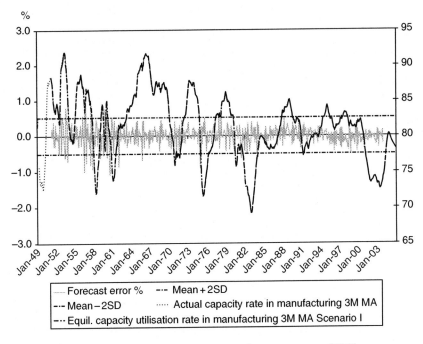

Figure 5.18c   Capacity utilisation rate (based on the momentum of PMI)

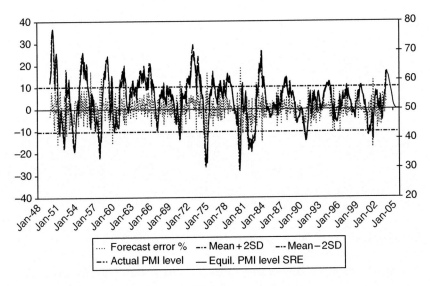

Figure 5.18d   US PMI – short-run equilibrium

net worth remain unchanged at their latest values in 2003:Q3. Second, there is no further news on economic fundamentals so that the PMI follows its own momentum. Figure 5.18d shows that in the absence of any further news on economic fundamentals the PMI would peak at the beginning of 2004 and would return to its equilibrium boom-bust dividing line of 50 by the end of 2005. Despite the early abating expectations, US industrial production would continue to gather steam in the course of 2004 and would peak in October at almost 10%, but it would decelerate from then on until the end of 2005 reaching zero growth (see Figure 5.18b). Profits would decelerate throughout the simulation period. Investment would accelerate even more in the first quarter of 2004, but would decelerate from then onwards (see Figure 5.18a). However, by the end of 2004, it would still be growing at almost 7%. In the course of 2005 investment would slowdown appreciably to less than 2% by the end of the year. Capacity utilisation will climb throughout 2004 and peak at 80 by the end of the year. However, it would decline moderately in the course of 2005 (see Figure 5.18c).

This experiment illustrates that the boost to investment from fiscal and monetary policy would ultimately fade away. Nonetheless, the current accommodating stance of fiscal and monetary policy is sufficient for the economy to be booming at the time of presidential election in November 2004. The new fiscal package that is in the pipeline for 2004 would certainly cause an even greater boom in the economy. However, it would also lead to higher interest rates in 2005 and beyond that would ultimately cause investment to tumble, but even later than these simulations suggest, in 2006 and beyond.

In the second set of simulations we have used (1) the investment model outlined above, but with industrial production being exogenous; (2) the profits model; and (3) the wage–price model. The K-Model is simulated under two alternative scenarios.

Scenario I (weak recovery in 2004): What would happen to investment if the current recovery were to falter in 2004 and became once again anaemic?

Scenario II (strong recovery in 2004): What would happen to investment if the recovery that started after the Iraq war continued to be strong throughout 2004?

6.1   Scenario I (weak recovery in 2004)

The essence of this scenario lies on the assumption that the strength of the second and third quarters of 2003 was due to one-off factors related to the fiscal package of the Bush Administration and rising confidence because of lower geopolitical risks after the end of the Iraq war. The stance of fiscal policy turned 1.6% of GDP easier with the 'Jobs and Growth Tax Relief Reconciliation Act of 2003'. The act provided for an additional first-year bonus depreciation write-off, increasing the immediate depreciation write-off from 30% (provided for in the 'Job Creation and Worker Assistance Act of 2002') to 50% for property acquired after 5 May 2003, and placed in service before 1 January 2005. The additional depreciation provided for by the 2003 act increased depreciation expenses in the second quarter by $83.7 billion and in the third quarter by $30.9 billion. In addition, the 2003 act provided for a reduction of $100.9 billion in July in personal tax and non-tax payments. The act reduced withheld federal taxes $45.8 billion as a result of new marginal tax rates, the expansion of the 10% income tax bracket, and acceleration in 'marriage-penalty' relief. Federal non-withheld taxes (payments of estimated taxes plus final settlements less refunds) were reduced by $55.5 billion because of advance payments of the child tax credit that began being mailed out 25 July 2003. The fiscal stimulus provided through the depreciation incentives and tax relief, ignoring the additional measures on dividend income, as they are controversial with respect to their effect on demand in the economy, is estimated to be 1.6% of nominal GDP.

In addition, monetary policy was eased once more at the end of June 2003 with the Fed funds rate cut to 1%. The accommodative stance of fiscal and monetary policy will keep the economy going, but the imbalances in all sectors will weigh down on the economy and the recovery will begin to falter during the course of 2004 from the torrid pace of 8% in the third quarter of 2003. Nonetheless, the economy will grow at the rate of potential output in 2004 and 2005 with industrial production growth averaging 3%. We expect the Fed to tighten monetary policy in the second quarter of 2004 with the prime-lending rate climbing to 4.5% from its current level of 4%. The rate of debt accumulation would continue to be less than the rate of growth of the economy, due to the budget deficit; so that, the DI would fall slightly to 615% from 624% in 2003:Q3 The continuous balance sheet restructuring, along with declining profitability will further erode the net worth of the corporate sector to 84% by the end of 2005 from 88.5% in 2003:Q3. Table 5.2 summarises the assumptions underlying Scenario I, along with their current values between September and December 2003. With these assumptions, and for the reasons explained in Chapter 3, profits would decelerate rapidly falling to −6.2% by the end of 2005 (see, Table 5.2). Investment would peak in 2004:Q1 and would decelerate rapidly for a year until 2005:Q1. However, it would start recovering thereafter. By the end of 2004 investment would be growing at the meagre rate of 1%. Capacity utilisation will continue to recover throughout the 2-year period.

The conclusion of this simulation is that investment is near its peak, as the buoyant rate of the previous six months was due to one-off factors. Economic fundamentals would deteriorate in the course of 2004, with the Fed likely to tighten its monetary policy, profitability declining and the corporate sector continuing the balance sheet restructuring. Part of the reason for this risk to investment lies in the assumption of falling profitability, which is due to

Table 5.2 The investment loop

	Current values Sep.–Dec.03	Real gross private domestic investment Scenario I (weak recovery)	Corporate profits % y-o-y	Capacity utilisation index Scenario II (strong recovery)	Monthly job creation 6M MA	Scenario I (weak recovery) true	Scenario II (strong recovery) false	Monthly job creation 6M MA
Assumptions								
Industrial production % y-o-y								
1st year	2.4	3.0		4.6		3.0	4.6	
2nd year		3.0		1.4	3.0	3.0	1.4	3.0
Corporate debt as % of investment								
1st year	623.5	615		630		615	630	
2nd year		615		600	615	615	600	615
Prime lending rate % y-o-y								
1st year	4	4.5		4.0		4.5	4.0	
2nd year		4.5		5.0	5	4.5	5.0	5

Corporate sector net worth as % of GDP

	88.5	86.2 / 84.0	88.5 / 81.7	85.1
1st year	88.5	86.2	88.5	85.1
2nd year		84.0	81.7	

	86.2 / 84.0	88.5 / 81.7	85.1	
Effects on the corporate sector				
Current level	3.6	33.1	74.5	12
Deviation from long-run equilibrium (LRE)	0.6	22.0	0.0	−5.2
Scenario I (weak recovery)				
12-M SRE (future short-run Equilibrium)	1.1	−4.0	76.0	171
24-M SRE (future short-run Equilibrium)	0.8	−6.2	77.5	222
12-M SRE and current level (difference)	−2.4	−37.1	1.5	160
24-M SRE and current level (difference)	−2.8	−39.3	3.0	210
Scenario II (strong recovery)				
12-M SRE (future short-run equilibrium)	4.2	0.5	77.3	225
24-M SRE (future short-run equilibrium)	−2.2	−13.2	77.0	182
12-M SRE and current level (difference)	0.6	−32.6	2.7	213
24-M SRE and current level (difference)	−5.8	−46.3	2.5	170
	−3.0	−4.5	−125.6	−5333.9
	3.1	7.0	51.7	3967.8

robust job creation (see Chapter 3). Although growth is assumed to be weak compared to the alternative scenario, it is still near potential output. According to the model such growth would be sufficient to induce companies to hire people at the rate of 170 thousand per month. However, this is still far away from the rate of just one thousand in December 2003. If companies were to be cautious in hiring people, then profits would not fall as much as in Scenario I, and the risk to investment would be much lower.

6.2   Scenario II (strong recovery in 2004)

The essence of Scenario II lies on the premise, which is largely true, that a combined fiscal and monetary stimulus will last for at least a year, and probably eighteen months, before it tapers off. Given that the US fiscal stimulus was introduced between May and July 2003, the US economy should remain strong until the end of 2004.

The role of the accommodative stance of monetary policy is to prevent long-term interest rates from rising and therefore prolong the effects of the fiscal stimulus. However, despite a record forty-year low short-term interest rates introduced by the Fed in the period from 2001 to 2003, long-term interest rates have risen since June 2003 and the yield curve is steep. If long-term interest rates stay at this level, or even rise further, which is very likely, the stimulus from fiscal policy will ultimately peter out. This means that growth will diminish in 2005 and beyond, other things being equal. Given that the average growth for the preceding four quarters before the fiscal stimulus was introduced was 2.6%, that the fiscal stimulus was 1.6% of GDP and that the first year multiplier is about unity, the central projection for average US growth until the second half, or the end, of 2004 should be 4.2%. This is very close to the consensus projection, as of December 2003, for 4.4% growth in 2004. Since the depreciation incentives on new structures will only count if premises are ready for service at the beginning of 2005, companies that would like to take advantage of the scheme should already have started spending. This explains the buoyant recovery of investment in the second quarter of 2003 that was responsible, to some extent, for the unexpectedly strong growth in that quarter. The other major factor that contributed to the unexpectedly strong second quarter was the explosion of defence spending because of the Iraq war.

The stunning 8.2% growth in the third quarter of 2003 was caused by the combination of two main reasons. The strong consumption, which was due to the income tax cuts that were introduced in that quarter, the last-wagon effect for those companies that wanted to take advantage of the depreciation incentives on new structures (which accounted for $30 billion). It was also due to the worldwide improving confidence because of lower geopolitical risks after the end of the Iraq war that boosted US exports in the third quarter. This implies that the stunning third quarter growth was due to one-off factors that are likely to dissipate in the first half of 2004. Nonetheless, the economy should still grow at 4.2% – central projection until the second half of 2004. Industrial production will average 4.6% growth in 2004, but will fall to 1.4%

in the course of 2005. The average rate of growth of industrial production over the two-year period will be 3%, the same as in Scenario I of weak recovery. However, in Scenario II growth would be stronger in 2004 and weaker in 2005 than in Scenario I, but with the same average growth for the two-year period (see Table 5.2 for the detailed assumptions of Scenario II).

Paradoxically, the higher growth rate of the economy implies that the Fed can afford to wait longer before it tightens monetary policy (see also Chapter 3). With Scenario I the Fed should tighten in the second quarter of 2004, but with strong growth the Fed should tighten after the presidential election. The explanation of this paradox is that with strong growth inflation would remain muted both in 2004 and 2005, whereas with slow growth inflation will fall more in 2004, but will rise sharply in 2005. Although there is no trade-off between inflation and growth, there is one between the volatility of growth and the volatility of inflation. Scenario I implies low growth volatility and high inflation volatility, which given the lags of monetary policy on inflation entails early tightening. In contrast, Scenario II implies high growth volatility and low inflation volatility. Hence, the Fed can afford to wait before it tightens monetary policy.

In Scenario II, therefore, the prime-lending rate would remain at 4% in 2004, but it would be raised to 5% in the course of 2005. Corporate profits in 2004 would fall less drastically than in Scenario I, but more strongly in 2005. The strong growth of the economy would induce companies to expand borrowing in 2004, but they would reduce it in 2005. Again the volatility of the DI is assumed to be higher in Scenario II than in Scenario I. The net worth of the corporate sector would remain unchanged in 2004, but would be dented in 2005 (see Table 5.2). Capacity utilisation would rise stronger in 2004, but will converge to Scenario I by the end of 2005 (see Figure 5.19a). The overall effect of these factors would be strong investment growth throughout 2004, although there would be some volatility. By the end of 2004 investment growth would be as strong as 9%. However, investment would decelerate rapidly in 2005, falling below the level of Scenario I (see Figure 5.19b).

The overall conclusion of the fast growth scenario for 2004 is that investment will remain very strong in this year, but will fall precipitously in 2005. Economic fundamentals would be much better than Scenario I in 2004, but worse in 2005 and that explains the stark difference in the risk to investment. The performance of investment under Scenario II is obviously better than the first simulation, as in the latter there is no change in economic fundamentals.

7   Sensitivity analysis

The plausibility of the scenario analysis depends on how sensitive the projections of investment are to their determinants. It is convenient in comparing the impact of the various determinants of investment to look at multipliers. The multiplier measures the ratio of the percentage change of

132

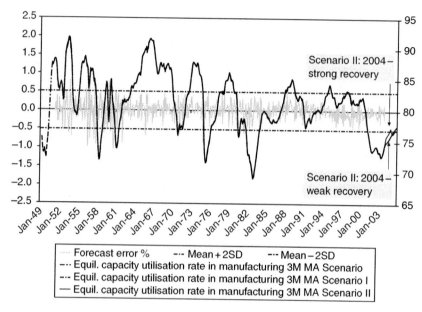

Figure 5.19a   Capacity utilisation – short-run equilibrium

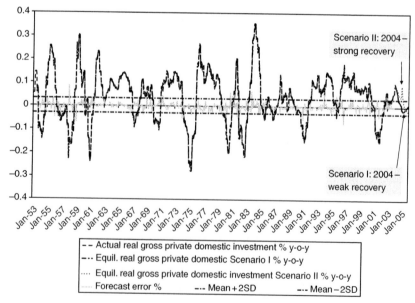

Figure 5.19b   Real gross private domestic investment – short-run equilibrium

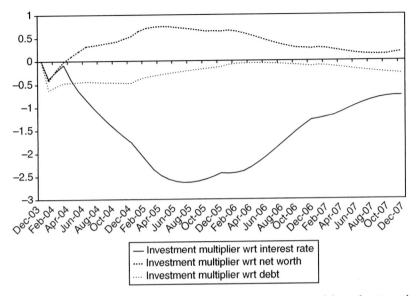

Figure 5.20 Investment multiplier with reference to interest rate, debt and net worth

investment to a given percentage change in one of its determinants, say, industrial production. Figures 5.20 and 5.21 show the investment multipliers with respect to all six determinants. The effect of industrial production on investment builds up to 1.5 in eighteen months and then begins to taper off. The effect of the interest rate on investment has a similar pattern to industrial production. The effect builds up for the first twenty months and then tapers off. The effect of the rest of the variables tapers off much faster.

8   Summary and conclusions

In the first year of the current recovery investment grew at the worst-ever anaemic pace. Both short- and long-run factors contributed to it. However, in the last six months, following the end of the Iraq war, both the short- and long-run factors that affect investment have improved. The short-run analysis suggests that the double-dip recession, in which the industrial sector fell in the recovery phase, has helped to turn positive all the short-run factors that affect investment. Labour cost has been dented yet again, profit margins and corporate profits have improved, lean inventories in the face of higher demand have induced increased industrial production, which should be boosted even more in the course of 2004 as demand is likely to remain high. Higher growth in the economy is taking care of the excess capacity that was installed in the euphoria years of the bubble and consequently

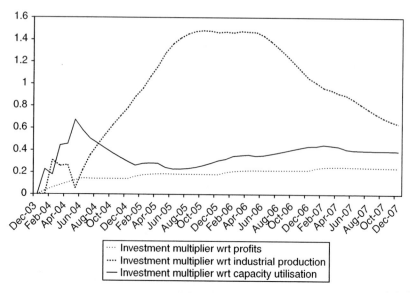

Figure 5.21   Investment multiplier with reference to profits, industrial production and capacity utilisation

capacity utilisation has started to improve. Hence, the short-run analysis suggests that investment should remain buoyant in 2004.

The long-run analysis suggests that in the current downturn debt levels and the degree of leverage are higher than ever before. The switch into long-term debt has helped in the downswing, but it became a hindrance in the recovery, as companies did not benefit from the low interest rates that the Fed had introduced. Credit risk soared after the burst of the bubble and the interest differential between capital market and bank interest rates widened. These problems contributed to the anaemic recovery of investment in the one-and-a-half-year of the new cycle. However, the long-run factors affecting investment improved dramatically in the last six months. The net worth of the corporate sector has deteriorated only slightly compared to the early 1990s downturn, as companies were very quick in restructuring their balance sheet. Debt levels as per cent of GDP have been reduced, as growth in the economy was very brisk. Moreover, interest rates are lower than in any other cycle and debt service is lower than the last thirty years. Credit risk has now somewhat abated. Moreover, interest rates remain low relative to previous downturns. This improvement in the long-run factors has paved the way for a sustained investment recovery.

In spite of the improvement of the short- and long-run factors that affect investment in the last six months, there are still long-term risks to a sustained investment recovery. In order to assess those risks we have conducted two sets of simulations. In the first it is assumed that economic fundamentals would not improve any further and that debt and corporate net worth would remain unchanged from their latest values. The conclusion of this simulation points to the risk that the boost to investment from fiscal and monetary policy would ultimately fade away, but investment would remain robust in 2004. In the second set of simulations investment is compared under two alternative scenarios. In Scenario I (dubbed 'weak growth') the economy enjoys a constant rate of growth in 2004–05 that is approximately equal to the rate of potential output. In Scenario II (dubbed 'strong growth'), the economy enjoys a much stronger growth in 2004, but weaker growth in 2005. However, over the 2-year period the average growth is the same in both scenarios, but with greater growth volatility in Scenario II compared to I.

The conclusion of Scenario I is that investment is near its peak, as the buoyant rate of the previous six months was due to one-off factors. Economic fundamentals would deteriorate in the course of 2004, with the Fed likely to tighten, profitability declining and the corporate sector continuing the balance sheet restructuring. Part of the reason for this risk to investment lies in the assumption of falling profitability, which is due to robust job creation (see, Chapter 4). Although growth is assumed to be weak compared to the alternative scenario, it is still near potential output. According to the model such growth would be sufficient to induce companies to hire people at the average rate of 170 thousand per month. However, this is still far away from the rate of just one thousand in December 2003. If companies were to be cautious in hiring people, then profits would not fall as much as in Scenario I and the risk to investment would be much lower.

The conclusion of Scenario II is that investment will remain strong in 2004, but it will fall precipitously in 2005. Economic fundamentals would be much stronger in 2004 but weaker in 2005 than Scenario I. This explains the stark difference in the performance of investment in 2004, but also the risk to investment in the long run. High volatility in growth would cause high volatility in investment.

The conclusion from the two sets of simulations, taken together, is that the current accommodating stance of fiscal and monetary policy is probably sufficient for the economy to be booming at the time of presidential election in November 2004, as there is sufficient momentum already built in. However, the long-term risk to investment stems from the fact that the current Administration is not willing to take the risk that the economy would only be growing at the rate of potential output in 2004 as investment growth may be subdued by then. It is therefore considering yet another fiscal package to stimulate the economy in the run-up to the presidential election. Although such package would ensure that the economy is booming at the time of the election, it will raise long-term interest rates even more and will foster the forces that would ultimately weaken investment in 2005 and beyond. Hence, the long-term risk to investment would not dissipate by the introduction of yet another fiscal package. Instead, it would raise such risk.

6
The Housing Market and Residential Investment

1 Introduction

The importance of the housing market and residential investment was highlighted by OECD (2000b), suggesting that 'In the United States...the contribution of real estate developments to the current economic expansion has been emphasised recently' (p. 169). In fact, it is argued that 'Over the 1996–99 period, the growth of housing wealth in excess of income growth in the United States may have contributed 0.4 percentage point to the total drop of the household saving ratio of some 2.4 percentage points' (p. 179). The same OECD study concludes that 'The link between house price developments and movements in aggregate demand suggests that monitoring developments in property markets can provide a useful input to the setting of economic policy' (OECD, 2000b, p. 181; see also, Greenspan, 1999).[1] The boom of the housing market since the burst of the equity bubble has raised some concerns. Greenspan (2004c) emphasised the importance of 'preventive actions' which 'are required sooner rather than later' in order to 'fend off possible future systemic difficulties, which we assess as likely if GSE expansion continues unabated' (p. 4).[2] Especially so, since 'the existence, or even the perception, of government backing undermines the effectiveness of market discipline' (p. 4). It is, therefore, suggested that 'the GSE regulator must have authority similar to that of the banking regulator', but also 'GSEs need to be limited in the issuance of GSE debt and in the purchase of assets, both mortgages and nonmortgages, that they hold' (p. 5).

The threat to the sustainability of the current recovery from the personal sector imbalances that were created by the boom and bust of the equity bubble can in principle be put at bay if the recovery were strong for some time. However, a strong recovery may cause a collapse in the housing market. The personal sector imbalances would then resurface and may threaten the sustainability of the current recovery. The very easy stance of monetary policy that was adopted by the Fed in order to deter the deflationary effects of the burst of the 'new-economy' bubble have fuelled the housing market boom of the last three years. The housing market is not yet a bubble, as it has not yet exceeded the peak of all previous cycles in the last thirty-five years, but it has all the characteristics of becoming one, if the boom were to continue. Although the problem is more acute in the Northeast, other regions would be infected through lower incomes and employment, if the market, which is near its peak, were to collapse. The risk of a collapse arises from the high levels of debt and the overstretched capacity of households to service their debts even at these low levels of interest rates. The damage to the property market in the next two years depends on the strength of the current recovery. A strong recovery in 2004 would lead to a collapse of the housing market in 2005 with dramatic falls in house prices, residential investment and the gross (and net) value of property. The recent round of refinance would not deter the collapse of the housing market; it would simply postpone it for a while. On the other hand, a weak recovery would lead to a slight further increase of house prices in 2004 and stabilisation in 2005. The reason for this stark contrast is that long-term interest rates would rise much more under a strong than a weak recovery. Between the two scenarios a strong recovery in 2004 seems more likely than a weak one because of the huge fiscal stimulus of 2003, and a new one planned for 2004, the very accommodative stance of monetary policy and high levels of confidence amongst businesses and consumers alike, triggered by the lower geopolitical risks after the end of the Iraq war.

We begin this chapter by looking at some length into the current realities of the US housing market (section 2). This enables us to propose a theoretical construct for the US housing market, in terms of the demand for it (section 3) and the supply of it (section 4). In section 5 we discuss the K-model of the housing market. A discussion of the likely future developments in this market is the focus of section 6. A final section summarises and concludes (section 7).

2 The housing market

Table 6.1 shows the changes in personal sector wealth since the burst of the equity bubble. Net wealth, defined as assets less liabilities, peaked in March 2000 at $43.5 trillion or 625% of disposable income and bottomed at $38.4 trillion or 488% of disposable income in September 2002, as equity prices plunged. The loss in net wealth between the peak and the trough of the equity bubble is $5.1 trillion or 137% of disposable income. The equity market rally since the end of the Iraq war has moderated these losses to $2.2 trillion or 115% of disposable income by the end of the second quarter of 2003 (the latest quarter for which data is available).

These shifts in net wealth obscure the risk of replacing the equity by the property bubble. Table 6.1 shows the breakdown of net wealth into its constituent components. By the end of the second quarter of 2003 the losses in total assets (defined as tangible and financial) between the peak and the trough of the bubble had been completely offset. However, this is entirely due to the gains in tangible assets (mainly property), which exactly offset

Table 6.1 Personal sector balance sheet

	Net wealth	Net wealth as % of nominal disposable income	Total assets	Total assets as % of nominal disposable income	Tangible assets	Tangible assets as % of nominal disposable income	Financial assets	Financial assets as % of nominal disposable income	Liabilities	Liabilities as % of nominal disposable income
Peak of equity bubble (Mar. 2000)	43 480	625	50 494	726	14 480	208	36 015	518	7 014	101
Bottom of equity bubble (Sep. 2002)	38 386	488	46 899	597	17 766	226	29 133	371	8 514	108
Latest quarter (Jun. 2003)	41 249	510	50 539	625	18 584	230	31 955	395	9 290	115
Loss between peak and bottom of bubble	−5 095	−137	−3 595	−129	3 286	18	−6 882	−147	1 499	7
Latest gain or loss since peak of bubble	−2 231	−115	44	−101	4 104	22	−4 059	−123	2 276	14

the losses in financial assets. Households, though, have continued to borrow heavily in the last three years of the order of $2.3 trillion or 14% of disposable income. This accounts for the deterioration in net wealth. The rate of debt accumulation in the last three years is unprecedented. There is no other three-year period, since records began in 1952, in which debt increased at such frenetic pace. The second highest rate is 10.2% of disposable income that occurred between April and September 1987, after the peak of the property market in April 1987. The rate of debt accumulation fell rapidly after the equity market crash in October 1987.

Table 6.2 shows the role of the property market in supporting consumer expenditure and cushioning the economy in its recent downturn. The boom in the residential property market has resulted in capital gains of the order of $3.4 trillion for households between the peak of the equity bubble and the second quarter of 2003. However, households continuously borrow against their property to finance consumer expenditure. Accordingly, the percentage of owner's equity in household real estate keeps falling. Between the peak of the equity bubble and the second quarter of 2003 the owner's equity in household real estate has fallen from 56.9% of disposable income to 54.3%. This represents $433 billion home equity extraction (i.e. realised capital gains), which accounts for 40% of the consumer expenditure in this period. The fiscal support to the personal sector in the form of tax cuts and other benefits account for an additional $170 billion during this period. Hence, taken together, the fiscal support and the home equity extraction account for 60% of consumer expenditure in the last three years. This explains why the consumer remained resilient throughout the recent downturn. This poses the question of what would happen if property prices were to fall. Would the consumer respond by saving more and cutting down on expenditure?

Although in the short run the ratio of house prices to disposable income can fluctuate widely, in the long run it should be trendless,[3] as it shows the number of years it takes to buy a house, which can neither be on an up-trend nor on a down-trend in the long run. Figure 6.1 shows the median price of existing homes for sale relative to per capita nominal disposable income during the last thirty-five years. This peaked in June 1980 at 733% of disposable income and bottomed in December 1990 at 512%. It recovered ever since and at the end of September 2003 it stood at 606%. Compared to the 1970s house prices seem low, but this is not correct when account is taken of the low inflation and interest rate environment of today.

The long-term decline in the median house price relative to disposable income in the 1980s reflects the fall in inflation and interest rates that made houses more affordable and moderated their demand as a hedge against inflation. Figure 6.2 confirms this conclusion by comparing nominal with real (deflated by CPI) house price inflation. Although nominal house price inflation was high in the 1970s and low since the 1980s, in real terms

Table 6.2 Source and uses of housing capital gains (billions of dollars)

	Real estate of households	Percentage of owner's equity in household real estate	Extracted home equity	Disposable personal income (nominal)	Personal income	Fiscal support	Consumption (nominal)
Peak of equity bubble (Mar. 2000)	10 658	56.9		6 955	8 212	1 256	6 552
Bottom of equity bubble (Sep. 2002)	13 430	56.4		7 860	8 959	1 099	7 361
Latest quarter (Jun. 2003)	14 093	54.3		8 086	9 172	1 086	7 596
Difference between peak and bottom of bubble	2 772	−0.5	479	905	747	157	809
Difference since peak of bubble	3 435	−2.6	433	1 131	961	170	1 043

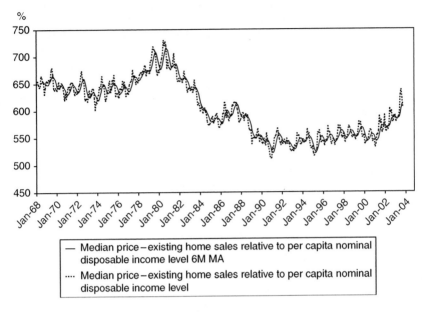

Figure 6.1 Median price of existing homes relative to nominal disposable income

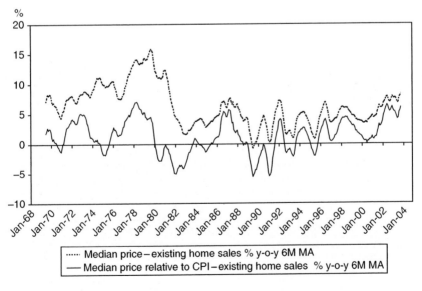

Figure 6.2 House price inflation

(deflated by CPI) it has been the same in the two periods (see Figure 6.2). Nominal house price inflation increased steadily in the 1970s, but declined in the early 1980s in line with inflation and interest rates. In September 2003 nominal house price inflation hit 8.4%, the highest since 1982, the period of low inflation. Real house price inflation does not suffer from the distortions of inflation and reflects more accurately the demand and supply forces of the housing market. In September 2003 real house price inflation hit 6.1%, only 1% lower than the all time high in the last thirty-five years of 7.1% reached in April 1978.

The housing market is not yet a bubble, but it has all the characteristics of becoming one. The boom is not nationwide, but concentrates largely in the Northeast, and to a lesser extent in the West (see Figure 6.3). In the Northeast house price inflation soared to 15% in September 2003, still lower than the all time high of the last thirty-five years of 25.5% observed in August 1987. The concentration of the housing boom in one area may be less worrisome than if it were nationwide, but it is still troublesome, since it is more vulnerable to a sudden collapse with possible chain reactions in the income and employment of the other regions. Changes in demand for housing are first reflected in the prices of existing homes, which then give the signal to developers to alter the supply of new houses. Because of gestation lags, the current supply of new homes reflects previous demand conditions. Hence, prices of new homes are more volatile than existing homes as they represent a small proportion of total homes for sale and reflect current demand

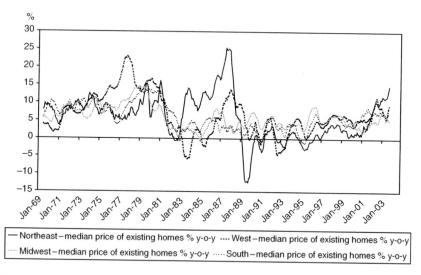

Figure 6.3   Regional house price inflation

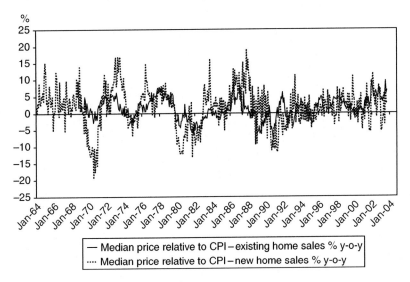

Figure 6.4   Relative median house prices

conditions, but supply of previous demand. Hence, the prices of existing homes for sale are a better indicator of market conditions than new homes. Figure 6.4 compares the price of existing homes with new homes and shows that the former is a better indicator of market conditions. House prices at the top end of the market are more volatile to fluctuations in demand than the low end. The median price is not affected as much as the average price by the top end of the housing market. Hence, the median price of existing homes is a better indicator of market conditions than the average price, as it is both less volatile and it is, at worst, a coincident indicator and, more often, a leading indicator of the housing market (see Figure 6.5).

3   The demand for housing

The demand for housing depends on the real disposable income of house-holds. This is a composite variable, as it is affected by both per capita real disposable income and population growth. On occasions, real personal income is a better proxy of income than real disposable income because the latter is affected by taxes and subsidies, which households may regard as temporary rather than permanent. Figure 6.6 shows the association of house prices with real personal and disposable income. An increase in income leads to higher demand for housing that pushes up house prices. The growth in disposable income accounts, to some extent, for the recent housing boom. The demand for housing is greatly affected by the mortgage rate, which is

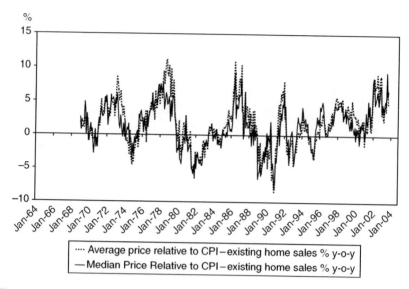

Figure 6.5 Relative existing house prices

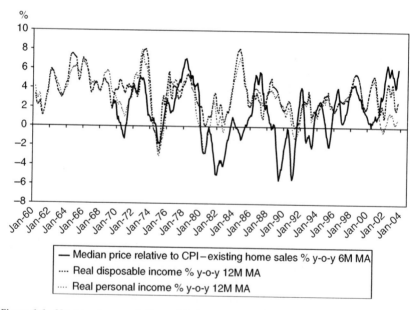

Figure 6.6 House prices, real disposable income and real personal income

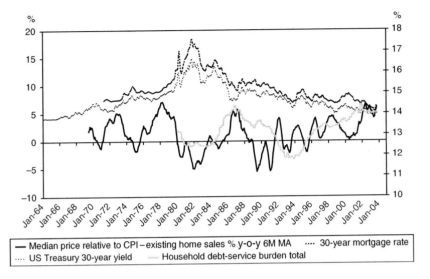

Legend:
— Median price relative to CPI – existing home sales % y-o-y 6M MA   ···· 30-year mortgage rate
····· US Treasury 30-year yield   ····· Household debt-service burden total

Figure 6.7 House prices, interest rates and debt service

closely associated with the 30-year Treasury yield (see Figure 6.7). Higher bond yields lead to increases in the mortgage rate that diminishes the demand for housing and lowers house price inflation. The boom of the housing market since the burst of the equity bubble is due to the lower mortgage rate. The risk to the housing market comes from this variable. Bond yields are bound to rise even more because of soaring budget deficits and faster economic growth. In fact, the more buoyant the current recovery is, the bigger the increase in the mortgage rate and therefore the higher the probability that the property market will tumble.

The debt service burden measures the ratio of interest payments on consumer debt to nominal disposable income. It is influenced by the mortgage rate, the size of consumer debt and nominal disposable income. The higher the mortgage rate or consumer debt is, the bigger the debt service burden. On the other hand, the higher the nominal disposable income is, the lower the debt service burden. But households are willing to accumulate more debt and withstand a heavier debt service burden, if house prices are expected to rise. Hence, house prices tend to rise with increases in the debt service burden, and vice-versa. This, of course, is destabilising in the short run, as it tends to fuel the boom or deepen the bust in the housing market. Confidence is driving these perverse expectations. In the upswing of the cycle confidence is rising and households are willing to accumulate more debt and withstand heavier debt service burdens. In the downswing of the cycle households are becoming increasingly scared and reduce their debts and service burden. Figure 6.7 shows the positive correlation of house prices with the debt service burden and the negative correlation with the mortgage rate.

The net real estate of households measures the value of property less the mortgage obligations. Higher house prices lead to capital gains in the property market that boost the value of the real estate of households. These capital gains and expectations that they will continue for some time lead households to accumulate more debt in the short run. Hence, there is a positive correlation between house prices and mortgage debt in the short run. However, at some point in time, the rate of debt accumulation exceeds the pace of house price increases and the net real estate of households begins to fall. This leads to lower demand for housing, other things being equal, since property is an asset and the net real estate of households measures the importance of the wealth effect in the demand for housing.

More often than not the net real estate is a leading rather than a co-incident indicator of the housing market. Figure 6.8a shows the positive correlation of house price inflation with both mortgage debt and net real estate growth. Figure 6.8b shows the gross and net real estate and mortgage debt as per cent of disposable income. Mortgage debt fluctuated around 40% for twenty years until 1985, but doubled since then to 80% of disposable income until the second quarter of 2003. Since the burst of the equity bubble in March 2000 mortgage debt has increased 14% of disposable income. Clearly, the rate of debt accumulation shows that households expect house prices to continue to rise for some time. Although the gross real estate of households is at an all time high at 175% of disposable income, the net real

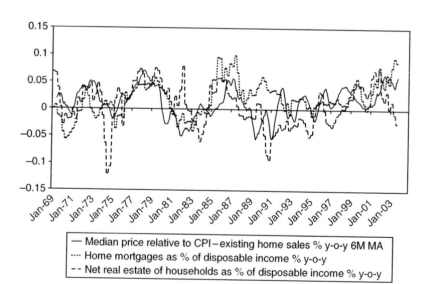

— Median price relative to CPI – existing home sales % y-o-y 6M MA
···· Home mortgages as % of disposable income % y-o-y
-- Net real estate of households as % of disposable income % y-o-y

Figure 6.8a   House prices, net real estate and mortgage debt

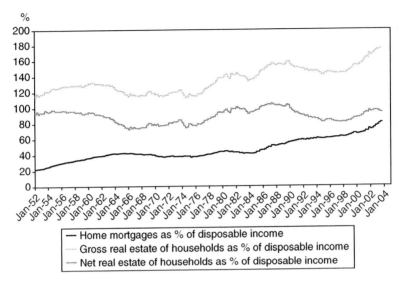

Figure 6.8b Gross and net real estate and mortgage debt

estate of households has already peaked and this does not augur very well for the continuation of the housing boom.

4 The supply of housing

The supply of houses is a positive function of house prices. Property developers and existing homeowners are willing to increase the supply of houses for sale, if house prices are rising. Figure 6.9 shows the positive correlation between house price inflation and existing homes for sale. Figure 6.10 shows that the supply of new homes is closely associated with the supply of existing homes for sale. This means that property developers behave in much the same way as existing homeowners – they increase the supply as house prices rise. House price inflation precedes turning points of the supply of houses by, on average, six months (see Figure 6.9). This implies that house price inflation provides the signal to property developers and existing homeowners to alter the supply. A rise in house price inflation leads after a few months to increased supply of houses, and vice-versa. The supply of existing- and new-homes is at an all time high (see Figure 6.10).

Once house price inflation begins to rise real residential investment picks up so that property developers can increase the supply of new homes. Although in the short run the correlation of house price inflation with real residential investment is positive, in the long run it is negative, as the higher supply leads, other things being equal, to lower prices. On the other hand,

148

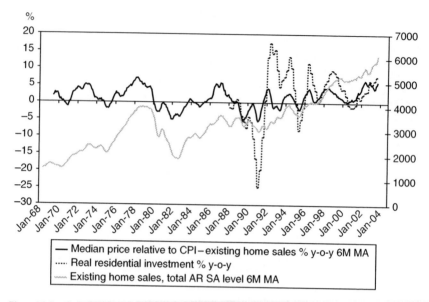

Figure 6.9   House prices, existing homes for sale and real residential investment

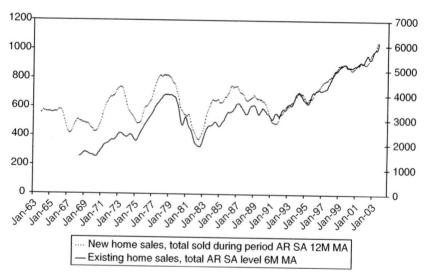

Figure 6.10   Housing units for sale

the positive correlation in the short run means that supply should increase with higher prices.[4] On some occasions, the reaction of real residential investment to changes in house price inflation is instantaneous, but most of the time it follows with a few months lag. This has been particularly true in the recent housing boom of the last five years (see Figure 6.9). The increased lag between house price inflation and real residential investment means that property developers are becoming increasingly wary that the boom in the housing market may not last much longer.

A rise in house price inflation leads after a few months to increases in housing starts. The average lag is three months (see Figure 6.11). Property developers regulate the pace of construction so that completions are in line with housing starts and the stock of houses for sale is close to the desired level (see Figure 6.12). Hence, despite the strong housing boom, property developers have refrained from becoming overenthusiastic and oversupplying the market with new houses, as the stock of houses available for sale has been kept unchanged. But the same cannot be said about homebuyers. The frenetic pace of house sales is evident in Figure 6.13, which shows that new home buyers are purchasing property which has either not yet started or is under construction.

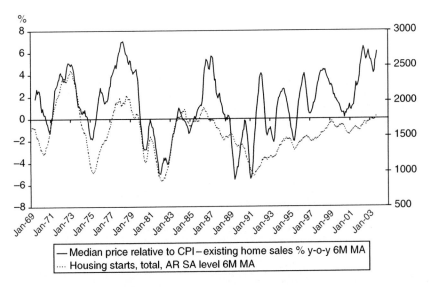

Figure 6.11 Housing starts and house prices

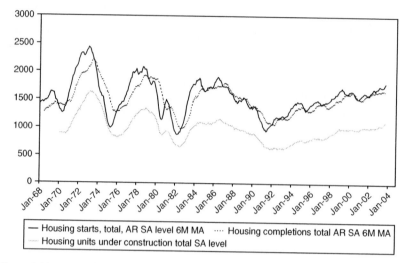

Figure 6.12   Housing starts, completions and under construction

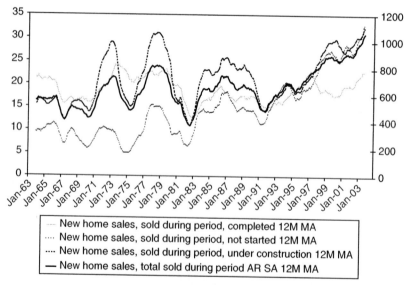

Figure 6.13   Sold during period – new home sales

5 The K-Model of the housing market

The K-Model of the housing market captures the above-mentioned principles through four equations. The first explains house prices through the forces of demand for and supply of houses. The second equation explains real residential investment. The third equation explains gross real estate (the value of property) and the fourth net real estate (the value of property net of mortgage debt).

In the steady state house prices are influenced by the following demand factors:

The level of real disposable income (RYD)
The mortgage rate (MR)
The debt service burden (DSB)
The net real estate of households (NREH)

The first two variables reflect the short-run factors that affect the demand for houses, while the last two variables the long-run factors, which are associated with personal sector imbalances. We may, therefore, express the demand for housing (HD) as:

$$HD = H_1(HP, RYD, MR, DSB, NREH) \tag{a}$$

House prices are also affected in the steady state by the following supply factors:

The level of housing starts (HST)
The level of real residential investment (RRI)

We may, therefore, stipulate the supply of housing (HS) as:

$$HS = H_2(HP, HST, PRI) \tag{b}$$

Combining demand and supply factors we are able to represent the long-run relationship for house prices as:

$$HP = H(RYD, MR, DSB, NREH, HST, PRI) \tag{1}$$

For the reasons explained in the demand for housing section the level of real disposable income, the debt service burden and the net real estate of households affect house prices positively, while the mortgage rate affects house prices negatively. The level of housing starts affects house prices positively, while the level of real residential investment negatively.

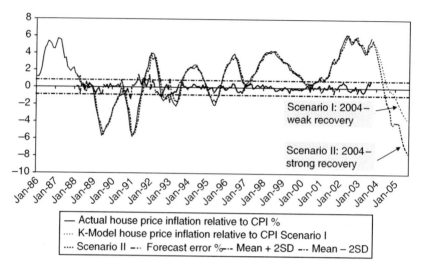

Figure 6.14   Relative median house price inflation – short-run equilibrium (SRE % y-o-y)

In the short run house price inflation responds negatively to previous disequilibria from the steady state. This implies that house price inflation moves to bring the housing market back to equilibrium in the long run. According to the K-Model it takes sixteen months to correct any given deviation from equilibrium. House price inflation responds with the same signs to the yearly rate of change of all aforementioned variables, with the exception of real residential investment. The rate of growth of real residential investment affects house price inflation positively in the short run, but the level of real residential investment affects the level of house prices negatively in the long run.

The forecast error in the K-Model of house price inflation is only 0.35%. This means that with an error of 0.7% the model can explain 95% of all past house price inflation fluctuations. Indeed, in the last 187 months there have been only five instances where the house price inflation error has exceeded 0.7% (see Figure 6.14). On that basis the forecasting ability of the model is such as to claim that with 95% probability house price inflation in the future will lie within the interval of the central projection plus or minus 0.7%. This assumes that the behaviour of house price inflation will continue to be governed by the same structure that is encapsulated in the K-Model. Although there are monthly data for all variables that go back to the 1960s, real residential investment is only available since the beginning of 1987. This prevents model testing from going back to the 1960s that would have enabled checking whether the model has a stable structure through different business cycles. Figure 6.15 shows the performance of the level of house prices in the last fifteen years.

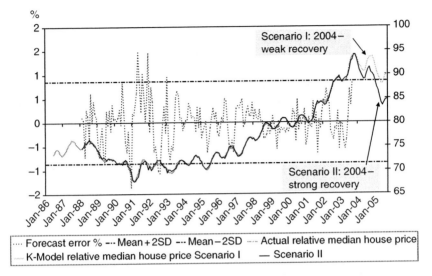

Figure 6.15 Relative median house price – short-run equilibrium

In the steady state the level of real residential investment depends on:

The year-on-year rate of growth of real disposable income (GRYD)
The level of house prices (HP)
The mortgage rate (MR)
The level of housing starts (HST)

With the exception of the mortgage rate, all variables affect positively the level of real residential investment.[5] The mortgage rate affects it negatively. In the short run the rate of growth of real residential investment is affected by the yearly change in all aforementioned variables with the same signs as in the steady state.

The long-run RRI relationship may be expressed as follows:

$$RRI = R(GRYD, HP, MR, HST) \tag{2}$$

The forecast error of real residential investment is 1.75%. Judged on its own this error is small, but it is five times bigger than the forecast error of the house prices model. However, the volatility of residential investment is much higher than the volatility of house prices. Hence if account is taken of the relative volatility the difference of the two models is much smaller. The model of house prices explains 83% of volatility, while the model of residential investment explains 78%. Figures 6.16 and 6.17 show the model performance of the rate of growth and level of real residential investment.

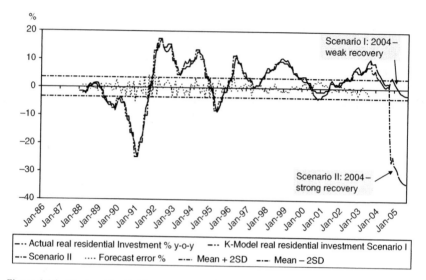

Figure 6.16   Real residential investment – short-run equilibrium % y-o-y

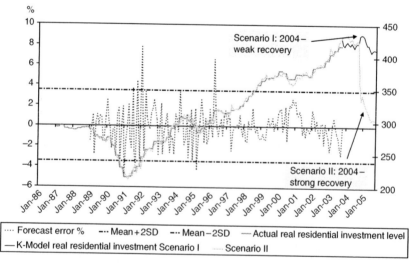

Figure 6.17   Real residential investment – short-run equilibrium (SRE) level

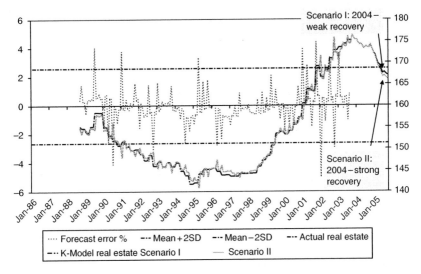

Figure 6.18 Gross real estate – short-run equilibrium level

Two further relationships complete the picture. The first is actually an identity:

$$NRE = GRE - MD \tag{3}$$

where NRE is net real estate, GRE is gross real estate, which is the value of property, and MD is total mortgage debt. GRE is explained as in equation (4):

$$GRE = G(HP) \tag{4}$$

where the value of gross real estate of households depends on house prices, as changes in prices cause capital gains or losses in the value of property. Figure 6.18 shows the model performance of gross real estate. The forecast error is 1.3%.

Figure 6.19 explains the rationale of the model for the housing market. A negative or positive shock in real disposable income or the mortgage rate affects the demand for houses and alters house prices, since the supply of houses is fixed at any point in time. This provides a signal to existing home-owners and property developers to alter the supply of houses. Accordingly, real residential investment is adjusted. The new balance of demand and supply of housing affects the capital gains (or losses) in the housing market and therefore the value of gross real estate. The new trend in house prices induces households to adjust their mortgages, which, in turn, affects the net real estate of households. The latter though affects the demand for housing and

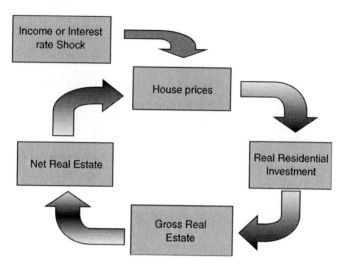

Figure 6.19 The housing market loop

the cycle is repeated leading to a spiralling effect, as the stimulus from each cycle is getting bigger in the initial phase of the process. However, at some point in time, the rate of debt accumulation exceeds the rate of capital gains and the net real estate begins to fall. This puts a brake to the process of expanding house prices at infinitum.

The housing boom of the last few years can be explained with the help of the model as follows. Rising real disposable income in the second half of the 1990s helped house price inflation to accelerate. But the tightening of monetary policy after the 1997–98 crisis reduced house price inflation to zero by June 2000. The easing of monetary policy in the aftermath of the burst of the equity bubble set up a spiral of house price inflation. Lower mortgage rates increased the demand for houses and spurred real residential investment. The new balance of demand and supply of housing led to capital gains in the property market that boosted the value of gross real estate. This induced households to borrow more and increase again the demand for houses. This cycle has been repeated several times in the last three years leading to accelerating house price inflation. The extremely low interest rates that the Fed put in place to combat the deflationary effects of the burst of the equity bubble have, unfortunately, fuelled the housing boom. The risk is that, if it continues, it will become a bubble, which if it bursts, will threaten to bring the economy down yet again. The pace of the current recovery increases this risk, as it pushes up long-term interest rates, which will ultimately reverse the spiral from positive to negative. The point cannot be repeated enough. The higher the pace of economic activity, the graver the danger that higher interest rates might prick the 'property bubble'. The bursting of the latter could have serious negative consequences for the economy. The critical factor for the reversal of the spiral is that the pace of debt accumulation exceeds the rate of capital gains in the property market. This is the condition that ensures that net real estate stops rising and begins to fall. This has already happened and in time it will lead to lower demand for housing. The down-spiral process will accelerate if the recovery continues to be buoyant and long-term interests rise.[6]

6 The likely course of the housing market

To shed light on the likely course of the housing market over the next two years we have used the K-Model to simulate two alternative scenarios:

Scenario I (weak recovery in 2004): What would happen to the housing market if the current recovery were to falter in 2004 and became once again anaemic?

Scenario II (strong recovery in 2004): What would happen to the housing market if the recovery that started after the Iraq war continued to be strong throughout 2004?

6.1 Scenario I (weak recovery in 2004)

The essence of this scenario lies on the assumption that the strength of the second and third quarters of 2003 was due to one-off factors related to the fiscal package of the Bush Administration and rising confidence because of lower geopolitical risks after the end of the Iraq war. The stance of fiscal policy turned 1.6% of GDP easier with the 'Jobs and Growth Tax Relief Reconciliation Act of 2003'. The act provided for an additional first-year bonus depreciation write-off, increasing the immediate depreciation write-off from 30% (provided for in the 'Job Creation and Worker Assistance Act of 2002') to 50% for property acquired after 5 May 2003, and placed in service before 1 January 2005. The additional depreciation provided for by the 2003 act is estimated to have increased depreciation expenses in the second quarter by $75.2 billion. In addition, the 2003 act provided for a reduction of $100.9 billion in July in personal tax and non-tax payments. The act reduced withheld federal taxes $45.8 billion as a result of new marginal tax rates, the expansion of the 10% income tax bracket, and acceleration in 'marriage-penalty' relief. Federal non-withheld taxes (payments of estimated taxes plus final settlements less refunds) were reduced by $55.5 billion because of advance payments of the child tax credit that were released on 25 July 2003. The fiscal stimulus provided through the depreciation incentives and tax relief, ignoring the additional measures on dividend income, as they are controversial with respect to their effect on demand in the economy, is estimated to be 1.6% of nominal GDP. In addition, monetary policy was eased once more at the end of June 2003 with the Fed funds rate cut to 1%. The accommodative stance of fiscal and monetary policy will keep the economy going, but the imbalances in all sectors will weigh down on the economy and the recovery will begin to falter during the course of 2004. The economy will average 3.0% growth in 2004 and will continue at this rate in 2005. Real disposable income growth will fall back to 2.5% both in 2004 and 2005. With the economy returning to its past anaemic pace, long-term interest rates will rise gently, but not substantially, with the mortgage rate climbing to 6.5% in 2004 from 6.15% in September 2003. Long-term interest rates are bound to rise, in spite of the return of the economy to its anaemic growth. However, as confidence evaporates long-term interest rates will fall back to an average of 6.0% for the mortgage rate in 2005 (see Table 6.3 for a summary of the current and assumed values for 2004 and 2005). Households will refrain from accumulating more debt, as the boom in the housing market is near its peak. Thus, mortgage debt, which stood at 81% of disposable income in September 2003, will fall to 80% and 79% in 2004 and 2005, respectively. The debt service burden will average 14% of disposable income over the next two years. Housing starts will abate somewhat, but will remain strong at 1.7 million units annual rate, compared to 1.8 in September 2003. With these assumptions the median house price will rise 1.9% in 2004 and will hardly increase any further in 2005 (see Table 6.3 for a summary of the results). Real residential investment will rise just 0.9% in 2004, but will fall 1.5% in 2005. The gross real estate (i.e. the value of property) of households will fall 1% and 4.6% in 2004 and 2005, respectively. The net real estate will decline even more to −0.6% and −6.3%.

The inevitable conclusion of this simulation is that a return to anaemic growth, will deter the collapse of the housing market. Tepid growth will prevent the surge in long-term interest rates and will curb the appetite of households in accumulating debt and tolerate ever-increasing debt service burdens in the hope of rising incomes.

6.2   Scenario II (strong recovery in 2004)

The essence of scenario II lies on the premise, which is largely true, that a combined fiscal and monetary stimulus will last for at least a year, and probably eighteen months, before it tapers off. Given that the fiscal stimulus was introduced between May and July 2003, the economy should remain strong until the end of 2004. The role of the accommodative stance of monetary policy is to prevent long-term interest rates from rising and therefore prolong the effects of the fiscal stimulus. However, despite low short-term interest rates introduced by the Fed over the period 2001–03, long-term interest rates have risen sharply since June 2003 and the yield curve is, currently, extremely steep. If interest rates stay at this high level, or even rise further, which is very likely, the stimulus from fiscal policy will ultimately peter out. This means that growth will diminish in 2005 and beyond, other things being equal. Given that the average growth for the preceding four quarters before the fiscal stimulus was first introduced in May 2003 was 2.6%, that the fiscal stimulus was 1.6% of GDP and that the first year multiplier is about unity, the central projection for average growth until the second half, or the end, of 2004 should be 4.2%. Since the depreciation incentives on new structures will only count if premises are ready for service at the beginning of 2005, companies that would like to take advantage of the scheme should already have started spending. This explains the buoyant recovery of investment in the second quarter of 2003 that was responsible, to some extent, for the unexpectedly strong growth in that quarter. The other major factor that contributed to the unexpectedly strong second quarter was the explosion of defence spending because of the Iraq war.

The stunning 8.2% growth in the third quarter of 2003 was caused by the combination of two main reasons. The strong consumption, which was due to the income tax cuts that were introduced in that quarter, was the last-wagon effect for those companies that wanted to take advantage of the depreciation incentives on new structures (which accounted for $30 billion). It was also due to the worldwide improving confidence because of lower geopolitical risks after the end of the Iraq war that boosted US exports in the third quarter. This implies that the stunning third quarter growth was due to one-off factors that are likely to dissipate in the first half of 2004. Nonetheless, the economy should still grow at 4.2% – central projection until the end of 2004. Such growth will most likely boost job creation and create the impression that the last three years following the burst of the equity bubble was simply a nightmare that belongs to the past.

Higher long-term interest rates, caused by strong growth, will probably induce lower business investment in 2005 and may trigger a collapse of the housing market that may not only cause residential investment to tumble, but also induce households to be more cautious in their spending. That is the essence of Scenario II. The effects of this scenario are simulated by assuming that the mortgage rate will climb to 7.5%, on average, in 2004, but will fall to 7.0% on average in 2005. The strong growth in 2004, coupled with a recovery of the equity market, will induce households to accumulate even more debt, in the hope that the housing boom will last forever. Mortgage debt is therefore assumed to continue soaring at the rate of the last three years bringing it up to 85% of disposable income from 81% in the third quarter of 2003. The collapse of the housing market and the fall in the equity market in 2004 will induce households to lower their mortgage debt to 83% of disposable income in the course of 2005. Consequently, the debt service burden will rise to an all time high of 15.5% of disposable income in 2004 from 14% in the third quarter of 2003, but the consumer retrenchment of 2005 and the repayment of debt will cause debt service burden to fall back to 13.8% in 2005.

Table 6.3 The effects of weak and strong recovery in 2004 on the housing market

	Current values	Scenario I (weak recovery)				Scenario II (strong recovery)				Sensitivity	
		Median house price (thousands of dollars)	Residential investment (billions of dollars)	Gross real estate of households (as % of disposable income)	Net real estate of households (as % of disposable income)	Median house price (thousands of dollars)	Residential investment (billions of dollars)	Gross real estate of households (as % of disposable income)	Net real estate of households (as % of disposable income)	House prices	Residential investment
Assumptions	Sep.-03										
30-year mortgage rate %	6.15										
1st year				6.5				7.5			
2nd year				6				7			
Debt service % of disposable income	14.03										
1st year				14				15.5			
2nd year				14				13.8			
Mortgage debt % of disposable income											
1st year	81.0			80				85			
2nd year				79				83			
Real disposable income % y-o-y											
1st year	2.4			2.5				4.5			
2nd year				2.5				1.5			
Housing starts units of houses											
6-month MA				1700				1800			
1st year	1 803			1700				1150			
2nd year											
CPI inflation % y-o-y				2				2			
1st year	2.3			2				2			
2nd year											
Effects on the housing market											
Current values		172.3	418.0	175.1	94.0	172.3	418.0	175.1	94.0	172.3	418.0
12-M SRE (future short-run fair value level)		175.6	421.7	173.4	93.4	171.7	425.2	173.4	88.4	168.3	411.4
24-M SRE (future short-run fair value level)		172.5	411.9	167.1	88.1	162.3	303.4	166.2	83.2	158.6	287.2
12-M SRE and current level (% difference)		1.9	0.9	−1.0	−0.6	−0.4	1.7	−1.0	−5.9	−2.3	−1.6
24-M SRE and current level (% difference)		0.1	−1.5	−4.6	−6.3	−5.8	−27.4	−5.1	−11.5	−8.0	−31.3
Sensitivity of 12-M SRE										−2.0	−3.3
Sensitivity of 24-M SRE										−2.2	−3.9

of Scenario II			Sensitivity of Scenario II													
Gross real estate of households	Net real estate of households	House prices	Residential investment	Gross real estate of households	Net real estate of households	House prices	Residential investment	Gross real estate of households	Net real estate of households	House prices	Residential investment	Gross real estate of households	Net real estate of households	House prices	Residential investment	Gross real estate of households
8.5																
8																
			14													
			12.4													
							93.5									
							91.3									
											3.5					
											0.5					
															1620	
															1035	
175.1	94.0	172.3	418.0	175.1	94.0	172.3	418.0	175.1	94.0	172.3	418.0	175.1	94.0	172.3	418.0	175.1
173.4	88.4	171.1	423.9	173.4	88.4	167.0	415.6	173.4	79.9	171.4	424.5	173.4	88.4	169.6	389.6	173.4
165.4	82.4	160.7	301.2	166.0	83.0	155.0	293.3	165.1	73.8	161.5	299.5	166.1	83.1	157.5	282.8	165.7
−1.0	−5.9	−0.7	1.4	−1.0	−5.9	−3.1	−0.6	−1.0	−15.0	−0.5	1.6	−1.0	−5.9	−1.5	−6.8	−1.0
−5.5	−12.4	−6.7	−28.0	−5.2	−11.7	−10.1	−29.8	−5.7	−21.5	−6.3	−28.4	−5.1	−11.6	−8.6	−32.3	−5.4
0.0	0.0	−0.4	−0.3	0.0	0.0	−2.7	−2.3	0.0	−9.0	−0.2	−0.2	0.0	0.0	−1.2	−8.5	0.0
−0.4	−0.8	−0.9	−0.5	−0.1	−0.2	−4.3	−2.4	−0.6	−10.0	−0.5	−0.9	0.0	−0.1	−2.8	−4.9	−0.3

Real disposable income growth will accelerate to 4.5% in 2004 from 2.4% in the third quarter of 2003, as a result of the stronger growth in the economy that will cause substantial job creation. However, the deceleration of growth in 2005, along with generalised collapse of confidence and the plunge of the equity and the housing market, will trigger job losses in the course of 2005 that will push growth in real disposable income down to 1.5%. Housing starts will maintain their upward momentum in 2004 remaining at 1.8 million units, on average, in 2004, the same as in the third quarter of 2003, but will tumble to 1.15 million units in 2005 (Table 6.3 offers a summary of all the assumptions in Scenario II).

With these assumptions the median house price will fall 0.4% in 2004, but will tumble 5.8% in 2005 (see Table 6.3). This may not sound a lot in absolute terms and also compared to losses in the equity market, but a cursory look at Figure 6.2 reveals that in the last thirty-five years house price inflation was negative only once, in June 1989, and only at −0.7%. Hence, a drop of the order of 5.8% in nominal house prices in 2005 would be unprecedented in the last thirty-five years. House price inflation relative to CPI will fall 7.6% by the third quarter of 2005, which would be the biggest decline of the last thirty-five years (see Figure 6.2). Figure 6.14 shows the decline in house price inflation relative to CPI under the two scenarios. It is obvious that house price inflation is near its peak and will fall under both scenarios. But the fall would be much sharper under Scenario II. Figure 6.15 compares the fall in the level of relative house prices under the two scenarios. With a weak recovery relative house prices would fall slightly, but they would fall a great deal under the scenario of a strong recovery.

Real residential investment will grow 1.7% in 2004 under the strong recovery scenario, but would collapse in 2005 by 27.4% (see Table 6.3). Figure 6.16 compares the growth rate of residential investment under the two scenarios. The strong recovery in 2004 is a recipe for disaster for real residential investment in 2005 – it would collapse at a rate of 33.7%, the highest since records began in 1987. Figure 6.17 confirms this result by comparing the level of real residential investment under the two scenarios. The gross real estate of households (the value of property) will fall 1% in 2004 and 5.1% in 2005, in line with the fall in house prices (see Figure 6.18). However, the value of net real estate will fall much sharper, as debt will accumulate in the course of 2004. Thus, in 2004 net real estate will fall 5.9% and 11.5% in 2005.

The conclusion from this simulation is that stronger growth in 2004 would most probably cause a collapse of the property market in 2005. The average rate of growth of the economy for the two years combined will be approximately the same under both scenarios. However, the large volatility of growth under the strong recovery scenario would induce households to accumulate even more debt and withstand higher debt service burden in the short run that will ultimately cause a collapse in the housing market. At the root of the problem under the strong growth scenario is the surge in long-term interest rates in the course of 2004, which will be initially shrugged off by households under the euphoria that the nightmare of the last three years is over. However, the strong growth of 2004, if it materialises, would aggravate the imbalances of the personal sector and trigger a huge retrenchment in 2005.

6.3 Sensitivity of Scenario II (strong recovery in 2004)

The plausibility of this scenario depends on how sensitive the projections for the housing market are to their determinants. Table 6.3 provides the results of this sensitivity analysis. For comparative purposes, every determinant that is expressed as growth rate (per cent over the year earlier period) has been perturbed by 1% of its value in Scenario II. Variables that are expressed as ratios have been perturbed by 10% of their value in Scenario II, a plausible magnitude. It is convenient in comparing the impact of the various determinants in the housing market to look at multipliers. The multiplier measures the ratio of the percentage change of, say, house prices to a given percentage change in one determinant, say, mortgage rate. The Summary Table below provides the second year multiplier of the housing market indicators with respect to each of the five determinants.

House prices are most sensitive to interest rates. Just one per cent increase in the mortgage rate lowers house prices by 2% after twelve months and 2.2% after twenty-four months. The interest rate effect, therefore, is long lasting. The second year multiplier is 2.2, almost the same as the first year multiplier. The second most important factor of house prices is the debt service burden. An attempt by households to reduce their debt service burden by 1% would lower house prices 0.4% in the first year and 0.9% in the second year. The third most important factor affecting house prices is real disposable income growth. One per cent fall leads to 0.2% fall in house prices in the first year, rising to 0.5% in the second year. The mortgage debt is the fourth most important factor affecting house prices. A ten per cent rise in the mortgage debt leads to a fall in house prices of 2.7% in the first year and 4.3% in the second. The second year multiplier is 0.4. The fifth most important factor is housing starts. A ten per cent fall leads to a fall in house prices of 1.2% in the first year and 2.8% in the second year. The second year multiplier is just 0.3.

The most important factor affecting real residential investment is the mortgage rate. A one per cent rise in the mortgage rate leads to a fall in real residential investment of 3.3% in the first year and 3.9% in the second year. The second most important factor is real disposable income growth, where a one per cent fall leads to 0.2% fall in real residential investment after one year and 0.9% after two years. The debt service burden and the housing starts occupy the third position, as they have the same impact in the same year. However, whereas the effect of housing starts dissipates through time with first year multiplier being 0.9 and the second year 0.5, the effect of the debt service burden increases through time. Mortgage debt has the smallest impact of all determinants of real residential investment. The second year multiplier is only 0.2. The most important factor affecting the gross real estate of households is the mortgage rate. All other factors are insignificant. The order for net real estate is: (1) Mortgage debt; (2) mortgage rate; (3) debt service; (4) real disposable income growth. Housing starts have a negligible effect. The overall conclusion of the sensitivity analysis is that the mortgage rate is the most important factor affecting the housing market. Real disposable income growth is the second or third most important factor in affecting house prices and real residential investment.

7   Summary and conclusions

The buoyancy of the housing market has been at the root of the resilience of the consumer throughout the bear market of 2000–03. The capital gains from the property market not only have they offset the losses from financial markets, but they have also accounted for 40% of consumer expenditure in the last three years. The tax cuts and other fiscal support to the personal sector accounts for another 17% of consumer expenditure in the three years following the burst of the equity bubble.

Despite these capital gains the net wealth of the personal sector has not recovered. It is still $2.2 trillion dollars (or 115% of disposable income) down compared with the level of net wealth at the peak of the equity bubble in March 2000. This loss in net wealth is due to the surge in household debt, which is equal to 14% of disposable income in the three years after the burst of the bubble. This is unprecedented! There is no other three-year period, since records began in 1952, in which debt increased at such frenetic pace. The second highest rate is 10.2% of disposable income that occurred between April and September 1987, after the peak of the property market in April 1987. The rate of debt accumulation fell rapidly after the equity market crash in October 1987.

This level of debt may become unsustainable, if house prices were to fall and long-term interest rates were to rise. Indeed, between June and September 2003 long-term interest rates have risen more than 1% and mortgage rates by almost 1%. If long-term interest rates rise further then the risk is high that house prices and residential investment will fall. Would this have a spiralling effect on consumer expenditure and prompt households to save more?

The answer depends on the extent to which house prices would fall in the next two years. House prices rose 8.4% in September 2003, the highest since 1982. Although the highest house price inflation occurred in September 1979, at 15.6%, CPI-inflation was also high at the time. If house price inflation is expressed relative to CPI, then it is a whisker lower from the all time high of 6.8% reached in April 1978. The property market is not yet a bubble, as relative house price inflation is near a peak that is similar to other cycles. However, house price inflation is not uniform across geographical regions. It concentrates in the Northeast, but even there it is less than the all time high of the late 1980s. Nonetheless, the possibility of a housing market collapse in the Northeast is still there because of the unprecedented high level of debt that was fuelled by the low interest rates in the aftermath of the burst of the equity bubble. Although the possible collapse of the housing market in the Northeast will not spread to the other regions, it will still affect them through a chain reaction in incomes and employment.

According to the K-Model the mortgage rate is the most important factor of the housing market with real disposable income as the second or third. The first- and second-year multiplier with respect to the mortgage rate is over 2. This means that for every percentage rate increase in the mortgage rate house prices would fall more than two percentage points. The increase in the mortgage rate sets in motion a spiral between four key variables: house prices, real residential investment, gross real estate (the value of property) and net real estate (the value of property net of mortgage debt).

A rise in the mortgage rate or a fall in real disposable income growth lowers the demand for housing and triggers a fall in house prices, as the supply of houses is fixed in the very short run. In time, this lowers the supply of houses by reducing real residential investment and inducing households to keep their property instead of putting it in the market for sale. The new balance of demand and supply of houses causes capital losses in property and lowers the gross real estate of households. With time households are induced to repay their mortgage debt or, at least, to accumulate debt at a smaller pace. Either way the net real estate of households falls and this diminishes once again the demand for housing. The cycle has been completed and triggers another one that is larger than the one before. The spiral of falling prices, residential investment, gross and net real estate goes on increasing in amplitude until the rate of debt repayment exceeds the rate of capital losses in property values. Net real estate stops falling, as households pay back their debt, and begins to rise and this, in time, will increase the demand for houses thereby putting an end to the free fall of house prices. The system is stable – a shock in the mortgage or real disposable income growth leads to a new steady state equilibrium with lower house prices, lower real residential investment and lower gross and net real estate.

The mortgage rate has already risen and will probably rise even more in the course of 2004, as it closely follows the 30-year Treasury bond yield, which is likely to rise further because of soaring budget deficits and faster economic growth. However, the extent to which the housing market will fall depends on the strength of the recovery that started after the Iraq war. This is supported by easy fiscal and monetary policy and rising confidence because of lower geopolitical risks. If the recovery is weak in 2004, then house prices will rise in 2004 and stabilise in 2005. Real residential investment will remain approximately the same, as the rise in the first year will be offset by a fall in the second.

If the recovery in 2004 is strong, then the housing market will fall slightly in 2004 but will collapse in 2005 with unprecedented declines in house prices, real residential investment and gross (and net) real estate. Nominal house prices may fall as much as 6%. The biggest fall was less than 1% in July 1989.

The reason why the two scenarios lead to such different consequences for the housing market is that the strength of the recovery will determine the extent to which long-term interest rates would rise. With the weak recovery scenario the mortgage rate will rise by less than 0.5%, whereas with the strong recovery scenario the mortgage rate will climb more than one per cent.

Although both scenarios seem plausible, as the strength of the economy in the second and third quarters of 2003 was due to one-off factors, the strong recovery scenario has a slightly higher probability than the weak scenario. The one-off factors will dissipate in the course of 2004, but the economy may still manage 1.5% higher growth in 2004 compared with 2003. The average rate of growth for the two-year period may be approximately the same under both scenarios, but with the strong recovery scenario the growth volatility will be high and this will trigger a collapse in the property market. The Fed is aware of the consequences of these personal sector imbalances and the threat to the sustainability of the current recovery. Therefore, it is expected to take it into account in tightening monetary policy.

The overall conclusion is that a strong recovery is not preferable to a weak recovery at this stage of the US business cycle. An excessive easy stance of fiscal policy would be mainly responsible, if the recovery in 2004 turned out to be very strong. But this may be driven by political expediency in view of the November 2004 presidential election. Unfortunately, monetary policy may have very little scope in moderating the excessive growth in 2004. If the Fed tightened monetary policy, like the Bank of England did, then it would precipitate the fall of the property market and it may be blamed for bringing the economy down once again. In a pre-election year the Fed would probably abstain from acting as the election date nears, so that it will not be accused of political bias. The Fed, therefore, can only be a spectator to the scene that will be set up by fiscal policy.

7
Long-term Risks of Robust Consumer Behaviour

1 Introduction

In the second half of 2003 consumption rebounded because of an improved outlook for the corporate sector, higher confidence because of lower geopolitical risks and in view of the new round of tax cuts and higher government deficit. The short-run factors that affect consumption improved over the same period, and expected to remain buoyant in the course of 2004. Employment prospects are much better, inflation will remain subdued for a while and real disposable income growth will remain buoyant. Moreover, further gains in the property market and recovering equity prices mean that the imbalance of the personal sector has narrowed, in spite of higher indebtedness that stands at an all-time high. Hence, the outlook for consumption in 2004 has markedly improved. However, there are still long-term risks to consumption, especially so if growth in 2004 turns out to be strong, boosted once more by easy fiscal policy. Interest rates would rise and would undermine the outlook for the corporate sector, which would adversely affect the short-run factors that affect consumption. In addition, higher interest rates would adversely affect the long-run factors that affect consumption. Higher rates would threaten to lower both house and equity prices once more. In this case the personal sector imbalance would widen once again and this time it may lead to retrenchment by households that may even develop into recession in 2005, unless, of course, sufficient government deficit is in place. Slow growth in 2004 is preferable than fast growth, as none of these risks would materialise.

Figure 7.1 shows the pattern of real consumer expenditure for eight quarters before and after the trough of the recession as percentage of the earlier year. To simplify comparisons only four lines are shown, the average of the five demand-led recessions in 1947–72, the average of the three supply-led business cycles in 1973–84, the early 1990s recession and the recent one. In the recent downturn, consumption fared better than in any other cycle, when it decelerated from 5.1% to 1.8% and then it began to grow again.

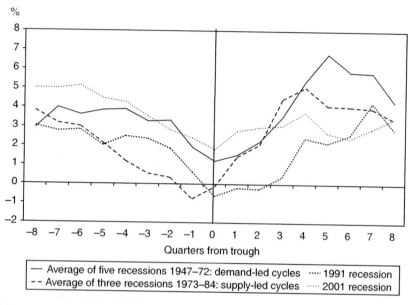

Figure 7.1   Consumption % y-o-y (for eight quarters before and after the trough)

Consumption never contracted and bottomed at the trough of the business cycle. Both features are typical in the average demand-led cycle. Consumption softened in the first half of the second year of the recovery, but regained its strength in the last two quarters of the same year. The softness of consumption in the second year of the recovery is typical in all business cycles. The rebound of consumption in the second half of 2003, coupled with rising consumer confidence raised hopes that the economy is on a sustainable path (Conference Board, 2003). In what follows in this chapter we examine the potential risks that lie dormant in the current environment of excessive optimism, which threaten the sustainability of the current recovery. We begin in Section 2 with an examination of the short-run factors that affect consumption, followed in Section 3 by a study of the long-run factors that influence consumption. We consider the K-Model and dwell on the theoretical background of consumer behaviour in Section 4. We assess the long-run risks to consumption in Section 5. Finally, we summarise and conclude in Section 6.

2   Short-run factors affecting consumption

Table 7.1 shows the sources and disposition of real and nominal disposable income. Personal income consists of earned and unearned income plus transfers payments (subsidies) from the government less personal contributions

Table 7.1 Sources and disposition of personal income

Oct. 03	Dollars in billions	%
1. Wages and salaries	5 120	
% of personal income		56
2. Other earned personal income	1 503	
(other labour income and		
proprietor's income)		
% of personal income		16
3. Unearned personal income	1 563	
(Rental, dividend and interest income)		
% of personal income		17
4. Transfer payments to persons	1 401	
% of personal income		15
5. Less: personal contributions for	397.9	
social insurance		
% of personal income		4
6. Personal income (sum of (1–4) − 5)	9 189	100
7. Less: Personal tax and non-tax payments	1 079.4	
% of personal income		12
8. Equals: disposable personal income	8 109	
% of personal income		88
9. Less: Personal outlays	7 772	100.0
9.1 Personal consumption expenditures	7 557	
% of personal outlays		97.2
9.2 Interest paid by persons	182	
% of personal outlays		2.3
9.3 Personal transfer payments to the	33	
rest of the world (net)		
% of personal outlays		0.4
10. Equals: personal saving	337	
11. Personal saving as a percentage of		4.2
disposable personal income		
12. Real disposable personal income	7 126	
(billions of chained 1996 dollars)		

for social insurance. Disposable income is equal to personal income less taxes, while real disposable income is adjusted for inflation in consumer prices. Figure 7.2 shows that although personal income and wages and salaries, which account for more than half of personal income, continue to recover from the recession of 2001, they are growing at a subdued pace, as they are still below the average of the previous business cycle. Figure 7.3 shows that although wages and salaries in the government sector, which account for only 17% of the total, have abated in the last two years (the rate of growth has been halved), those in the private sector producing industries have continued to recover, although they remain below the average of the

170

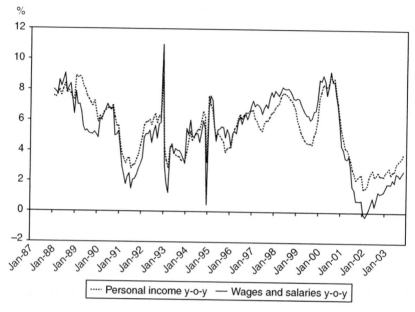

Figure 7.2 Personal income and wages and salaries (nominal)

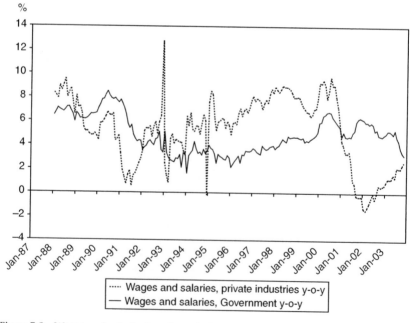

Figure 7.3 Wages and salaries in private industries and government (nominal)

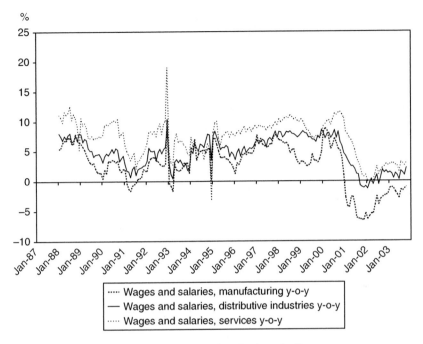

Figure 7.4 Wages and salaries in various industries (nominal)

last business cycle. Figure 7.4 shows that the recovery in wages and salaries is uniform across services, distributive industries and manufacturing, although in the latter they are still falling even in nominal terms. Other earned personal income, which accounts for 16% of personal income, is still growing satisfactorily. Among the components of other earned personal income, other labour income growth has slowed somewhat from extremely high to more sustainable levels, while proprietor's income has recently exceeded the average of the last business cycle (see Figure 7.5). Unearned personal income, which accounts for 18% of personal income, has improved in the last few months (see Figure 7.6).

Figure 7.7 shows that although in the first year of the recovery disposable personal income growth was more pronounced than personal income, the two are now converging. Thus, although personal income grew only 2.4% y-o-y in November 2002 (the end of the first year recovery), disposable personal income grew as much as 7.3%. Since then the gap of nearly 5% has been narrowed to less than 1%. The wide gap in the first year of the recovery is due to the fiscal support of the personal sector, which has now narrowed. The net transfers to persons (transfers less personal contributions to social security) rose from 3.3% y-o-y at the peak of the bubble in March 2000 to 16.8% in November 2001. However, they declined since then to 8.7% y-o-y in October 2003 (see Figure 7.8). Taxes as per cent of disposable income

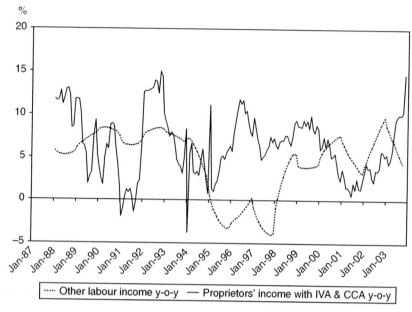

Figure 7.5 Other earned personal income (nominal)

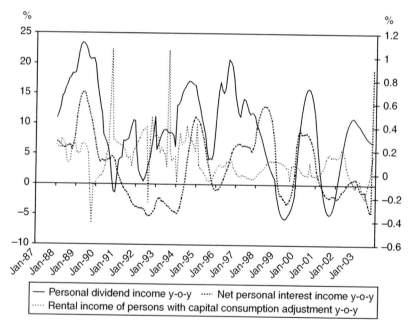

Figure 7.6 Unearned personal income (nominal)

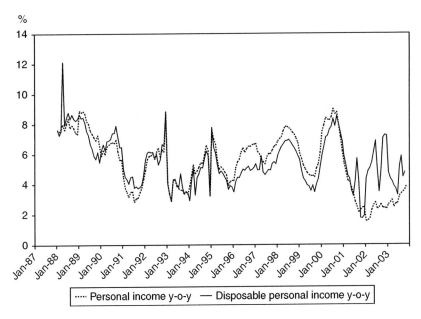

Figure 7.7 Personal income and disposable personal income (nominal)

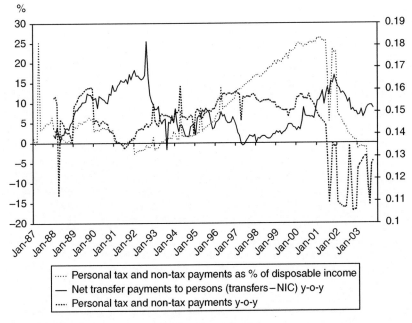

Figure 7.8 Fiscal support to personal sector

have been cut continuously from the peak of 18.3% in March 2001 to 12.6% in October 2003 (see Figure 7.8). Hence, the difference between disposable income and personal income growth in the first of the recovery was entirely due to the fiscal support of the personal sector.

As inflation in consumer prices, measured by the deflator in consumption expenditure, has been rather low and stable relative to the fluctuations in income the difference between nominal and real disposable income has also been small and stable (see Figure 7.9a). Hence, fluctuations in nominal disposable income have been transmitted to corresponding fluctuations in real disposable income. The pattern of consumption in the current downturn has largely followed that of real personal disposable income, although the latter has been much more volatile, as households attempt to smooth their consumption in the face of large swings in their income, partly caused by the business cycle and partly by changes in taxes and subsidies. Real disposable income peaked at 5.6% a year before the trough and bottomed at 0.3%, a quarter after the trough (see Figure 7.9b). Throughout the recovery real disposable income growth has been very volatile. The pattern of real personal disposable income in the recovery phase has not been dissimilar to the average demand- or supply-led business cycle. Moreover, it has been more buoyant than the early 1990s downturn, but largely because of fiscal injections. In the first year of the recovery real disposable income growth was spectacular

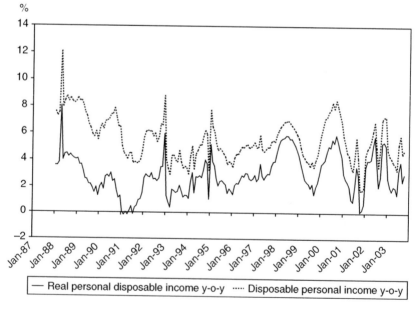

Figure 7.9a   Real and nominal personal disposable income

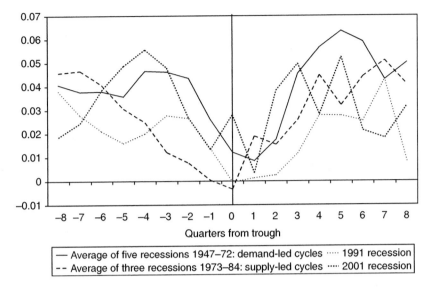

Figure 7.9b Real personal disposable income (for eight quarters before and after the trough)

and this explains why the consumer was so resilient during that period of time.

During the second round of retrenchment by the corporate sector real disposable income growth was more than halved from 5.7% in November 2003 to 2.4% in April 2003. However, real disposable income growth accelerated in the second half of 2003, but again because of new tax cuts. We may be able to throw some light on the prospects for real disposable income growth by decomposing wages and salaries in the private industries (which account for something less than half of personal income) into the product of its constituent components: (a) average hours per week, (b) employment, and (c) real hourly earnings. Companies usually cut the working week in the downswing, but restore it in the upswing of the cycle (see Figure 7.10). In the current cycle, the average weekly hours were cut 1.5 hours during the downswing. This is not dissimilar to previous business cycles. Companies cut 1.2 hours in the early 1990s downturn, 1.7 hours in the average demand-led cycle and 1.4 hours in the average supply-led cycle. However, during the early stages of the current recovery the average weekly hours increased by just 0.7 hours, the slowest pace than in any other cycle. Even worse, the average weekly hours were cut yet again for most of the current recovery hitting twice the low reached at the trough. In their attempt to restore profitability and healthy balance sheets in the second round of retrenchment, companies reverted not only to cutting the average weekly hours, but also employment.

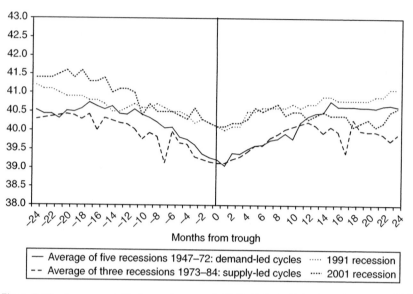

Figure 7.10   Average weekly hours in manufacturing (for twenty-four months before and after the trough)

In the downswing of the recent cycle job losses have been more pronounced than in any other cycle (see Figure 7.11). Job creation peaked nineteen months before the trough at 305 thousand new jobs per month and bottomed two months after the trough at 234 thousand job losses per month, the steepest decline in all last ten cycles. However, in the recovery phase job creation has been more anaemic than ever before, outstripping even the early 1990s cycle. On a six-month moving average basis, there was hardly any job creation in the current recovery. Even worse, job losses were resumed during the second round of retrenchment by the corporate sector. The second round of retrenchment by the corporate sector was successful in restoring profitability and improving balance sheets. Job creation resumed by the end of 2003 as a result, and should continue in the course of 2004.

Not only have companies cut the working week and laid off workers to restore profitability and healthy balance sheets in this second round of retrenchment in the current cycle, but they have also managed, for the first time, to reduce the earnings of the labour force. Real hourly earnings peaked at 4.2% a year before the trough and bottomed at the trough at −0.9% (see Figure 7.12). This is the first time that companies have managed to cut the earnings of the labour force and it may be the result of the flexible labour markets that were introduced in the late 1980s and early 1990s. It could also be the result of fiscal surpluses reducing aggregate demand. In the average demand-led cycle real hourly earnings simply fluctuated mildly around their

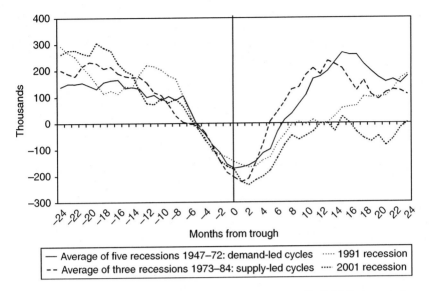

Figure 7.11 Monthly job creation/losses in non-farm payroll, 6M MA (twenty-four months before and after the trough)

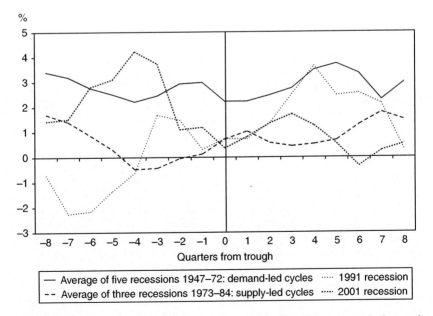

Figure 7.12 Real hourly earnings in non-farm business (for eight quarters before and after the trough)

mean value, without falling in the downswing or rising in the upswing. During the recovery of the current cycle, real hourly earnings rose by only 2% from their bottom to 1.1% in just three quarters from the trough. However, during the second round of retrenchment by the corporate sector real hourly earnings fell yet again to a new low. In the second half of 2004 they have started to increase providing even more evidence of the sustainability of the recovery.

Overall, the recent recession was very mild thanks to the resilience of the consumer. This is partly due to the buoyancy of real disposable income, which was boosted through easy fiscal policy. Had it not been for the fiscal injection, real disposable income would have fallen thereby pulling the rug under the consumer feet. Wages and salaries fell not only in real, but also in nominal terms. In most private industries they have fallen in real terms even during the recovery. But personal income has fared better than wages and salaries partly because wages and salaries in the government sector have been growing at a brisk pace and partly because other earned and unearned income has not suffered as much as wages and salaries. During the double-dip recession of the industrial sector, caused by a second round of retrenchment, companies cut the average working week, laid off workers, managed to reduce the hourly earnings of their workers and slashed investment. The slower growth in real disposable income during the double-dip recession caused a deceleration in consumption growth. However, the picture has changed markedly in the second half of 2003. The second round of retrenchment by the corporate sector was successful in restoring profitability and improving balance sheets. Hence, wages have begun to rise, job creation has been resumed, albeit sluggishly so far, and average weekly hours have increased. The 2003 round of tax cuts also bolstered real disposable income in the second half of the same year. The tax cuts have now a better chance of boosting consumption, as all the short-run factors that affect it have improved. Any risks to consumption, therefore, would only come from the long-run factors. We turn our attention to this issue in the section that follows.

3   Long-term forces restraining consumption – personal sector imbalances

During the upswing of the average demand- and supply-led business cycle, savings as percentage of nominal disposable income (what is usually called the *savings ratio*) fell 1.6% thereby fostering the pace of the recovery, due to some extent to the fiscal surplus (see Figure 7.13). In contrast, the savings ratio increased gradually by 2% almost throughout the downturn of the early 1990s, when budget deficit prevailed. This was the first time that the savings ratio did not fall in the recovery phase of the business cycle. This increase in the savings ratio contributed to making the recovery of the early 1990s anaemic. In the current downturn the savings ratio rose by nearly the

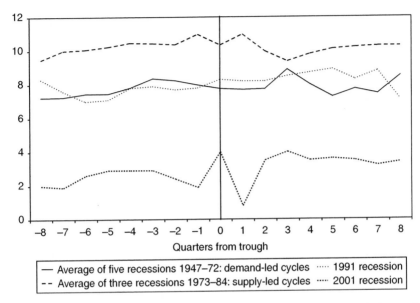

Figure 7.13 Personal savings as % of disposable income (for eight quarters before and after the trough)

same amount as in the early 1990s, from 1.9% seven quarters before the trough to 3.5% now, eight quarters after the trough (see also Figure 7.13). What the outlook for the savings ratio might be over the next two years or so, would determine not only the fate of the latest tax cuts, but also how much of the new boost to income from employment would stimulate consumption.

In the very long run consumption and real disposable income are growing at the same rate so that the ratio of consumption to income (the *average propensity to consume*) is equal to unity. But in the short run consumption can deviate substantially from income. In the Permanent Income – Life-cycle hypotheses the role of savings is to absorb the swings in income and allow for a smooth consumption pattern. Consumers save in good years and tap on these savings in bad years. Hence, the savings ratio moves pro-cyclically, it rises in booms and falls in recessions. However, the validity of this relationship has been questioned. Frowen and Karakitsos (1996) suggest that in a leveraged economy the savings ratio moves counter-cyclically (i.e. it falls in a boom and rises in a recession). In boom years asset prices rise faster than usual as consumers borrow against these assets to invest even more (leveraging). Faster than usual rising asset prices make people feel rich inducing them to relax on their effort to save as they believe that they can meet more easily their targets for savings (e.g. provide for pension, leave to their heirs). Hence, the savings ratio falls in a boom. In a recession asset prices fall and people are left with an overhang of debt. In order to repay their debt people cut on consumption out of current income and intensify on their effort to save in order to rebuild their wealth. Hence, the savings ratio increases in a recession. That is exactly what happened in the recent and the early 1990s downturn because the consumer has become much more leveraged than in the average demand- and supply-led business cycle.

In the short run, therefore, consumption depends on real disposable and the savings ratio. The forces that determine the savings ratio are net wealth and uncertainty about job security and income growth prospects. For the aforementioned reasons, a rise in net wealth lowers the savings ratio and vice versa (see, also, OECD, 2000b). An increase in uncertainty about job security and income growth prospects makes people more cautious inducing them to refrain from spending out of current income, thereby raising the savings ratio. Figure 7.14a shows the relationship between net wealth and the savings ratio, while Figure 7.14b shows net wealth in the various business cycles. When net wealth is above its long-term average the savings ratio is low, and vice versa. For example, in the 1950s and 1960s, the golden years of demand-led business cycles, net wealth was above its long-term average and the average savings ratio was low. In the 1970s and the 1980s, the supply-led business

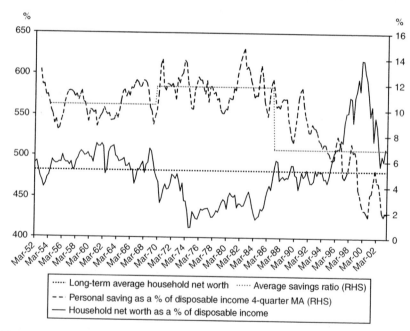

Figure 7.14a   Household net wealth

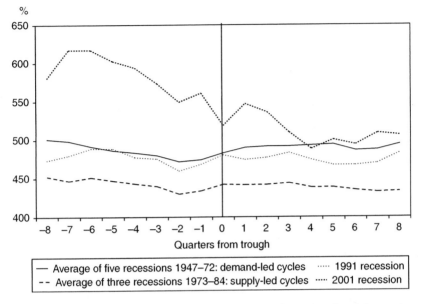

Figure 7.14b Personal sector net wealth as % of disposable income (for eight quarters before and after the trough)

cycles associated with the two oil shocks, net wealth fell below its long-term average and consequently the average savings ratio was increased. In the longest bull market from 1982 to 2000 net wealth steadily increased leading to steady decline in the savings ratio. During the bubble years in the second half of the 1990s net wealth rose to unprecedented levels and the savings ratio fell precipitously reaching rock bottom at the peak of the bubble. As equity prices declined steadily for three years, from March 2000 to March 2003, net wealth fell, reducing its long-term average of 480%, while the savings ratio increased to 4%. This rise in the savings ratio reflected increased cautiousness on the part of consumers in the face of falling asset prices with continuously rising debt. Figure 7.15 shows one measure of the personal sector imbalance. Between the peak of the bubble in March 2000 and the trough in September 2002 financial assets fell $6.8 trillion, but these were partially offset by rising property prices that boosted the value of tangible assets by $3.3 trillion, thereby limiting the erosion of gross wealth to $3.5 trillion (see Table 7.2). With the latest figures, 2003:Q3, the picture changed from negative to positive. The losses in financial assets narrowed to $3.6 trillion, while the gains in tangible assets soared to $4.6 trillion, so that gross wealth at $1 trillion stood higher than it had been at the peak of the bubble (see Table 7.2). Hence, the losses in financial assets have been more than offset by gains in property. This is impressive and one would have concluded that there is now

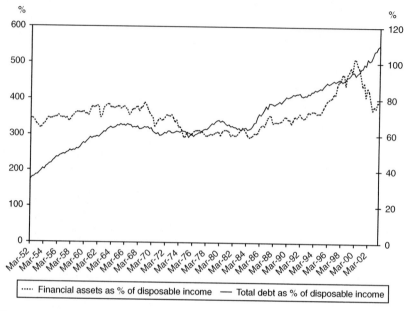

Figure 7.15 Financial assets and debt of the personal sector

Figure 7.15   Financial assets and debt of the personal sector

no problem for consumption. However, it is net rather than gross wealth that matters for consumption and this has not yet recovered.

The real estate of households as percentage of disposable income is at an all time high at 191% (see Figure 7.16). Unfortunately, the property boom has been financed by continuous debt accumulation, which as percentage of disposable income has reached 110% in the third quarter of 2003 (see Figure 7.15). Since the peak of the equity bubble debt has increased $2.5 trillion, as a result of which the $1 trillion gains in gross wealth is translated into $1.5 trillion loss in net wealth. Although this imbalance has narrowed from $5 trillion at the bottom of equity prices, it is still worrisome. This imbalance can be corrected in either of two ways: (a) a retrenchment by the personal sector that will raise the savings ratio further or (b) a rebound in asset prices. Throughout the recent downturn households never responded by retrenchment to this imbalance, presumably because they believed that the fall in asset prices was transient rather than permanent. Now that the recovery is under way it is still less likely that they will respond to this imbalance with retrenchment. However, if property prices were to decline, then the value of financial assets is also likely to fall. In this case net wealth would fall and the imbalance would widen once more. The risk of retrenchment by the personal sector would then rise. How much would the savings ratio rise depends also on the other factors that affect it, namely job security and incomes.

Table 7.2 Personal sector balance sheet

	Total assets	Total assets as % of nominal disposable income	Tangible assets	Tangible assets as % of nominal disposable income	Financial assets	Financial assets as % of nominal disposable income	Liabilities	Liabilities as % of nominal disposable income	Net worth	Net worth as % of nominal disposable income
Peak of equity bubble (March 2000)	50 571	727	14 489	208	36 082	519	7 011	101	43 560	626
Bottom of equity bubble (Sep. 2002)	47 071	599	17 825	227	29 245	372	8 536	109	38 534	490
Latest quarter (Sep. 2003)	51 598	639	19 129	237	32 470	402	9 546	118	42 052	521
Loss between peak and bottom of bubble	−3 500	−128	3 336	−18	−6 837	−147	1 525	8	−5 025	−136
Latest gain or loss since peak of bubble	1 027	−88	4 640	29	−3 612	−117	2 535	17	−1 508	−105

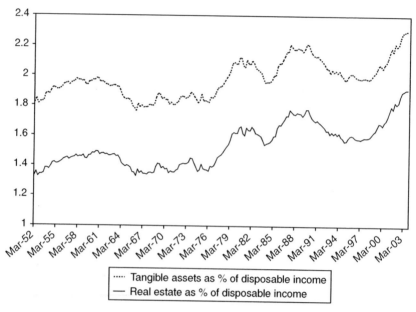

Figure 7.16   Tangible assets and real estate

Job security and income growth prospects depend on the outlook for the corporate sector. We have argued in Chapters 3 and 4 that although the outlook for both corporate profits and investment has improved, there are still substantial risks. For although the new fiscal package would actually enable investment to boom, the higher long-term interest rates that would ensue may weaken it in 2005. Moreover, if the boom of 2004 leads to strong pace of job creation then corporate profits growth would decline. Both factors may dent consumer confidence in 2005. Rising long-term interest rates would also threaten to tumble the property boom. The combination of worsening business and consumer outlook may then induce households to curb spending and raise the savings ratio. This risk is unlikely to materialise in 2004, but it is non-negligible for 2005. Unemployment has declined to 5.7% of the labour force from its peak of 6.3% in June 2003. It may fall more, especially if growth in 2004 is strong. However, the official measure of unemployment may hide the strength of job creation because many discouraged workers during the downturn would probably return to the labour force, thereby mitigating the fall in the official measure of unemployment. Hence, the savings ratio is unlikely to be raised in 2004, but if the risk factors materialise, then it would rise in 2005. Household debt service is extremely worrisome. In spite of low interest rates, household debt service is at an all time high because of high indebtedness (see Figure 7.17). The debt service ratio is

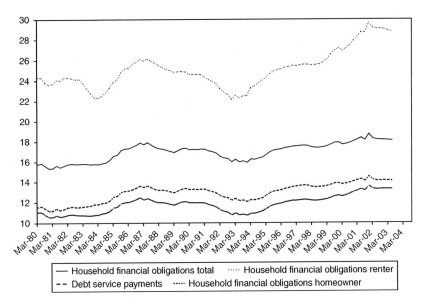

Figure 7.17 Debt service burden

an estimate of the ratio of debt payments on mortgages and consumer credit to disposable income. This stands at an all time high, despite the huge refinancing that has taken place in the last few years. The financial obligations ratio (FOR) is a broader measure than the debt service ratio. The FOR includes automobiles lease payments, rental payments on tenant-occupied property, homeowner's insurance and property tax payments. Most measures are at an all time high (see Figure 7.17). If interest rates were to rise, then households would find it difficult to service their debt and the savings ratio would climb. As the Fed is aware of these problems, it may be dissuaded from hiking rates this year. With growth at potential output the Fed should tighten in the second quarter of 2004, but with fast growth it can afford to wait. The required degree of tightening though would be larger in 2005, if the Fed chose to wait. Rising interest rates in 2005 would precipitate the retrenchment of the personal sector with the savings ratio rising even more.

Overall, despite the rally of equities in the last year or so, financial assets are still 10% lower than they were at the peak of the bubble. These losses amount to $3.6 trillion. The phenomenal boom in the property market has produced capital gains that more than offset the losses in financial assets, so that gross wealth is now 2%, or $1 trillion, higher than the peak of the equity market in March 2000. Although this is encouraging, net wealth, which matters for consumption decisions, is still 3.5%, or $1.5 trillion, lower because the property boom has been financed by debt accumulation that now stands at 110% of disposable income, an all time high. Although this imbalance has narrowed from $5 trillion at the bottom of equity prices, it is still worrisome, as it might be corrected by retrenchment. On the positive side consumers did not respond by retrenchment when the imbalance was much bigger, so that now that the economy is recovering it is even less likely to do so. However, there is a risk to consumption if growth in 2004 turned out to be very strong, boosted once more by fiscal policy. In this case investment would soften in 2005 because of higher long-term interest rates, and profitability would decline. The worsening outlook for the corporate sector in 2005 may induce caution on the part of consumers and raise the savings ratio. Higher long-term interest rates may also cause lower house prices, which would lead to falling financial asset prices. In this case the personal sector imbalance would widen once more and retrenchment may be the inevitable price. The situation would be aggravated by difficulties in debt servicing, which even at these low interest rates, stands at an all time high. In order to assess the likelihood of this risk we have simulated the K-Model under the alternative scenarios of fast and slow growth in 2004 and gauge the consequences for the 2-year period of 2004–05. To appreciate these results we first discuss the K-Model of consumption.

4   The K-Model of consumption

The analysis so far enables us to construct a theoretical model of US consumption. This particular framework we estimate and use for further investigation as shown below. We begin with our theoretical framework. In the very long run consumption and real disposable income are growing at the same rate so that the ratio of consumption to income (the *average propensity to consume*) is constant. But in the short run consumption can deviate substantially from income. In the Permanent-Income hypothesis (Friedman, 1957) and Life-Cycle hypothesis (Modigliani and Brumberg, 1954; Ando and Modigliani, 1963) consumers smooth their consumption patterns in the business cycle by basing their expenditure on their estimate of their permanent or trend income. Hence, the saving rate should rise in a boom and fall in a recession as consumers interpret the fluctuations in current income as temporary. In booms consumers regard the high current income as temporary and save the excess over permanent or trend income for the rainy days. In a recession consumers regard the drop in their current income as temporary and try to safeguard their standard of living by drawing down their savings (wealth). Thus, the saving ratio (the fraction of saving over disposable income S/YD) moves pro-cyclically, thereby rising in booms and falling in recessions. The validity of this relationship, however, has been questioned, based on two arguments.

The first is that consumer behaviour is myopic in the sense that the marginal propensity to consume out of transitory income is not zero, as the

Permanent-Income hypothesis suggests. The second is that consumers in formulating their desired consumption are constrained in terms of achieving the desired level, simply because capital markets are imperfect. Consumers, thus, face liquidity constraints in that they cannot borrow to finance their consumption. Flavin (1985) finds that the response of consumption to current income is due to liquidity constraints rather than myopia. Direct estimates of the importance of liquidity constraints suggest that countries with high reliance of consumption on current income are those where consumers rely less on capital markets (Jappelli and Pagano, 1989; Zeldes, 1989a; see, also, Carroll, 2001).[1] Campbell and Mankiw (1991) find that consumption for a number of countries can be accounted for by changes in permanent as well as current income suggesting that some households follow the Permanent-Income hypothesis or Life-Cycle hypothesis, while others, the Keynesian consumption-function. Indeed, the proportion of households who base their consumption on current income, varies between 20% for Canada to almost 100% for France with Sweden (35%), the US (35%) and the UK (35%)[2] falling in between (the result for the US is consistent with the finding in Campbell and Mankiw, 1990). These findings are consistent with the notion that countries with less developed credit markets should have a higher proportion of households whose consumption depends on current income.[3]

A further argument focuses on another important ingredient of the Life-Cycle hypothesis. This relates to the motive for saving, which is to provide for retirement so that the consumers can smooth out their consumption plans for their entire life. Kotlikoff and Summers (1981), however, found that the amount of wealth in the economy is by far too large to finance consumption in retirement thereby rejecting this form of the hypothesis. They conclude that people are saving to leave bequests to their heirs. Hence, the theory should be revised to allow for bequests as an additional motive for saving. In their own words, 'Intergenerational transfers appear to be the major element determining wealth accumulation in the United States' (p. 730). Modigliani (1988), however, argues that there are definitional and methodological problems with studies like Kotlikoff and Summers (1981). Once these have been accounted for, 'the role of bequest motivated transfers... seem to play an important role only in the very highest income and wealth brackets. Some portion of bequests, especially in lower income brackets, is not due to a pure bequest motive but rather to a precautionary motive reflecting uncertainty about the length of life, although it is not possible at present to pinpoint the size of this component' (p. 39).

It follows from this analysis that, although there may very well be arguments that contradict the Life-Cycle hypothesis, the main tenet of the theory that wealth is an important determinant of consumption and that households smooth out their consumption expenditure through time, remains valid under conditions of uncertainty (Zeldes, 1989b). The consumption 'smoothing' approach has received a great deal of attention recently and a growing number of contributions, an area reviewed recently by Browning and Crossley (2001). Under these conditions the motives for saving are also to provide for rainy days. In other words, saving is also *precautionary* and does not just provide for retirement or even for bequests.[4] The larger share of saving of the old people is consistent with increased risk aversion as people age. Old people are more cautious than the young, they take less risk, and are wary of large medical bills and the possibility of low income during their retirement. Thus, under conditions of uncertainty saving acts as a *buffer stock* (Deaton, 1991; Carroll, 1994, 1997) to enable households to maintain their consumption pattern even when their current income drops below their permanent income, as for example would be the case if an individual becomes unemployed or the income of a self-employed person drops substantially in a recession.[5] Consequently, and as Carroll and Samwick (1997) put it, 'wealth is higher for households with greater income uncertainty' (p. 42), so that 'consumers spend most of their lifetimes trying to maintain a modest "target" wealth-to-income ratio' (p. 68) and save for retirement later in their lives.[6] Uncertainty and 'buffer-stock' saving behaviour contain the implication of a concave consumption function, with the interesting characteristic that there are differences between marginal propensities to consume out of different income brackets (higher income groups have a lower marginal propensity to consume than lower income groups), a characteristic noted some time ago by Keynes (1936).

These developments entail interesting implications, which can be highlighted as follows. We may begin by writing consumer behaviour as:

$$C = c(YP) \tag{1}$$

where C is consumption, c is marginal propensity to consume out of permanent income (YP). We may also write disposable income of the personal sector (YD) as:

$$YD = C + S \tag{2}$$

where S stands for savings. Substituting (2) into (1) we may arrive at (3):

$$(S/YD) = 1 - c(YP/YD) \tag{3}$$

In a boom current income exceeds permanent income and the ratio (YP/YD) falls which leads to a rise in the saving ratio (S/YD). In a recession current income falls short of permanent income the ratio (YP/YD) rises which leads to a fall in the saving ratio. However, if we re-write (1) as in (1a):

$$C = c_1(YP) + c_2(NW) \tag{1a}$$

where NW is net wealth, and substitute (1a) into (2), we can arrive at equation (4):

$$(S/YD) = 1 - c_1(YP/YD) - c_2(NW/YD) \qquad (4)$$

It is clear from equation (4) that the saving ratio depends not only on the ratio of permanent to current income in the business cycle, but also on the wealth–income ratio. Thus, although in a boom the permanent to current income ratio falls, the wealth–income ratio may rise sufficiently to cause a fall instead of a rise in the saving ratio. This can be easily explained. Consumers have a target level for their wealth so that they can finance their own future consumption as well as that of their children in the form of bequests. Hence, households determine the optimal rate of their annual saving on the basis of their expectations about future income, asset prices, interest rates and inflation. In addition consumers take into account their precautionary saving for the rainy days. If plans turn out as expected there is no need for adjusting their saving rate. However, if wealth is rising faster than expected their need to save is reduced, while if wealth is falling short of its target then consumers need to save more. Wealth can rise faster than expected if asset prices increase or income is growing faster or if inflation falls more than anticipated. Hence, the saving ratio varies in a way to achieve the target wealth in the face of unexpected developments in the main determinants of the future path of wealth. Hence, in order to analyse the behaviour of the saving ratio in the business cycle we must examine the determinants of the wealth–income ratio.

Wealth is created by the accumulation of past savings. But wealth is kept or invested in various assets (tangible and financial) and consumers can additionally borrow using as a collateral their assets in order to increase the value of their wealth through investment. Thus, wealth is properly defined as *net* wealth, which is the value of assets resulting from the accumulation of past savings and capital gains (losses) from their investment less the liabilities of consumers. The value of assets and liabilities can increase or decrease as their prices change through time thereby altering the net wealth of consumers. At any point in time, consumers would have a target wealth, which is computed on the required consumption for the remainder of their life expectancy taking into account that one of the spouses may outlive to become very old, the bequests consumers would like to leave to their heirs, and the amount of precautionary saving in case they are faced with large medical bills during retirement. Since the target level of wealth would finance future consumption for themselves or their children, consumers would attempt to estimate their permanent or lifetime resources and the desired level of consumption.

Furthermore, actual wealth would fluctuate around its target level as asset prices fluctuate in the course of the business cycle and consumers take advantage of low or high interest rates to borrow or repay their debts. Moreover, other variables, like consumer confidence influenced by the level and rate of change of unemployment, inflation, wage-settlements and interest rates, the length and depth of the recession or the extent of the boom may affect the level of precautionary saving and consumers' estimate of their permanent income. In good periods, like a boom in the property or the equity market, wealth may exceed its target prompting consumers to spend more thereby reducing their savings ratio, as they feel wealthier. This situation may be accentuated if economic activity is buoyant in which consumer confidence is rising, prompting consumers to borrow more as their estimate of their permanent income is also rising. In bad periods, after a bust in the property or equity market or because their debt increased wealth may fall short of its target prompting consumers to spend less thereby raising their saving ratio as they feel poorer. This situation may be aggravated if falling wealth is accompanied by a recession in which consumer confidence is eroded, precautionary saving is increased and the estimate of their permanent income is reduced thereby prompting consumers to repay their debt. Hence, the adjustment of the saving ratio in the course of the business cycle requires an evaluation of all components of net wealth as well as the factors, which affect permanent income. In this framework the interest rate becomes a very important variable because it affects directly (through valuation) or indirectly (through other macro-variables) all components of the personal sector net wealth. Thus, in periods of high interest rates the value of bonds falls, house prices and the value of shares decline, servicing the debt increases or the value of debt increases through the restructuring of loans. Accordingly, consumer net wealth declines as the value of assets falls, whereas the liabilities increase. Consumer wealth falls short of its target prompting consumers to spend less and rebuild their wealth by saving more as they feel poorer. In contrast, in periods of low interest rates the value of bonds rises, house prices and the value of equities increase, servicing the debt becomes easier or the value of debt is reduced through the restructuring of loans. Accordingly, consumer net wealth exceeds its target prompting consumers to lower their savings ratio.

We may now use these propositions and the analysis, as in, for example, Frowen and Karakitsos (1996), to clarify the point that in a leveraged economy the savings ratio moves counter-cyclically, so that it falls in a boom and rises in a recession. In boom years asset prices rise faster than usual as consumers borrow against these assets to invest even more (leveraging). To the extent that consumers save to achieve a desired volume of wealth, then faster than usual rising asset prices make people feel wealthier inducing them to relax on their effort to save as they believe that they can meet their targets for savings (e.g. provide for pension, leave to their heirs, etc.) more comfortably in this way. Hence, the savings ratio falls in a boom. In a recession asset prices fall and people are left with an overhang of debt. In order to repay their debt people cut on consumption out of current income and intensify on their effort to save in order to rebuild their wealth. Hence, the savings ratio increases in a recession. We may also think of the rate of interest as an important determinant of consumption. Changes in the rate of interest can affect consumption in two ways. A higher rate of interest, for example, means higher returns on savings, so that consumers increase their consumption due to this income effect. At the same time, however, a higher rate of interest and the higher returns on savings this implies, causes consumers to substitute consumption for savings; there is, thus, a substitution effect in addition to the income effect referred to earlier. *Mutatis mutandis* in the case of a lower rate of interest being the object of analysis. The overall impact of a change in the rate of interest, then, depends crucially on the relative strength of the two effects to which we have just referred.

In the short run, therefore, consumption depends on real disposable, the savings ratio and the rate of interest. Our analysis clearly suggests that consumption may be written formally as in equation (5):

$$C = C(DY, SR, R) \tag{5}$$

where C is as defined above, DY is real disposable income of the personal sector, SR is the savings ratio as defined above (i.e. S/YD), and R is the rate of interest.

The long-run forces that determine the savings ratio are net wealth and uncertainty about job security and income growth prospects. For the reasons discussed earlier, a rise in net wealth lowers the savings ratio and vice versa. An increase in uncertainty about job security and income growth prospects makes people more cautious inducing them to refrain from spending out of current income, thereby raising the savings ratio. This analysis, then, leads us to hypothesise that the savings ratio is determined as in equation (6):

$$SR = SR(NW/YD, UN, CNF) \tag{6}$$

where NW/YD is the ratio of net wealth (NW) to YD of the personal sector, UN is unemployment and CNF is consumer confidence.

The structure of the two relationships just portrayed captures the rationale of the short- and long-run factors affecting consumption in the way explained above. Appropriate substitution of equation (2) into equation (1) yields our estimable equation (3):

$$C = C(DY, NW/YD, UN, CNF, R) \tag{7}$$

An increase in real disposable income growth raises the rate of growth of real consumption by the same rate in the very long run (steady state). However, in the short run consumption rises less than income. An increase

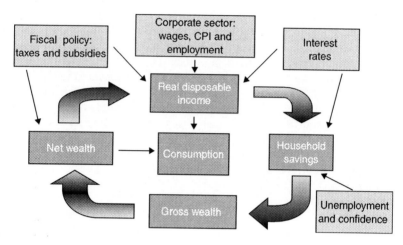

Figure 7.18   The income–consumption loop

in net wealth lowers the savings ratio, thereby increasing real consumption growth. The wealth effect is very important in this theoretical framework and has long lasting effects. An increase in unemployment or a decline in consumer confidence increases uncertainty regarding job security and income growth prospects, hence raises the savings ratio, which, in turn, lowers consumption growth. An increase in the rate of interest lowers real consumption growth, if the substitution effect is higher than the income effect. Equation (7) is precisely the equation that is estimated for the purposes of our analysis.

The rationale of the K-Model is summarised in Figure 7.18. The medium grey boxes illustrate the variables that belong to the income loop that affects consumption. The light grey boxes illustrate the variables that cause a shock to the income spiral. Shocks to the income spiral are introduced by monetary policy through changes in interest rates, fiscal policy through taxes and subsidies, and the corporate sector through wages, employment and CPI (Consumer Price Index). Assume that the economy is in long run equilibrium so that the income spiral is idle. Consider now a shock in policy or the state of the corporate sector that stimulates real disposable income. This would lead to higher savings that would increase gross wealth. The extra wealth would be invested in financial and/or tangible assets, which, in time, through capital gains would further boost gross wealth. But higher gross wealth would lead to more borrowing, which if it grows at a smaller pace than assets, will lead to an increase in net wealth. Realised capital gains from assets would boost real disposable income and a second round would be set in motion. In every round higher real disposable income and higher net wealth will stimulate consumption. In the new long-run equilibrium consumption, income, savings, gross and net wealth are higher than the initial equilibrium. The savings ratio would also be affected by unemployment and consumer confidence. The increase in consumption from any shock is not explosive. This means that the income–consumption loop is stable. The stability is ensured if the extra boost to consumption out of a given small increase in disposable income (what is called the marginal propensity to consume) and net wealth is less than unity.

5   An assessment of the long-term risks to consumption

In order to assess the long-term risks to consumption we have simulated simultaneously: (1) the consumption model, outlined above; (2) the wage–price model (see Chapter 2); and (3) the house price model (see Chapter 6). The wage–price model is essential, as it makes wages and salaries in private industries, which accounts for more than half of personal income, as well as CPI, which is used in the calculation of real disposable income, endogenous to the model. The housing model is also essential because it relates the housing market to the computation of net wealth, which is a crucial determinant of consumption. Since the consumption model is linked to the wage–price model, as well as to the housing market, the assumptions are the same as in Chapters 2 and 6. The K-Model is simulated under two alternative scenarios. These scenarios are the same as in previous chapters (e.g. Chapter 3 that discusses the implications for the wage–price sector and Chapter 6, the effect on the housing market). The reason for that is that we want to examine the implications of these two scenarios for the various sectors of the economy and financial markets.

Scenario I (weak recovery in 2004): What would happen to consumption if the current recovery were to falter in 2004 and became once again anaemic?

Scenario II (strong recovery in 2004): What would happen to consumption if the recovery that started after the Iraq war continued to be strong throughout 2004?

5.1   Scenario I (weak recovery in 2004)

The essence of this scenario lies on the assumption that the strength of the second and third quarters of 2003 was due to one-off factors related to the fiscal package of the current Administration and rising confidence because of lower geopolitical risks after the end of the Iraq war. The stance of fiscal policy turned 1.6% of GDP easier with the 'Jobs and Growth Tax Relief Reconciliation Act of 2003'. The act provided for an additional first year bonus depreciation write-off, increasing the immediate depreciation write-off from 30% (provided for in the 'Job Creation and Worker Assistance Act of 2002') to 50% for property acquired after 5 May 2003, and placed in service before 1 January 2005. The additional depreciation provided for by the 2003 act increased depreciation expenses in the second quarter by $83.7 billion and in the third quarter by $30.9 billion. In addition, the 2003 act provided for a reduction of $100.9 billion in July in personal tax and non-tax payments. The act reduced withheld federal taxes $45.8 billion as a result of new marginal tax rates, the expansion of the 10% income tax bracket, and acceleration in 'marriage-penalty' relief. Federal non-withheld taxes (payments of estimated taxes plus final settlements less refunds) were reduced by $55.5 billion because of advance payments of the child tax credit that began being mailed out 25 July 2003. The fiscal stimulus provided through the depreciation incentives and tax relief, ignoring the additional measures on dividend income, as they are controversial with respect to their effect on demand in the economy, is estimated to be 1.6% of nominal GDP.

In addition, monetary policy was eased once more at the end of June 2003 with the Fed funds rate cut to 1%. The accommodative stance of fiscal and monetary policy will keep the economy going, but the imbalances in all sectors will weigh down on the economy and the recovery will begin to falter during the course of 2004 from the torrid pace of 8% in the third quarter of 2003. Nonetheless, the economy will grow at the rate of potential output in 2004 and 2005 with industrial production growth averaging 3%. For the reasons explained in Chapter 2, the Fed should tighten monetary policy in the second quarter of 2004 and bond yields will rise with the 30-year mortgage rate rising to 6.5% at the end of 2004, but would fall back to 6% by the end of 2005 in view of the weakness of the housing market. Financial assets are assumed to grow modestly this year at 5%, after the frenetic pace of the last nine months, and to remain flat in 2005. Tangible assets other than property are assumed to grow at the same pace as in the recent past. Debt accumulation is assumed to slowdown over the next two years. Other personal income is assumed to grow at the same pace as in the last few years, while wages and salaries in the government sector are assumed to follow their recent downward trend. Net transfer payments (subsidies less personal contributions for social security) are hypothesised to grow at the same rate as last year because it is assumed that the two houses would resist pressure to lower subsidies to lower income groups in an election year. On the further assumption that the 2003 temporary tax cuts would become permanent, the ratio of personal taxes to personal income is assumed to remain unchanged. Table 7.3 summarises the assumptions underlying Scenario I, along with their current values between September and December 2003. With these assumptions the fiscal burden, defined as taxes less subsidies, would diminish gradually throughout the two-year period (see Table 7.3 and Figure 7.19).

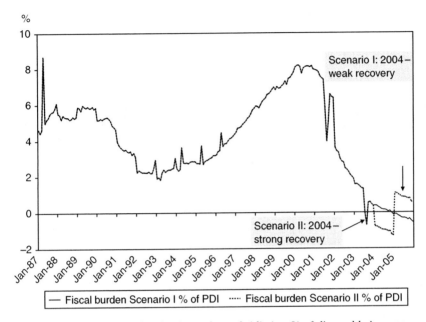

Figure 7.19 Personal fiscal burden (taxes less subsidies) as % of disposable income

With growth averaging potential output in the two-year period, the pace of job creation would be strong, around 170 thousand jobs per month. Wage inflation will continue to decline in 2004 partly because of abating CPI-inflation and partly because the real wage rate was higher than in equilibrium. This trend would be reversed in 2005, as inflation picks up and excess demand for labour begins to put upward pressure on wages (see Table 7.3 and Chapter 3, for more details). As a consequence of these developments in wages and employment, wages and salaries in private industries will grow faster, but mainly in 2005 (see Figure 7.20). However, real disposable income growth would decelerate from August 2004 onwards, as the effect of the previous tax cuts unwinds (see Table 7.3 and Figure 7.21). The net wealth of the personal sector would increase in the course of 2004, but would decline in 2005. The rate of growth of consumer confidence would peak in the spring of 2004 and would fall thereafter (see Figure 7.22). Unemployment would remain steady, as the extra job creation would bring back to the labour force many discouraged workers (see Figures 7.23a and b). With these assumptions about real disposable income growth, net wealth (see Figure 7.24), unemployment, confidence and interest rates, consumption growth would soon peak and would decelerate until the end of 2005 (see Table 7.3, and Figure 7.25). Nonetheless, consumption would still be growing at 3% by the end of 2004.

Table 7.3 Effects on consumption

	Current values Sep.–Dec. 03	Real consumption % y-o-y	Average hourly earnings, total private, SA, % y-o-y	Monthly job creation non-farm payrolls 6M MA	Unemployment as % of labour force	Unemployment plus marginally attached to the labour force	Fiscal burden as % of disposable income	Real disposable income, % y-o-y	Consumer confidence % y-o-y	Net wealth as % of disposable income
		Scenario I (weak recovery)				Scenario II (strong recovery)				
Assumptions										
Other personal income % y-o-y										
1st year	3.0	3.0				4.0				
2nd year		3.0				2.0				
Net transfer payments % y-o-y	7.3									
1st year		7.3				8.3				
2nd year		7.3				6.3				
Personal taxes as % of personal income	11.2									
1st year		11.2				10.2				
2nd year		11.2				12.2				
Wages and salaries in government % y-o-y	3.2									
1st year		2.5				3.0				
2nd year		2.5				2.0				
Financial assets % y-o-y	5.3									
1st year		5.0				10.0				
2nd year		0.0				–5.0				

Tangible assets other than property													
% y-o-y													
1st year	0.1		2.0							2.0			
2nd year			2.0										
Liabilities other than mortgages as % of disposable income	1st year		2.4										
30-year mortgage rate													
% y-o-y	5.9												
2nd year			1.0			1.0%							
1st year			6.5			7.5%							
2nd year			6.0			7.0%							

Current Level	3.6	2.4%	1	5.7	9.5	0.5%	3.3%	12.3%	506.3%
Deviation from long-run equilibrium (LRE)	−0.8	−0.5%	−5.2%	0.0	0.0%	0.0%	0.0%	−2.9%	25.3%
Scenario I (weak recovery)									
12-M SRE (future short-run Equilibrium)	2.9	0.0%	171	5.7	9.6	−0.1%	2.1%	1.4%	537.8%
24-M SRE (future short-run equilibrium)	1.0	1.9%	222	5.7	9.5	−0.5%	1.3%	0.2%	531.8%
12-M SRE and current level (difference)	−0.7	−2.4%	170	0.1	0.1	−0.6%	−1.1%	−11.0%	31.5%
24-M SRE and current level (difference)	−2.6	−0.5%	221	0.0	0.0	−1.0%	−2.0%	−12.1%	25.6%
Scenario II (strong recovery)									
12-M SRE (future short-run equilibrium)	4.8	1.0%	225	5.5	9.2	−1.3%	3.7%	1.4%	579.3%
24-M SRE (future short-run equilibrium)	−1.0%	0.7%	180	5.8	9.8	0.5%	−0.8%	0.2%	548.5%
12-M SRE and current level (difference)	1.2	−1.3%	224	−0.2	−0.3	−1.8%	0.5%	−11.0%	73.1%
24-M SRE and current level (difference)	−4.6	−1.6%	179	0.1	0.3	0.0%	−4.1%	−12.1%	42.3%

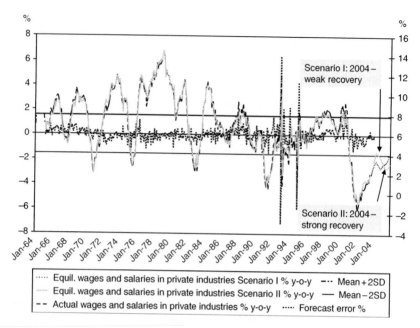

Figure 7.20 Wages and salaries in private industries

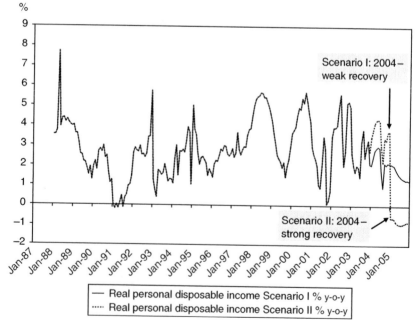

Figure 7.21 Real personal disposable income

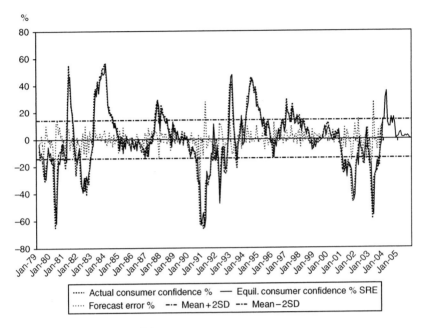

Figure 7.22 Consumer confidence

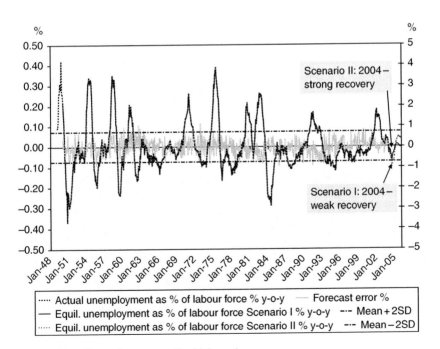

Figure 7.23a Unemployment as % of labour force

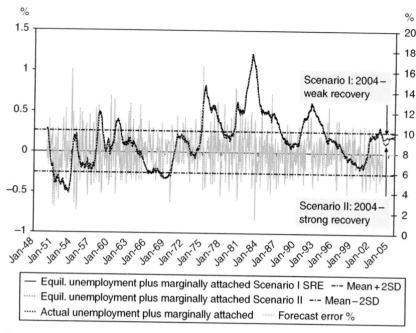

Figure 7.23b Unemployment plus marginally attached to the labour force

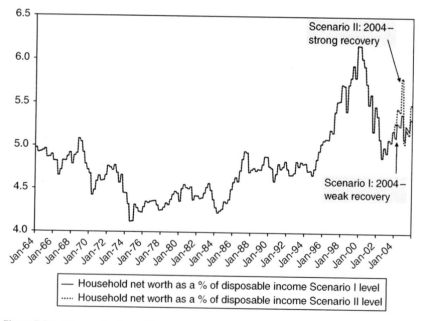

Figure 7.24 Personal net wealth

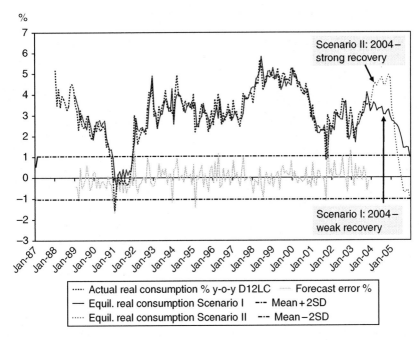

Scenario II: 2004 –
strong recovery

Scenario I: 2004 –
weak recovery

..... Actual real consumption % y-o-y D12LC	...... Forecast error %
— Equil. real consumption Scenario I	--- Mean + 2SD
..... Equil. real consumption Scenario II	--- Mean – 2SD

Figure 7.25 Real consumption

5.2 Scenario II (strong recovery in 2004)

The essence of Scenario II lies on the premise, which is largely true, that a combined fiscal and monetary stimulus will last for at least a year, and probably eighteen months, before it tapers off. Given that the US fiscal stimulus was introduced between May and July 2003, the US economy should remain strong until the end of 2004. The role of the accommodative stance of monetary policy is to prevent long-term interest rates from rising and therefore prolong the effects of the fiscal stimulus. However, despite forty-years low short-term interest rates introduced by the Fed in the last three years, long-term interest rates have risen sharply since June 2003 and the yield curve is extremely steep. If interest rates stay at this high level, or even rise further, which is very likely, the stimulus from fiscal policy will ultimately peter out. This means that growth will diminish in 2005 and beyond, other things being equal. Given that the average growth for the preceding four quarters before the fiscal stimulus was introduced was 2.6%, that the fiscal stimulus was 1.6% of GDP and that the first year multiplier is about unity, the central projection for average US growth until the second half, or the end, of 2004 should be 4.2%. Since the depreciation incentives on new structures will only count if premises are ready for service at the beginning of 2005, companies that would like to take advantage of the scheme should already have started spending. This explains the buoyant recovery of investment in the second quarter of 2003 that was responsible, to some extent, for the unexpectedly strong growth in that quarter. The other major factor that contributed to the unexpectedly strong second quarter was the explosion of defence spending because of the Iraq war.

The stunning 8.2% growth in the third quarter of 2003 was caused by the combination of strong consumption, due to the income tax cuts that were introduced in that quarter, the last-wagon effect for those companies that wanted to take advantage of the depreciation incentives on new structures. This accounted for $30 billion and was due to the worldwide improving confidence because of lower geopolitical risks after the end of the Iraq war that boosted US exports in the third quarter. This implies that the stunning third quarter growth was due to one-off factors that are likely to dissipate in the first half of 2004. Nonetheless, the economy should still grow at 4.2% – central projection until the second half of 2004. Industrial production will average 4.6% growth in 2004, but will fall to 1.4% in the course of 2005. The average rate of growth of industrial production over the two-year period will be 3%, the same as in Scenario I of weak recovery. However, in Scenario II growth would be stronger in 2004 and weaker in 2005 than in Scenario I, but with the same average growth for the two-year period (see Table 7.3 for the detailed assumptions of Scenario II).

Paradoxically, the higher growth rate of the economy implies that the Fed can afford to wait longer before it tightens monetary policy (see Chapter 3 for more details). With Scenario I the Fed should tighten in the second quarter of 2004, but with strong growth the Fed should tighten after the presidential election. The explanation of this paradox is that with strong growth inflation would remain muted both in 2004 and 2005, whereas with slow growth inflation will fall more in 2004, but will rise sharply in 2005. Although there is no trade-off between inflation and growth, there is one between the volatility of growth and the volatility of inflation. Scenario I implies low growth volatility and high inflation volatility, which given the lags of monetary policy on inflation entails early tightening. In contrast, Scenario II implies high growth volatility and low inflation volatility. Hence, the Fed can afford to wait before it tightens monetary policy.

Net transfer payments are assumed to grow at almost the same rate as in Scenario I. However, personal taxes are assumed to be cut further in 2004, but to rise in 2005 to curb the ballooning budget deficit. On these assumptions about fiscal policy the fiscal burden of the personal sector would diminish much more than Scenario I in 2004, but will rise in 2005, as some of these relief measures would be reversed in the first post-election year (see, Table 7.3 and Figure 7.19). Similarly, wages and salaries in the government sector will fall less in 2004, but more in 2005, than Scenario I, although the average for the two-year period is assumed to be the same. Other personal income is assumed to grow faster than Scenario I in 2004, in line with a more buoyant economy, but to slow in 2005, as growth decelerates, but with the two-year average assumed to be the same as in Scenario I (see Table 7.3). Financial assets and tangible assets other than property are assumed to grow even faster in 2004 than in Scenario I, but to fall in 2005, as house prices decline and the economy slows. Again the average for the two-year period is assumed to be the same as in Scenario I, but with volatility in Scenario II having been higher than in Scenario I (see Table 7.3).

With these assumptions wage earnings will increase more in 2004, but less in 2005 than Scenario I, in line with inflation and excess demand for labour. Similarly, employment growth will be higher in 2004 and lower in 2005 than Scenario I, in line with growth. Therefore, wages and salaries would follow a similar pattern. Although inflation will be higher in 2004 and lower in 2005, its effect would be more than offset by the growth in nominal income. Given that the fiscal burden would be lighter in 2004, but heavier in 2005, real disposable income growth would be higher in 2004, but much lower in 2005 than Scenario I. Unemployment would fall more in 2004 than Scenario I, because of faster growth. But it will rise again in 2005. House prices would carry on rising in 2004, but would fall sharper than Scenario I in 2005. The combination of falling house and financial asset prices would reduce gross wealth in 2005, but it would also induce households to repay their debts and therefore the net wealth would be higher than Scenario I. As a result of these developments in real disposable income, unemployment, confidence and interest rates consumption would be stronger in 2004 than Scenario I, but would fall precipitously in 2005 dragging the economy into recession towards the end of 2005. This simulation illustrates the long-term risk to consumption from strong growth in 2004. If this growth is the result of another fiscal stimulus, then long-term interest rates would rise and the Fed would finally tighten, albeit somewhat later than the markets assume. Higher interest rates in 2004 may lead to lower house prices, falling financial asset prices and lower investment (see Chapter 5 for more details). Gross wealth would fall as a result and the worsening outlook for the corporate sector and reduce real disposable income growth. Since the economy would be strong at the end of 2004, policymakers would have an incentive to tighten fiscal policy in the first post-election year to curb the budget deficit. If this were to happen, then the combination of a slowing economy with tight fiscal policy would turn the slowdown into recession. In this downturn consumption would not be as resilient as it was in the 2001 recession, but it would either lead the economy into recession or it would fall along with investment. The conclusion of this simulation is that slow growth in 2004 is better than fast growth. Growth at around potential output would keep a cap on long-term interest rates and would not jeopardise investment growth and the housing market in 2005. A dramatic slowdown, which might even develop into recession in 2005, would be avoided with slow growth in 2004. High growth volatility in the next two years would cause high volatility in real disposable income growth, gross and net wealth and therefore consumption. The long-term risk to consumption stems from pro-cyclical fiscal policy (i.e. continuous easing in the upswing of the cycle).

6   Summary and conclusions

The recent recession was very mild thanks to the resilience of the consumer. This is partly due to the buoyancy of real disposable income, which was boosted through easy fiscal policy. Had it not been for the fiscal injection, real disposable income would have fallen thereby pulling the rug under the consumers' feet. Wages and salaries fell not only in real, but also in nominal terms. In most private industries they have fallen in real terms even during the recovery. But personal income has fared better than wages and salaries partly because wages and salaries in the government sector have been growing at a brisk pace and partly because other earned and unearned income has not suffered as much as wages and salaries. During the double-dip recession of the industrial sector, caused by a second round of retrenchment, companies cut the average working week, laid off workers, managed to reduce the hourly earnings of their workers and slashed investment. The slower growth in real disposable income during the double-dip recession caused a deceleration in consumption growth. However, the picture has changed markedly in the second half of 2003. The second round of retrenchment by the corporate sector was successful in restoring profitability and improving balance sheets. Hence, wages have begun to rise, job creation has been resumed, albeit sluggishly so far, and average weekly hours have increased. The latest round of tax cuts has also bolstered real disposable income in the second half of 2003. The tax cuts have now a better chance of boosting consumption, as all the short-run factors that affect it have now improved.

Despite the rally of equities in the last nine months, financial assets are still 10% lower than they were at the peak of the bubble. These losses amount to $3.6 trillion. The phenomenal boom in the property market has produced capital gains that more than offset the losses in financial assets, so that gross wealth is now 2%, or $1 trillion, higher than the peak of the equity market in March 2000. Although this is encouraging, net wealth, which matters for consumption decisions, is still 3.5%, or $1.5 trillion, lower because the property boom has been financed by debt accumulation that now stands at 110% of disposable income, an all time high. Although this imbalance has narrowed from $5 trillion at the bottom of equity prices, it is still worrisome, as it might be corrected by retrenchment. On the positive side consumers did not respond by retrenchment when the imbalance was much bigger, so that now that the economy is recovering it is even less likely to do so. However, there is a risk to consumption if growth in 2004 turned out to be very strong, boosted once more by fiscal policy. In this case investment would soften in 2005 because of higher long-term interest rates and profitability would decline, if job creation were strong in 2004. The worsening outlook for the corporate sector in 2005 may induce caution on the part of consumers and raise the savings ratio. Higher long-term interest rates may also cause lower house prices, which would lead to falling financial asset prices. In this case the personal sector imbalance would widen once more and retrenchment may be the inevitable price. The situation would be aggravated by difficulties in debt servicing, which even at these low interest rates, stands at an all time high.

In order to assess the likelihood of this risk we have simulated the K-Model under the alternative scenarios of fast and slow growth in 2004 and gauged the consequences for the two-year period of 2004–05. This simulation illustrates the long-term risk to consumption from strong growth in 2004. If this growth is the result of another fiscal stimulus, then long-term interest rates would rise and the Fed would finally tighten, albeit somewhat later than the markets assume. Higher interest rates in 2004 may lead to lower house prices, falling financial asset prices and lower investment. Gross wealth would fall as result and the worsening outlook for the corporate sector and reduce real disposable income growth. Since the economy would be strong at the end of 2004, policymakers would have an incentive to tighten fiscal policy in the first post-election year to curb the budget deficit. If this were to happen, then the combination of a slowing economy with tight fiscal policy would turn the slowdown into recession. In this downturn consumption would not be as resilient as it was in the 2001 recession, but it would either lead the economy into recession or it would fall along with investment. The conclusion of this simulation is that slow growth in 2004 is better than fast growth. Growth at around potential output would keep a cap on long-term interest rates and would not jeopardise investment growth and the housing market in 2005. A dramatic slowdown, which might even develop into recession in 2005, would be avoided with slow growth in 2004. High growth volatility in the next two years would cause high volatility in real disposable income growth, gross and net wealth and therefore consumption. Hence, the long-term risk to consumption stems from pro-cyclical fiscal policy (i.e. continuous easing in the upswing of the cycle).

8
Foreign Demand

1 Introduction

The buoyancy of the US economy since the end of the Iraq war and the spectacular recovery of exports in the US, the euro area[1] and Japan, and we refer to them as (G-3) in what follows, in the third quarter of 2003 have raised hopes of a US-led world recovery. The OECD index of leading indicators has continued to rise and this heralds further strengthening of (G-3) exports in the months ahead. However, the conclusion of a world recovery over a longer horizon depends on the strength of the US economy and the extent of previous changes in competitiveness. In this respect, the US and Japan have gained competitiveness in the last two years, while the euro area has suffered a great loss. However, if the US economy were to grow as fast as potential output in the next two years, then the world economy would recover.[2] Such growth would be sufficient to offset previous losses in competitiveness and allow the euro area to enjoy an export-led recovery. Steady growth in the US at potential output is preferable to fast growth in 2004 and weak growth in 2005, but with the same average, because the world recovery would falter. The implication is that domestic demand in the euro area and Japan should be boosted by accommodative economic policy. Although the same effect can be achieved by easy fiscal policy in the US, this may not be desirable at this phase of the US business cycle.

The improved outlook for the US economy after the end of the Iraq war has raised hopes of a strong US-led world recovery. The argument is that buoyant US growth would first stimulate the exports of US's main trading partners. This would spur production in the rest of the world and after a while there would be job creation in the export-industry. Later on, companies would have to expand capacity and therefore investment would be boosted. Through higher investment the recovery in the rest of the world would become widespread with gains in employment and incomes, which finally would boost consumption. During this process, which may take around two years, the US would lead the rest of the world to recovery. The argument is very powerful because the overall stimulus to world trade is greater than the initial stimulus – the multiplier or magnifying effect is greater than unity. However, there are some concerns with this scenario regarding, first, the strength of the US economy and, second, the dollar weakness, which in some cases (for example against the euro) was of the order of almost 50% in the period from 2001 to 2003. This is sufficiently long time to allow for the effects of competitiveness on exports to work themselves out. In particular, the concern is whether the US recovery would be sufficiently strong in boosting world demand to offset the effects of the previous losses in competitiveness on the exports of the US main trading partners. In the six months following the end of the Iraq war the US economy went from strength to strength hitting more than 8% growth, the highest since 1984. However, this excessive growth was, to some extent, due to one-off factors. The economy is poised to decelerate to a more sustainable level in the course of 2004, but there are doubts as to what would be that level. The return to an anaemic US recovery might fail to spur the rest of the world exports and the world recovery might fade away in the course of 2004.

The validity of these concerns depends, first, on the extent to which the dollar weakness has translated into losses in competitiveness in the US main trading partners; second, on the degree of importance of these losses in competitiveness on the rest of the world exports; and third on the feedback to US exports. We begin in Section 2 by reviewing the performance of exports in the (G-3) economies. Section 3 highlights the properties of exports in (G-3), as these are encapsulated in the K-Model. In Section 4 we make use of the K-Model to simulate the effects on (G-3) exports of two alternative scenarios regarding the US economy – weak and strong growth, while in Section 5 we summarise the arguments and offer some conclusions.

2 The recent track record and the determinants of (G-3) exports

We begin with the US economy.

2.1 The US case

US real exports peaked in the second quarter of 2000, three quarters before the onset of the recession, and turned into negative growth in the fourth quarter of 2000. With the exception of the first three quarters of 2002, exports contracted for nearly three years, until the second quarter of 2003. However, in the third quarter of 2003 they staged a spectacular recovery climbing to 10.5% relative to the previous quarter (q-o-q) from −1% in the second. The tremendous rise of exports in the third quarter has allayed fears that the US recovery would depend exclusively on domestic demand and has raised hopes of a strong US-led world recovery with further multiplying effects on US exports.

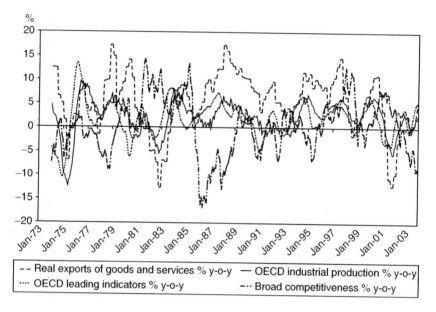

Figure 8.1   US exports determinants

Figure 8.1 shows the main determinants of the demand for US real exports of goods and services. Real exports depend positively on world demand, approximated by OECD industrial production, and negatively on competitiveness – an index that compares domestic with foreign producer prices expressed in domestic currency. The OECD industrial production is, most of the time, a coincident indicator of real exports. The OECD index of leading indicators precedes changes in the OECD industrial production, on average, by six months. Hence, a rise in the leading indicators suggests increases in world demand with a few months lag, which are translated into a boost in exports.

The OECD index of leading indicators bottomed in April 2003 at −1.2% (y-o-y) and has increased to 5.1% last November (see Figure 8.1). The OECD industrial production bottomed in May 2003 at −0.1% (y-o-y) and rose to 1.8% in October. Although US real exports staged a stupendous recovery in the third quarter of 2003, they only increased by 0.5% relative to the year earlier (y-o-y) from −0.9% in the second quarter. The dollar peaked against a broad basket of currencies in February 2002 and depreciated 11.5% by December 2003. This fall in the dollar was translated into 12% gain in competitiveness in the same time period (see Figure 8.2). The rise in the OECD index of leading indicators augers well with further increases in the OECD industrial production in the course of 2004 and this raises hopes that US

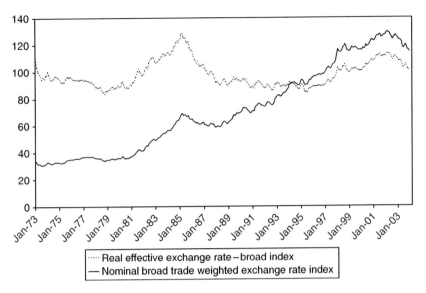

Figure 8.2 US nominal and real effective exchange rate

exports would continue to pick up steam on a year-to-year basis. The gains in competitiveness should also boost exports in 2004. Hence, there is great support for the view that exports would contribute to the strength of the US recovery.

2.2 The euro-area case

The euro-area exports peaked one quarter earlier than the US exports, that is, in March 2000, but remained more resilient, as they began to contract two quarters later than the US, that is, in the second quarter of 2001. Euro-area exports had a similar pattern to their US equivalents in the recent downturn. With the exception of the first three quarters of 2002, in line with the US they contracted for more than two years. Euro-area exports bottomed in the second quarter of 2003, in line with the US exports, and rose by 8.9% (q-o-q) in the third quarter of 2003, slightly less than US exports. This may imply a US-led recovery for the euro area, too, a question we try to tackle in what follows. We may note, though, at this stage that many euro-area companies have operations based in the US, and profit directly from the US domestic economy.

The behaviour of the euro-area equity markets certainly supports this view. They have rallied relentlessly since the end of the Iraq war on the belief that evidence of a strong US recovery would pull the euro area out of its misery. Indeed, the spectacular recovery of exports in the third quarter of 2003 bolstered such hopes.

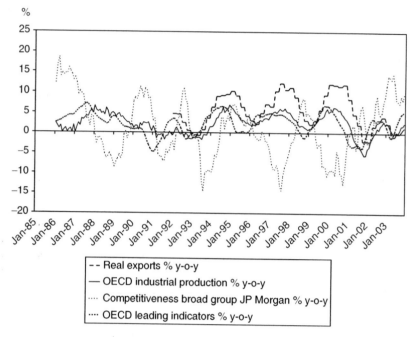

Figure 8.3   EU exports determinants

Figure 8.3 shows the determinants of euro-area exports. Not surprisingly, euro-area exports have the same determinants as the US – world demand and competitiveness. The OECD industrial production is also a coincident indicator of euro-area exports, as in the case of the US. The rise in the last six months of OECD leading indicators suggests further increases in OECD industrial production which, other things being equal, should boost euro-area exports in the course of 2004. However, whereas the US has gained competitiveness in the last few years, the euro area has lost competitiveness because of the strong appreciation of the euro. The euro bottomed in October 2000 against the dollar at $0.85 and rose to $1.26 in December 2003, which translates into 48% appreciation (see Figure 8.4). During that time the euro area lost 27% in competitiveness, whereas the US gained 12% (see Figure 8.4). This huge loss in the euro-area competitiveness raises doubts as to whether the US recovery would pull the euro area out of its problems in the course of 2004, as the markets have priced it in.

This risk is exacerbated by the weakness of domestic demand in the euro area. Whereas exports recovered strongly in the third quarter of 2003, domestic demand in the euro area contracted 2.5% (q-o-q) in the third quarter. The underlying reason for the weak domestic demand in euro area is due to the relatively tight stance of economic policy. Fiscal policy has turned

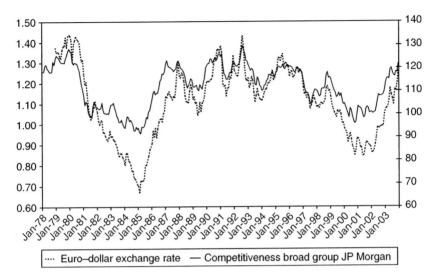

Figure 8.4 EU exchange rate and competitiveness

easy since 2001, but the stimuli have been small compared to the US. The stimulus was only 0.8% of GDP in 2001, 0.9% in 2002 and is projected at 1.4% in 2003 (see Figure 8.5a). However, fiscal policy would turn easy in 2004 once the planned tax cuts in various countries, including France and Germany, are implemented. Although the ECB has cut rates and domestic monetary conditions are accommodative, the appreciation of the euro has more than offset the cuts in interest rates (see Figure 8.5b). Hence, overall monetary conditions have become tighter since April 2002, in spite of the cuts in rates by the ECB, because of the strong euro. In the last three months monetary policy has been tightened even further because of the appreciation of the euro that has resulted in 27% loss in competitiveness since October 2000. The stance of monetary policy was tightened during the period September to November 2003, from zero in September 2003 to 0.6% by the end of November. Hence there are doubts as to whether sufficient domestic demand is in place that can lead the economy to recovery in the fourth quarter of 2003. But there are good reasons to expect that domestic demand would strengthen in the course of 2004. Hence, the case for an early recovery in euro area relies, to a large extent, on an export-led recovery. In the meantime, confidence is rising and the most important factor that would determine growth with a six-month view is demand for exports. There is little doubt that sustained strong growth in the US would ultimately lead the euro area to recovery. Rising exports would spur production, then investment and, finally, consumption. The real issue is the speed that this might materialise and whether there is a chance of disappointment in

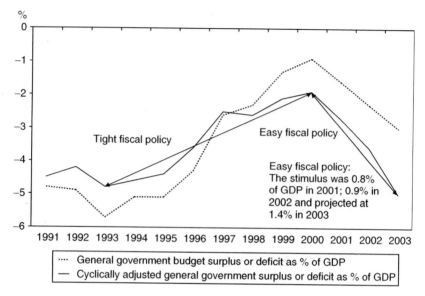

Figure 8.5a The stance of EU fiscal policy

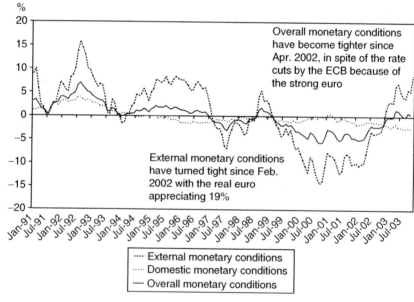

Figure 8.5b The stance of EU monetary policy

the short run. The markets have taken the view that the recovery is already on its way taking heart from the revival in exports in the third quarter and shrugging off the poor performance of domestic demand, as it is a lagging indicator of future economic growth.

2.3 The Japanese case

Japan's exports peaked one quarter earlier than the US, that is, in the first quarter of 2000, but contracted for only four quarters – from the second quarter of 2001 till the first of 2002. They recovered strongly from the second quarter of 2002, supported by buoyant growth in Asia, mainly China. However, Japan's exports may háve already peaked at 27.4% (q-o-q) in the second quarter of 2002. They were boosted in the third quarter of 2003, in line with the recovery of US and euro-area exports, but they might resume the deceleration in the course of 2004 (y-o-y), although they might continue to improve (q-o-q). Figure 8.6 shows that Japan's exports determinants are the same as in the other two economies. The OECD industrial production is a coincident indicator of Japan's exports, but slightly less reliable than in the US or the euro area. The occasions when the OECD index of leading indicators, which precedes changes in OECD industrial production by approximately six months, fails to predict turning points of Japan's exports, are all related to substantial movements over protracted periods of the yen

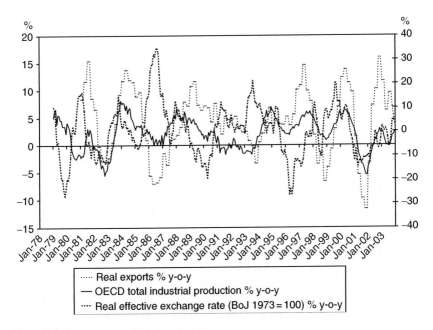

····· Real exports % y-o-y
— OECD total industrial production % y-o-y
···· Real effective exchange rate (BoJ 1973 = 100) % y-o-y

Figure 8.6 Japan – exports determinants

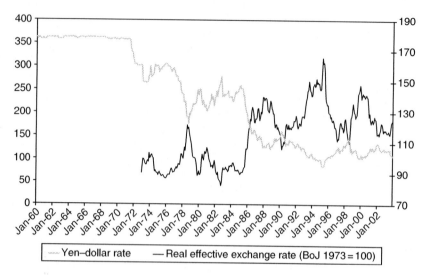

Figure 8.7   Japan – nominal and real exchange rate

real exchange rate – a measure of Japan's competitiveness. Thus, although the OECD index of leading indicators bottomed in March 1991, after the Gulf War and the beginning of the US recovery, exports continued to slow and bottomed in December 1993, as the exchange rate was appreciating resulting in losses of competitiveness. In the three-year period 2001 to 2003, during which the euro appreciated 48% against the dollar, the yen was effectively unchanged. The yen stood at ¥109.1 against the dollar in October 2000; it depreciated to ¥132.4 in March 2002 (i.e. a month after the dollar peaked) and then it appreciated again to ¥107.1 in December 2003 (see Figure 8.7). These fluctuations in the yen have been translated into 11.3% gains in competitiveness as opposed to 27% losses in euro-area competitiveness (see Figure 8.7).

We may summarise this section by observing that all cases considered in this section imply that we are able to represent real exports (RX_i) where the subscript i refers to UK, the euro area, and Japan as appropriate, as follows:

$$RX_i = X(WD, COMP) \tag{a}$$

where WD stands for world demand and COMP for competitiveness.

In what follows (1) is utilised within the K-Model framework. There is, however, an important characteristic that ought to be highlighted. The K-Model reveals that real exports have the following properties. First, there is a very strong relationship between OECD industrial production and (G-3) real exports. The impact of world industrial production on real exports is greater than unity in the long run, implying a multiplier effect – one country's trade gives a boost to another country's trade that has further impact on the first country. The multiplier measures the percentage change in real exports for a given percentage change in world industrial production. Consequently, (a) as above should be better represented by equation (1):

$$RX_i = X(IPOECD, COMP) \tag{1}$$

where IPOECD is industrial production of the OECD countries.

3 The properties of the (G-3) exports

We begin this section with Figure 8.8 which shows the multiplier of (G-3) real exports with respect to the OECD industrial production through time. The six-month multiplier is 1.7 for the US implying that one per cent increase in world industrial production leads to 1.7% increase in US real exports in the first six months. For the euro area, the six-month multiplier is 1.4, whereas for Japan it is only 1. The multiplier for Japan remains near unity for a four-year period, whereas common sense dictates that it should be greater than unity. This raises the question of why Japan does not appear to benefit from the boost in world industrial production as other countries. This paradox is resolved by distinguishing between exports from mainland

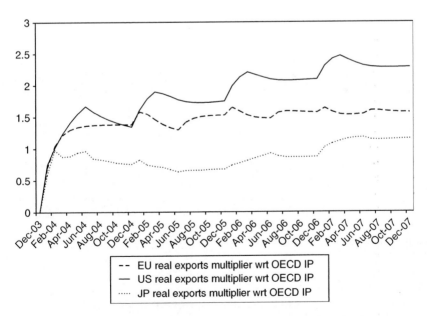

Figure 8.8 Exports multiplier with reference to OECD industrial production

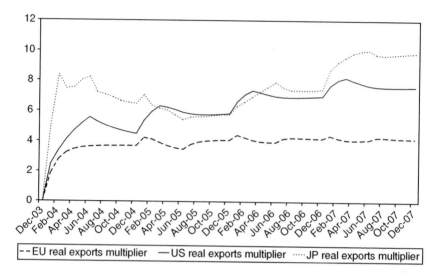

Figure 8.9   Exports multiplier with reference to OECD industrial production adjusted for share of exports to GDP

Japan – the only exports according to national accounts statistics – and exports from worldwide corporate Japan. Japan takes advantage of a pickup in world industrial production, but only part of the stimulus comes back to mainland Japan with the rest stimulating Japanese companies located overseas.

Japan's (mainland) exports account for only 11.7% of GDP, on par with the US exports, which are 11% of GDP. But this figure grossly understates the full exporting capacity of Japan. For example, euro-area exports as a per cent of GDP account for 37.4%. Japan's worldwide industrial base may be even bigger than the euro area, but it is difficult to measure it. Japan's Foreign Direct Investment (FDI) has been negative, meaning that they invest abroad more than others invest in Japan. Cumulative FDI since 1980 has reached 111% of GDP. But it is difficult from such measures to get the full picture of Japan's worldwide industrial base and the impact of an increase in world industrial production. An indirect way of resolving the issue is to normalise the effect of world industrial production by measuring its impact on exports per unit of GDP. Figure 8.9 shows the multiplier adjusted for the relative size of exports to GDP for the US, euro area and Japan. Although the pattern of adjusted multipliers is the same as the unadjusted ones the former not only is greater than unity for all three countries, but the multiplier of Japan is always bigger than the US and euro area in the first two years (see Figure 8.9). This means that Japan is the main beneficiary amongst (G-3) of a pickup in world demand. The huge worldwide industrial base of Japan explains the paradox of Japan's exports multiplier being near unity. This has implications for corporate profits. Japan's corporate profits would increase much more than those of the euro area or the US from a boost in world industrial production and therefore its stock market would outperform the other two markets, in the short run. However, the impact of world industrial production on jobs and incomes in Japan would be limited by the fact that the unadjusted multiplier is near unity. The OECD industrial production does not reflect the boost in industrial production in Asia, with the exception of Korea that has joined OECD. The share of Japan's exports to Asia accounts for 42% and therefore the effect on exports from a boost in world industrial production may be grossly understated. Despite this drawback, the engine for growth is the US. If the US were to lose some of its momentum, both the OECD industrial production and Asia industrial production would be affected.

The second property of exports is that they bear a strong relationship with competitiveness. Figure 8.10 shows the (G-3) real exports multiplier with respect to competitiveness. For convenience, the US competitiveness is assumed to improve, while for the euro area and Japan competitiveness is harmed. In the first six months the multiplier is zero for the US and the euro area, but −0.1 for Japan. This means that a change in competitiveness has no effect on US and euro-area exports for the first six months, while 10% loss in competitiveness in Japan leads to just 1% fall in exports. After the first six months the effect of competitiveness on US and euro-area exports builds up. In the long run the US multiplier reaches 0.64 in just over

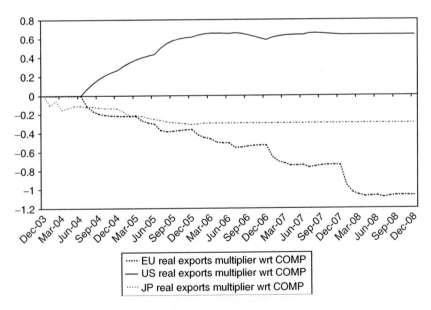

Figure 8.10 Exports multiplier with reference to competitiveness

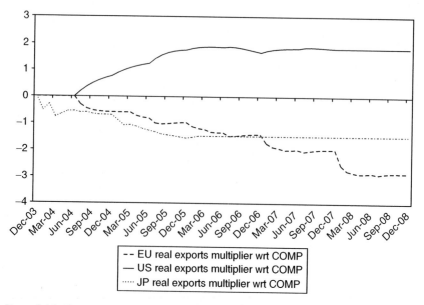

Figure 8.11 Exports multipliers with reference to competitiveness adjusted for share of exports to GDP

two years, while in the euro area the multiplier keeps rising for five years reaching 1.24. This means that the overall effect of a permanent change in competitiveness on euro-area exports is almost double that of the US and its effects last for more than double the time compared to the US. This, in turn, implies that the US is able to absorb the effects of a permanent loss in competitiveness much faster than the euro area – in just over two years, whereas it gradually builds up in euro area for five years. Thus, a permanent 10% gain (or loss) in competitiveness leads to 6.4% higher (or lower) US exports in two years, while it leads to 12.4% higher (or lower) euro-area exports in five years. Two years after the shock in competitiveness, euro-area exports are only 3.6% higher (or lower).

As in the case of the multiplier with respect to world industrial production, these figures grossly understate the full effects of competitiveness on Japan's exports, since they only measure the effect on mainland Japan and ignore the effect on the industrial base of Japan overseas. Figure 8.11 shows the multiplier adjusted for the relative size of exports to GDP for the US, Japan and the euro area. Although the pattern of adjusted multipliers is the same as the unadjusted ones, the overall effect on Japan's worldwide industrial base is much bigger and the differential with the US and the euro area is much smaller. Whereas the unadjusted long-run effect of a permanent loss in competitiveness is one-fourth of euro area and half of the US the adjusted one is only half of the former and 20% smaller than the US. This is a huge

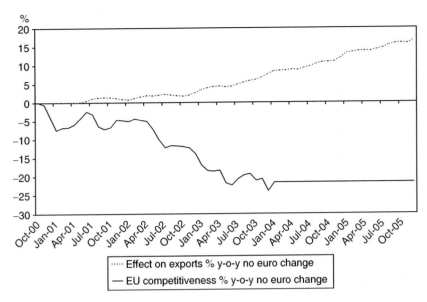

Figure 8.12 Effect on EU exports – no euro change (unchanged at Oct. 2000 value)

difference and shows that the euro area is not 75% worse than Japan in adjusting to competitiveness, but only 50%. Japan is also 20% better than the US in adjusting to competitiveness. The vulnerability of the euro area to changes in competitiveness is due to its inflexible labour markets that create rigidities in price adjustments. A country's ability to absorb changes in the nominal exchange rate depends on how much and how quickly companies can induce productivity gains, by a combination of job cuts, cost cutting and increased capital spending. Such adjustments aim at reducing unit labour cost and therefore export prices so that the effect of changes in the nominal exchange rate on competitiveness is minimal. From this point of view, Japan is the best followed by the US, while the euro area is the laggard.

Figure 8.12 illustrates in a more explicit way the properties of euro-area real exports according to the K-Model. The index of euro-area competitiveness bottomed in October 2000 at 95.8 and started to rise reaching 121.8 in December 2003. This implies a loss in competitiveness of 25.9 index points or 27% in the last three years. In order to assess the dynamic impact of this loss in competitiveness on real exports it is assumed that the euro did not appreciate in the last three years, but instead the index of competitiveness remained unchanged at its October 2000 value of 95.8 not only until now but for ever after (i.e. long enough so that a new steady state can be reached). Hence, the experiment assumes that in the last three years there was no gradual loss in competitiveness of the order of 27%. Figure 8.12 shows that after a year (i.e. in October 2001) if competitiveness had not been lost of the order of 7%, real exports would have been higher than they actually were by only 1.4%, a trivial amount. By the end of the second year (in October 2002) if competitiveness had not been lost of the order of 13%, real exports would have been higher than they were by 1.7%, still an insignificant amount. By the end of the third year (in October 2003) if competitiveness had not been lost of the order of 23%, real exports would have been higher than they were by 6%. If the exchange rate were to stabilise so that the total losses would be limited to 24%, then the effect on exports would reach 11% in the fourth year (in October 2004) and 16% in the fifth year (in October 2005). This implies that euro-area exports would be hit by 5% and 10% after one and two years, respectively, compared to what they would have been if competitiveness had not been lost.

The simulation illustrates a very important point, namely that after three years of a gradual loss in competitiveness just over one-third of the five-year impact on real exports has been felt and that the remainder has yet to be felt. Hence, although world industrial production is rising, it is likely that the effects of a major part (almost two-thirds) of the loss in competitiveness have yet to be felt over the next two years. Hence, world industrial production would need to rise much more if the euro area is to have an export-led recovery.

4   The likely course of (G-3) exports

The role of the US as a leader of the world economy suggests that world demand would depend on US demand. In particular, fluctuations in US industrial production should explain fluctuations in OECD industrial production. Figure 8.13 provides support for this hypothesis by making the OECD industrial production a function of US industrial production. So another relationship is in order:

$$IPOECD = IP_1(IPUS) \qquad (2)$$

where IPUS is US industrial production. The forecast error of the K-Model for OECD industrial production is only 0.5% in nearly thirty years of monthly data that span six business cycles, which were both demand- and supply-led.

The total Purchasing Management Index (PMI) of the Institute for Supply Management (ISM) is geared to gauge developments in the US economy over the next six months.[3] In particular, the PMI can explain fluctuations in US industrial production. Figure 8.14 provides support for this hypothesis by making US industrial production a function of PMI. The forecast error of the K-Model of US industrial production is only 1.15% in the last ten business cycles that cover more than half a century.

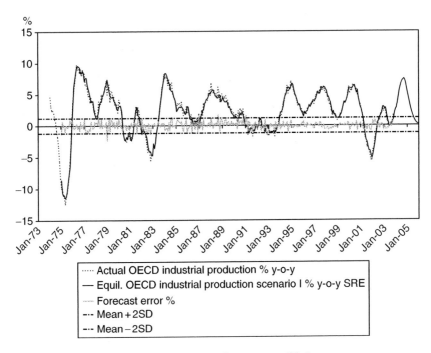

Figure 8.13 OECD industrial production – short-run equilibrium

In view of the arguments just presented, US industrial production can be represented as:

$$IPUS = IP_2(PMI) \qquad (3)$$

where PMI is as defined above.

The PMI is based on a survey of business intentions. These expectations are affected by economic developments, but in the absence of news on economic fundamentals such expectations would follow their own momentum with optimism building first up, then fading away and followed by a similar cycle of pessimism. In the long run such expectations would peter out and the PMI would reach long run equilibrium. Figure 8.15 provides support for the hypothesis that the momentum of business expectations can explain the PMI. So that:

$$PMI = M(BEXP) \qquad (4)$$

where BEXP stands for business expectations.

222

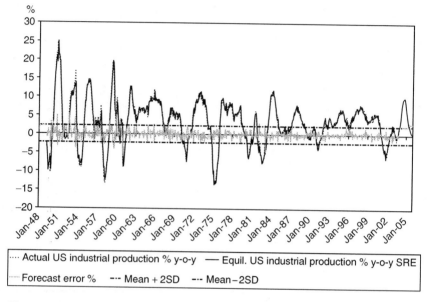

Figure 8.14 US industrial production – short-run equilibrium

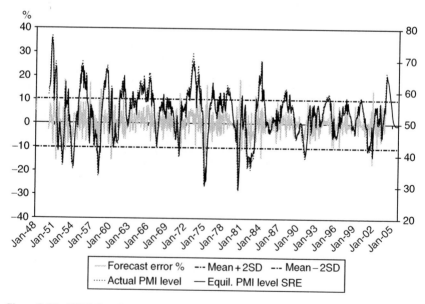

Figure 8.15 US PMI – short-run equilibrium

The forecast error of the K-Model for PMI is 5%. Although this sounds big when compared to the forecast error of US industrial production, which is only 1.2%, it is quite small when account is taken of volatility. Whereas the standard deviation of US industrial production since 1948 is only 5.8%, the standard deviation of the PMI, during the same time period, is 23.3%, therefore four times larger. Since the forecast error of the PMI is four times as large as the forecast error of US industrial production, the K-Model for the PMI is as good as the industrial production model.

These three equations (PMI, US industrial production and OECD industrial production) can be combined with the exports model to generate projections for (G-3) exports on two assumptions. First, unchanged competitiveness; and second, there are no further news on economic fundamentals and the PMI follows its own momentum. Figure 8.15 shows that in the absence of any further news on economic fundamentals the PMI would peak at the beginning of 2004 and would return to its equilibrium boom–bust dividing line of 50 by the end of 2005. Despite the early abating expectations, US industrial production would continue to gather steam in the course of 2004 and would peak in October at almost 10%, but it would decelerate from then on until the end of 2005 reaching zero growth (see Figure 8.14). The world economy would follow the US and the OECD industrial production would accelerate in the course of 2004 hitting a peak at just over 7% by next October. However, the OECD industrial production would decelerate since then reaching zero growth by the end of 2005. Given this pattern of world demand and with unchanged competitiveness US exports would soar to 17% by the time of the US presidential election (see Figure 8.16). If this were to materialise it would be a spectacular recovery that was only repeated twice in the last thirty years – in the fourth quarter of 1978 and the first quarter of 1988 (see Figure 8.16). However, US exports would decline after the presidential election, but by the end of 2005 they would still be growing at 4.5% (see Figure 8.16).

The strong US recovery would lift euro-area exports, which would peak in October 2004 at 10%. But they would decelerate from then onwards very rapidly. Unlike the US, euro-area exports would contract in the second half of 2005 hitting −2.5% by the end of that year, as the previous losses in competitiveness take their toll (see Figure 8.17). In spite of the strong US recovery, mainland Japan, as opposed to worldwide corporate Japan, would not be able to benefit from the world recovery, as the momentum of exports is down on a year-to-year basis (see Figure 8.18). Quarter-on-quarter growth, however, may still be positive. Although the assumptions of this simulation are unrealistic, because there would be plenty of news on economic fundamentals and competitiveness would change in the course of the next two years, the conclusions are not just interesting, but very important. First, even if economic fundamentals were not to improve any further the world economy would have sufficient momentum for exports to become stronger

224

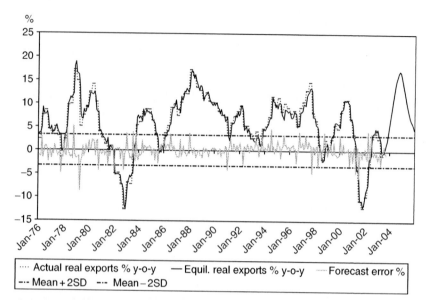

Figure 8.16 US real exports (based on the momentum of US PMI)

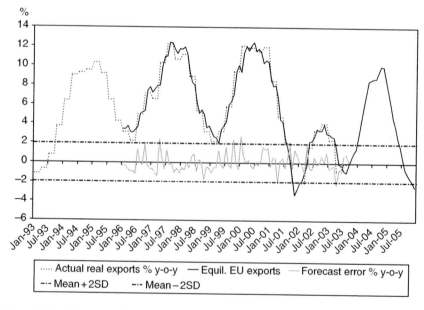

Figure 8.17 EU exports (based on the momentum of US PMI)

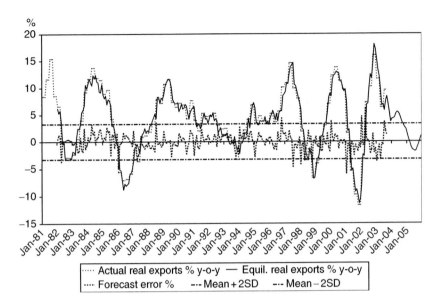

Figure 8.18 Japan – real exports (based on the momentum of US PMI)

in 2004. However, the world economy would weaken substantially in 2005. Second, the US would be the main beneficiary of its own export-led world recovery with euro area being the second and mainland Japan being the laggard. However, again a distinction should be made about mainland Japan and worldwide corporate Japan. The latter would stand to gain the most from the US-led world recovery over the next two years. These have implications for corporate profits and hence for the stock market, as profits are repatriated or at least are reported on a consolidated basis. However, income and employment in mainland Japan would be the least beneficiary of this world recovery. Third, despite its huge losses in competitiveness euro area can still enjoy an export-led recovery, if US growth is very strong. However, unless domestic demand in euro area recovers in 2004, the export-led recovery would peter out in 2005. Therefore, economic policy in euro area should become more accommodative in the course of 2004 to turn the export-led into widespread recovery.

Given the aforementioned drawbacks of the above simulation and in order to throw more light on the likely course of (G-3) exports over the next two years we have cut the dependence of US industrial production on the PMI and have just used the exports K-Model to simulate two alternative scenarios regarding the strength of the US economy – weak and strong growth.

Scenario I (weak US recovery in 2004): What would happen to (G-3) exports if the current US recovery were to falter in 2004 and become once again anaemic?

Scenario II (strong US recovery in 2004): What would happen to (G-3) exports if the US recovery that started after the Iraq war continued to be strong throughout 2004?

4.1   Scenario I (weak US recovery in 2004)

The essence of this scenario lies on the assumption that the strength of the second and third quarters of 2003 was due to one-off factors related to the fiscal package of the current US Administration and rising confidence because of lower geopolitical risks after the end of the Iraq war. The stance of fiscal policy turned 1.6% of GDP easier with the 'Jobs and Growth Tax Relief Reconciliation Act of 2003'. The act provided for an additional first-year bonus depreciation write-off, increasing the immediate depreciation write-off from 30% (provided for in the 'Job Creation and Worker Assistance Act of 2002') to 50% for property acquired after 5 May 2003, and placed in service before 1 January 2005. The additional depreciation provided for by the 2003 act increased depreciation expenses in the second quarter by $83.7 billion and in the third quarter by $30.9 billion. In addition, the 2003 act provided for a reduction of $100.9 billion in July in personal tax and non-tax payments. The act reduced withheld federal taxes $45.8 billion as a result of new marginal tax rates, the expansion of the 10% income tax bracket, and acceleration in 'marriage-penalty' relief. Federal non-withheld taxes (payments of estimated taxes plus final settlements less refunds) were reduced by $55.5 billion because of advance payments of the child tax credit that began being mailed out 25 July 2003. The fiscal stimulus provided through the depreciation incentives and tax relief, ignoring the additional measures on dividend income, as they are controversial with respect to their effect on demand in the economy, is estimated to be 1.6% of nominal GDP.

In addition, monetary policy was eased once more at the end of June 2003 with the Fed funds rate cut to 1%. The accommodative stance of fiscal and monetary policy will keep the economy going, but the imbalances in all sectors will weigh down on the economy and the recovery will begin to falter during the course of 2004 from the torrid pace of 8% in the third quarter of 2003. Nonetheless, the economy will still grow at the rate of potential output in 2004 and 2005 with industrial production growth averaging 3%. The competitiveness index in (G-3) is assumed to remain unchanged. No further gains or losses in competitiveness are assumed to take place over the next two years. These two assumptions about the strength of the US industrial production and (G-3) competitiveness are sufficient to generate projections on (G-3) exports, as world industrial production can be accurately explained by its US equivalent. Table 8.1 summarises all the assumptions underlying Scenario I, along with their current values between September and December 2003.

Table 8.1 G-3 exports

		Current values Sep.–Nov. 2003	US real exports % y-o-y	EU real exports % y-o-y	JP real exports % y-o-y	OECD industrial production % y-o-y	US industrial production % y-o-y	PMI total level
			Scenario I (weak recovery)			Scenario II (strong recovery)		
Assumptions								
OECD industrial production % y-o-y	1st year	1.8	4.0			7		
	2nd year		4.0			1		
EU competitiveness level	1st year	117.9	119.0			119		
	2nd year		119.0			119		
JP competitiveness level	1st year	124.8	125.0			125		
	2nd year		125.0			125		
US broad competitiveness level	1st year	101.1	101.0			106.0		
	2nd year		101.0			96.0		
US industrial production % y-o-y	1st year	1.6	3.0			4.6		
	2nd year		3.0			1.4		
OECD leading indicators level	1st year	123.0	127.0			129.0		
	2nd year		127.0			125.0		
US PMI level	1st year	66.2						
	2nd year							
Current level			0.5	−0.1	9.6	1.8	1.6	66.2
Deivation from long-run equilibrium (LRE)			−1.7	1.1	6.2	0.7	−2.2	5.0

Table 8.1 Continued

	Current values Sep.–Nov. 2003	US real exports % y-o-y	EU real exports % y-o-y	JP real exports % y-o-y	OECD industrial production % y-o-y	US industrial production % y-o-y	PMI total level
		Scenario I (weak recovery)			Scenario II (strong recovery)		
Scenario I (weak recovery)							
12-M SRE (future short-run equilibrium)		10.3	3.6	−0.5	2.6	6.4	51.9
24-M SRE (future short-run equilibrium)		6.6	0.1	3.5	2.3	−0.3	49.6
12-M SRE and current level (difference)		9.8	3.7	−10.0	0.8	4.8	−14.3
24-M SRE and current level (difference)		6.0	0.2	−6.1	0.5	−1.9	−16.6
Scenario II (strong recovery)							
12-M SRE (future short-run equilibrium)		11.7	4.9	0.3	3.6	6.4	51.9
24-M SRE (future short-run equilibrium)		5.7	−1.0	2.7	1.4	−0.3	49.6
12-M SRE and current level (difference)		11.1	5.0	−9.3	1.8	4.8	−14.3
24-M SRE and current level (difference)		5.1	−0.9	−6.9	−0.4	−1.9	−16.6

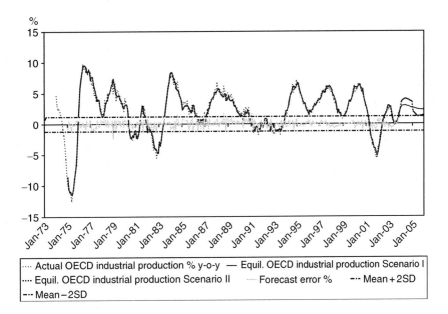

Figure 8.19 OECD industrial production – short-run equilibrium

With US industrial production growing at the steady rate of 3% world industrial production would grow 2.6% in 2004 and 2.3% in 2005 (see Table 8.1 for a summary of the two-year effects and Figure 8.19 for the full trajectory under the two alternative scenarios). With (G-3) competitiveness assumed unchanged over the next two years, US exports would soar 10.6% in 2004 and 6.6% in 2005 (see Table 8.1 and Figure 8.20). US exports would peak at the end of 2004 and they would decelerate in the course of 2005 to 6.5% by the end of 2005. Euro-area exports would continue to expand until May 2004 hitting 5.1% growth; they would decelerate for a few months and then pick up steam until the US presidential election, but they would taper off gradually in the course of 2005 with growth declining to zero by the end of that year (see Figure 8.21). Japan's exports growth would continue to decline until the US presidential election and then they would start recovering hitting 3.5% by the end of 2005 (see Figure 8.22).

The conclusion of this simulation is that the US would be the main beneficiary of its own recovery, partly because its exports are 1.7% lower than their long-run equilibrium and partly because of the momentum that would build up in US exports over the next two years. The effects on euro-area exports would be more muted than the US, partly because exports are 1.1% higher than their long-run equilibrium, but mainly because the beneficial effect of higher world demand would be largely offset by previous losses in

230

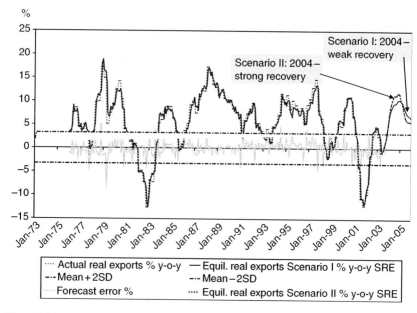

Figure 8.20   US real exports – short-run equilibrium

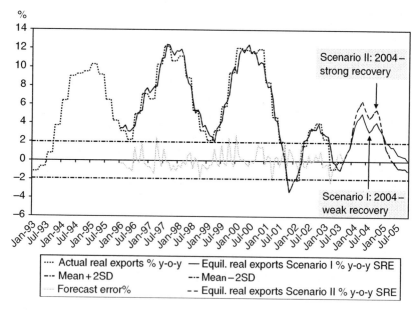

Figure 8.21   EU exports – short-run equilibrium

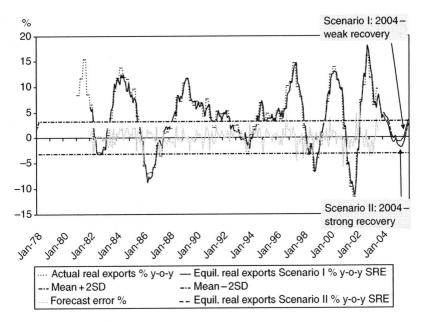

Figure 8.22 Japan – real exports – short-run equilibrium

competitiveness. Japan would be the least beneficiary of this boost in world trade, mainly because its exports are 6.2% higher than their long-run equilibrium and partly because of a declining momentum in its exports in the next twelve months. However, in contrast to its other two rivals, Japan's exports would begin to recover when the exports of its rivals begin to fade away.

4.2 Scenario II (strong US recovery in 2004)

The essence of scenario II lies on the premise, which is largely true, that a combined fiscal and monetary stimulus will last for at least a year, and probably eighteen months, before it tapers off. Given that the US fiscal stimulus was introduced between May and July 2003, the US economy should remain strong until the end of 2004. The role of the accommodative stance of monetary policy is to prevent long-term interest rates from rising and therefore prolong the effects of the fiscal stimulus. However, despite forty-years' low short-term interest rates introduced by the Fed in the last three years, long-term interest rates have risen sharply since June 2003 and the yield curve is extremely steep. If interest rates stay at this high level, or even rise further, which is very likely, the stimulus from fiscal policy will ultimately peter out. This means that growth will diminish in 2005 and beyond, other things being equal. Given that the average growth for the preceding four quarters before the fiscal stimulus was introduced was 2.6%, that the fiscal stimulus was 1.6% of GDP and that the first year multiplier is about unity, the central projection for average US growth until the second half, or the end, of 2004 should be 4.2%. This is very close to the consensus projection for 4.4% growth in 2004. Since the depreciation incentives on new structures will count only if premises are ready for service at the beginning of 2005, companies that would like to take advantage of the scheme should already have started spending. This explains the buoyant recovery of investment in the second quarter of 2003 that was responsible, to some extent, for the unexpectedly strong growth in that quarter. The other major factor that contributed to the unexpectedly strong second quarter was the explosion of defence spending because of the Iraq war.

The stunning 8% growth in the third quarter of 2003 was caused by the combination of strong consumption, due to the income tax cuts that were introduced in that quarter, the last-wagon effect for those companies that wanted to take advantage of the depreciation incentives on new structures, which accounted for $30 billion and worldwide improving confidence because of lower geopolitical risks after the end of the Iraq war that boosted US exports in the third quarter. This implies that the stunning third quarter growth was due to one-off factors that are likely to dissipate in the first half of 2004. Nonetheless, the economy should still grow at 4.2% – central projection until the second half of 2004. Industrial production will average 4.6% growth in 2004, but will fall to 1.4% in the course of 2005. The average rate of growth of industrial production over the two-year period will be 3%, the same as in Scenario I of weak recovery. However, in Scenario II growth would be stronger in 2004 and weaker in 2005 than in Scenario I, but with the same average growth for the two-year period (see Table 8.1 for the detailed assumptions of Scenario II).

The effect of strong US growth in 2004 implies that world demand would grow 3.6% in 2004 and 1.4% in 2005 (see Figure 8.19). With faster growth in the world economy and unchanged competitiveness, US exports would grow even faster than Scenario I in 2004, but would decline slightly more in 2005. US exports would peak at the end of 2004, in line with Scenario I, but at the slightly higher rate of 12%. However, by the end of 2005 would be just less than one per cent lower than in Scenario I (see Figure 8.20). The higher volatility of US industrial production under Scenario II compared with Scenario I implies also higher volatility for US exports. Euro-area exports would grow even stronger than in Scenario I, but would follow a similar pattern. They would peak at the end of 2004 and would decline in 2005 even more than in Scenario I (see Figure 8.21). Hence, the volatility of euro-area exports would be higher in Scenario II than in Scenario I. Japan's exports would also follow a similar pattern under the two scenarios, but again with higher volatility (see Figure 8.22).

5 Summary and conclusions

The (G-3) exports have a common structure in which world demand and competitiveness are the key determinants. Despite the common structure there are important differences in (G-3) export performance stemming from the quantitative importance of each determinant and the time it takes for their effects to be felt on exports. Three important conclusions have emerged from this analysis. First, the US is the main beneficiary of a boost in world trade, followed by the euro area, while Japan is the laggard. The effect on exports is greater than the initial stimulus in the world economy – the multiplier effect is greater than unity – as one country's trade gives a boost to another country's trade that has further impact on the first country, and so on.

Second, the conclusion that Japan is the least beneficiary of a boost in world trade is counterintuitive. But the paradox is resolved when account is taken of the worldwide industrial base of Japan and not just the industrial base in mainland Japan. With this adjustment Japan comes right at the top, followed by the US, while the euro area is now the laggard. The distinction between mainland Japan and its worldwide industrial base has diverse implications for corporate profits, on the one hand, and jobs and incomes, on the other. Japan's corporate profits would increase much more than those of euro area or the US from a boost in world industrial production and therefore its stock market would outperform the other two markets, in the short run. However, the impact of world industrial production on jobs and incomes in Japan would be limited by the fact that the unadjusted multiplier is the smallest of the three.

Third, Japan is in a far better position than its rivals to absorb changes in the nominal exchange rate on competitiveness. Japan is around 20% better than the US in adjusting to competitiveness, while euro area is half as good as Japan. Moreover, Japan and the US can absorb the effects of nominal exchange rate on competitiveness in around two years, while it takes five years for this adjustment to take place in the euro area.

The buoyant recovery of the US economy after the end of the Iraq war and the spectacular performance of (G-3) exports in the third quarter of 2003 has raised hopes of a strong US-led world recovery. The OECD index of leading indicators, which precedes changes in world demand by six months, bottomed in April 2003 and continued to rise until November, thereby suggesting further improvement in (G-3) exports over the following few months. But over a longer horizon the conclusion of a US-led world recovery depends on the strength of the US economy and the extent of previous changes in (G-3) competitiveness. The depreciation of the dollar in the last two years has led to gains in US competitiveness. Despite the roller-coaster of the yen in the last three years, Japan's competitiveness has also improved. However, the euro area has suffered significant losses in competitiveness because of the strong appreciation of the euro in the last three years and its slow adjustment of competitiveness to changes in the nominal exchange rate. These developments in (G-3) competitiveness augur well for a rise in US and Japan exports and a world recovery, but they cast doubts on whether the euro area can benefit from it.

To throw more light on the likely course of (G-3) exports we have conducted a number of simulations. In one of them it is assumed that (G-3) competitiveness remains unchanged over the next two years and that there is no further improvement in US economic fundamentals. The US economy is allowed to proceed on the momentum of expectations that has been built in the previous nine months. This is sufficient to enable the economy to gather steam in 2004, and lead to an export-led recovery of the world economy. However, the US would lose steam in 2005 in the absence of any further improvement in economic fundamentals and the world recovery would fade away. The conclusions of this simulation are that the US is the main beneficiary of its own export-led recovery, as its exports would rise more than its rivals, the euro area and Japan. The euro area is the second beneficiary and Japan is the laggard in terms of incomes and employment, but not in terms of profits, as these are generated from the worldwide industrial base of Japan, which, as has already been argued, is the primary beneficiary, higher than the US or the euro area. In spite of previous losses in competitiveness, euro-area exports would rise significantly and the region would be able to enjoy an export-led recovery in 2004. However, unless euro-area domestic demand picks up in 2004 the export-led recovery would peter out in 2005. This suggests that economic policy in the euro area should become more accommodative in 2004.

In the second set of simulations exports are gauged under the alternative scenarios of weak and fast US growth. In the first scenario growth is steady throughout the two-year period, while in the second scenario growth is fast in 2004, and weak in 2005, but with the same average growth as in the first scenario. The conclusions of this second set of simulations are as follows. First, if the US economy were to grow as fast as potential output in the next two years there would be world recovery. The US would be again the main beneficiary, followed by the euro area and finally with Japan, with the same caveat as before about profits on the one hand, and jobs and incomes on the other. Second, such growth in the US would be sufficient to offset the previous losses in euro-area competitiveness and allow the region to enjoy an export-led recovery. Third, volatility in US growth would induce undesired volatility in (G-3) exports. Fast growth in 2004 would boost (G-3) exports, but if that were to be followed by weak growth in 2005, then export growth would fall as well. The implication of this analysis is either that domestic demand in the euro area and Japan ought to be boosted or that US growth should not be allowed to weaken if the world recovery is not to falter in 2005. This may seem to justify another fiscal injection in the US in 2004. However, in spite of its beneficial effects on (G-3) exports it would have other undesirable effects on the US domestic economy.

9
The US External Imbalance and the Dollar: A Long-term View

1 Introduction[1]

The finance of the huge US current account deficit has so far been met very easily, as the residents in the Rest of the World (ROW) have been willing to lend the US the necessary funds to cover this deficit. This process has turned the US into a serious net debtor to the ROW in the last twenty years. However, the debt is in US dollars and there are no immediate good reasons why residents in the ROW should lose their confidence in the ability of the US to service this debt. There is a risk, though, that ROW residents may lose their appetite to hold US assets, if they continue to suffer huge losses on their holdings of US assets. As we argued in Chapter 1 above, during September and October 2003 there was a temporary drop in the desire of foreign investors to accumulate US assets, but this was restored subsequently. The risk that foreigners may, at some point in time, lose their appetite implies that it would be better that the US should balance or, at least, reduce its current account deficit. The dollar is on declining trend and that would help the current account deficit, because the economy is operating with spare capacity and needs to boost its exports to foster the recovery.

The deficit in the US current account, which records transactions in goods and services, has progressively widened since the recession in the early 1990s. In the 1980s it was also in deficit, but it narrowed with the dollar depreciation following the Plaza Accord in 1985 and was closed with the recession of 1990–91. Under free floating, the capital account, which records transactions in assets and Foreign Direct Investment (FDI), is the mirror image of the current account and represents the finance of the current account deficit. The discrepancy, if any, between the current account and the capital account reflects changes in foreign exchange reserves, which on occasions may arise from central bank intervention in the foreign exchange market.

The current account deficit (the external imbalance) stood at the historical record of 5.2% of nominal GDP in October 2003, and rising, bigger than the

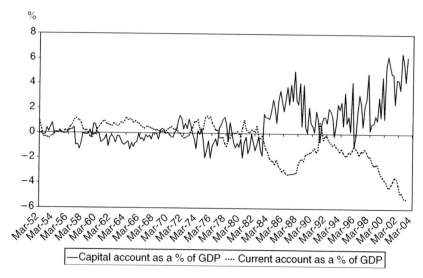

Figure 9.1   US balance of payments

3.3% recorded in the early 1990s recession, which was the previous record deficit in the last fifty years (see Figure 9.1). The finance of the current account deficit, so far, has not been a problem (save for the period since September/October 2003) since the surplus in the capital account has exceeded the deficit in the current account. For example, in the second quarter of 2003 the surplus in the capital account was 6.2% of GDP, outstripping the deficit in the current account by 1%. And yet the dollar has been falling and in 2004 rather dramatically. There is, thus, a serious problem with the huge US current account deficit. The purpose of this chapter is to delve into this problem. Section 2 examines the long-term consequences of the external imbalance. Section 3 poses the question of whether the US needs to worry about the current account imbalance. Section 4 examines the relationship between the dollar and the current account imbalance at the theoretical level, where a new way of looking at the determinants of the exchange rate is discussed; in doing so we make extensive use of the game theoretic approach as this is applied in the foreign exchange market. This section also looks into this relationship at the more empirical level. It emerges that the empirical evidence provided supports the theoretical premise as postulated in the same Section. Finally Section 5 summarises and concludes.

2   The long-term consequences of the external imbalance

The accumulation through time of the external imbalance measures the degree of the US indebtedness. Figure 9.2 shows the net worth of ROW,

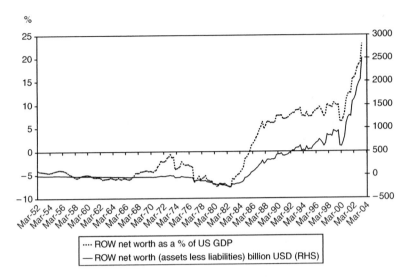

Figure 9.2 Rest of the world (ROW) net worth (US assets held by ROW less ROW assets held by US)

defined as ROW holdings of US assets less holdings of ROW assets. The ROW net worth measures the indebtedness (if positive) or creditworthiness (if negative) of the US economy. The US became for the first time net debtor to the rest of the world at the end of 1985 and this debt has continued to grow ever since. At the end of the second quarter of 2003 the US net debt to ROW was of the order of 23% of US GDP or 2.5 trillion US dollars. What are the long-term consequences of this indebtedness? To some extent the answer depends on how this debt is used. Does it represent acquisition of US tangible assets by ROW or US borrowing, and if so, for what purpose? Examining the composition of ROW net worth provides a clue.

The ROW net worth consists of ROW holdings of US money market instruments, credit market instruments, equities, FDI and miscellaneous assets less the corresponding US holdings of ROW assets. By far the biggest component of ROW net worth is the net credit market position (ROW holdings of US government and corporate bonds less US holdings of ROW bonds). At the end of the second quarter of 2003 the net credit market position of ROW was 26% of US GDP (see Figure 9.3). The US government as well as the corporate sector have been heavily borrowing from ROW by issuing bonds. The US became indebted to ROW at the end of 1981 and this debt has continued to grow ever since (see Figure 9.3). In the 1950s, 1960s and 1970s the ROW net money market position was positive, meaning that foreign residents were attracted by US deposits. However, since 1982, with the exception of 1993–96, the ROW net money market position has been negative

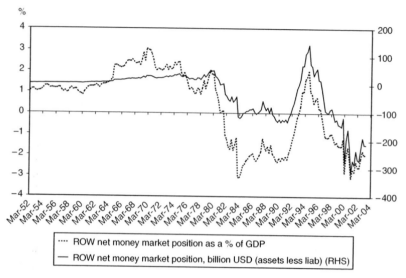

Figure 9.3   ROW net money market position (US assets held by ROW less ROW assets held by US)

(see Figure 9.4). In the second quarter of 2003 the ROW net money market position was −2% of US GDP. Hence, ROW residents are not anymore so much attracted by US deposits. Instead, US residents are now more attracted by ROW deposits.

The ROW net equity position (ROW holdings of US equities less US holdings of ROW equities) in the second quarter of 2003 was −1.4% of US GDP (see Figure 9.5). Since 1993 the appetite of US residents to acquire foreign equities has exceeded that of ROW residents to acquire US equities. The irony is that the ROW relative appetite for US stocks peaked just before the crash of 1987 and bottomed in March 2000, that is, throughout the biggest bull market (see Figure 9.5). The ROW appetite for US equities has resurfaced during the bear equity market of the last three years. This shows that US residents have a much better sense of equity markets than foreigners. Figure 9.6 shows the ROW net FDI position (ROW direct investment in the US less US direct investment in ROW). This has been negative in the last fifty years meaning that US buying of foreign companies has always exceeded ROW buying of US companies. From the ROW point of view this trend bottomed at the end of 1979 at −10% of US GDP. The gap narrowed very fast until June 1990 (at the onset of the recession) at −1.5% of US GDP. However, it widened again until June 1998 to − 3.4% of US GDP. The gap has marginally narrowed ever since to just −2.3% in the second quarter of 2003.

The conclusion from the FDI figures is that in the thirty years to 1983 the US had been buying ROW companies through the surpluses in the current

239

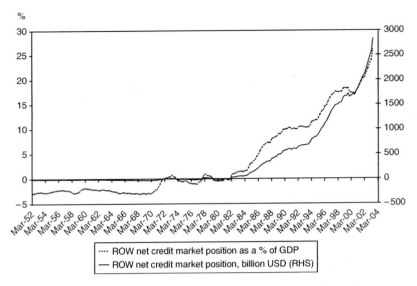

Figure 9.4   ROW net credit market position (assets held by ROW less assets held by US)

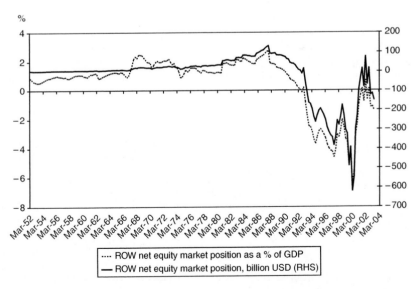

Figure 9.5   ROW net equity position (assets held by ROW less assets held by US)

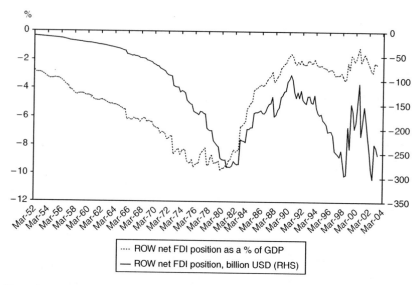

Figure 9.6   ROW net FDI position (assets held by ROW less assets held by US)

account. Since 1983 it has been borrowing from ROW to buy ROW companies. Clearly, this is not a problem if foreign residents are willing to lend the US to buy their companies; indeed, they must be doing so because they believe that they would be more profitable under US management. But the US borrows from ROW not only to buy foreign companies. The ROW net worth at the end of the second quarter of 2003 stood at 23.2% of US GDP. It consists of 26.2% of bonds, −2% of money market instruments, −1.4% of equities, −2.3% of direct investment and 2.6% of miscellaneous assets. Hence, only a small part of US borrowing is devoted to buying foreign companies, the rest is financing the excess expenditure over its income. The overall conclusion is that US has been borrowing from ROW by issuing bonds partly to buy ROW companies, but mainly to finance the excess expenditure over its income. However, to some extent the US is importing products from its own factories abroad. The question that needs to be addressed is whether this is typical and indeed sustainable. We address this particular issue in the section that follows.

3   Does the US need to balance its current account?

In the small open economy paradigm this is neither typical nor sustainable. A country with a surplus in the current account will invest the proceeds in ROW by buying tangible assets. A country with a current account deficit will sell its tangible assets to ROW or borrow from ROW in ROW currency.

If confidence in the ability of the economy to service its external debt is shaken the currency will fall and the country in question will become insolvent, as its debt will soar by the degree of currency depreciation. Therefore, in theory, although a deficit in the current account can be financed in the short run either by a corresponding surplus in the capital account or by running down foreign reserves, this cannot go on forever. In the long run (steady state) the current account must be zero, because otherwise it implies that domestic residents can forever sell their assets or indefinitely borrow from overseas to finance their excess expenditure over their income. Clearly, this cannot last forever, as domestic residents will ultimately run out of assets, or foreign residents will lose their appetite to acquire such assets. Hence, in the long-run (steady state) equilibrium the current account must be balanced.

The US case is interesting from this perspective, because the dollar is a reserve currency, and the US debt is simply domestic rather than foreign. This means that any crisis in the US must come from lack of confidence in its ability to service its domestic debt. But this is not possible! Although foreign residents hold more than half of the US general government debt, this is smaller than any other G7 economy. Moreover, although the US corporate debt is large (46% of US GDP), foreign residents hold only one quarter. Hence, there is no compelling reason why foreign residents should lose their confidence in the ability of the US to service its debt. However, foreign residents may lose their appetite to lend the US, if they continuously suffer losses from their holdings of US assets. One factor that has contributed to such losses is the dollar and the other is the bad timing of foreign residents in buying US assets. From this point of view the huge current account deficit (the external imbalance) is one of the problems that face the US economy. Figure 9.7 shows that as per cent of GDP direct holdings of equities by the personal sector increased from 44% in 1952 to 87% in 1968, but then declined to just 20% in 1982 and then recovered to a peak of 98% in March 2000. In the last three years direct holdings fell to 39%, but have recovered recently (second quarter of 2003) to 46% of GDP. However, such large swings reflect changes in the value of equities, which can be seen if direct holdings are expressed as per cent of the total. The proportion of equities held directly by the personal sector has been on long-term downtrend from 91% in 1952 to 38% lately (see Figure 9.7). This reflects a portfolio shift by the personal sector from direct to indirect holding through life insurance companies, pension funds and mutual funds. The proportion of total holdings of equities by the personal sector (both direct and indirect) declined merely 5%, from 98% in 1952 to 93% in the mid 1990s (see Figure 9.8). However, since the burst of the bubble in March 2000 the proportion of total holdings by the personal sector has fallen by 5%, which was almost entirely bought by foreign residents.

Figure 9.9 shows that the proportion of ROW holdings of US equities has increased from just 2% of US GDP in 1952 to just over 8% in September 1990,

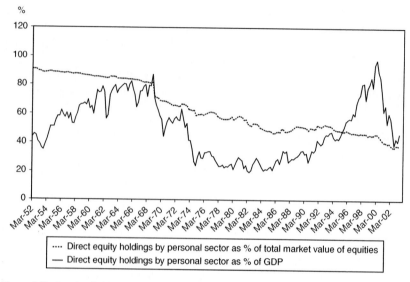

Figure 9.7   Stock of direct equity holdings by personal sector

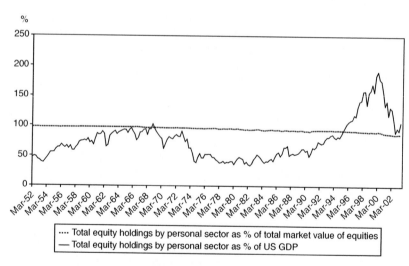

Figure 9.8   Total holdings of equities by the personal sector

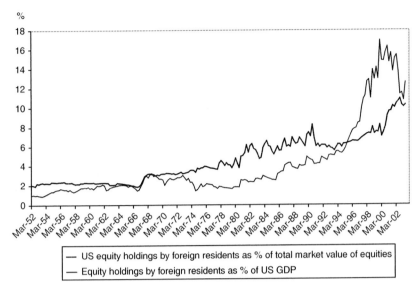

%

Figure 9.9 US Stock equity holdings by foreign residents

but it remained low throughout the major bull market of the 1990s. The proportion of ROW holdings of US equities increased during the bear market by 4% from March 2000 till September 2002. This means that foreign residents not only missed the major bull market of the 1990s, but also were net buyers during the bear market. During the bear market of 2000–03 the US personal sector sold its stock holdings to ROW residents who foolishly believed that this was simply an opportunity to buy US shares. Figure 9.10a confirms this conclusion by showing the net purchases by the US and ROW residents. Figure 9.10b shows that foreign residents have not only suffered losses in their holdings of US equities, but also in bonds. In the second quarter of 2003 foreign residents bought aggressively the US bond market, which started one of its biggest collapse. Therefore, foreign residents have suffered capital losses in the past from holding US assets and the dollar has plunged in the last three years, which may have aggravated such losses. Sustained losses in US assets may dry the appetite of ROW to hold such assets. Hence, the huge current account deficit is one of the problems that face the US economy. The current account deficit has persisted for far too long. This means that the US lacks the foundations for a sustainable new business cycle, since the current account deficit is bound to grow even bigger in the case of a recovery.

In theory, the current account can be corrected in one of two ways. The US economy should expand at a smaller rate of growth than the rest of the world for a considerable period of time, until the current account deficit

244

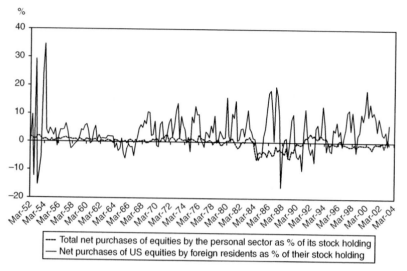

Figure 9.10a Net purchases of US equities by US and foreign residents

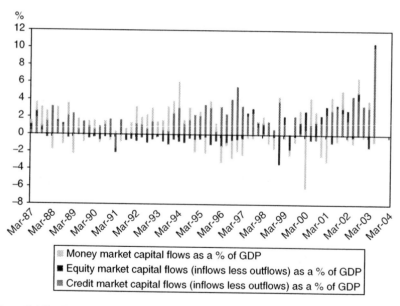

Figure 9.10b Capital flows money, bonds and equities (inflows less outflows) as a % of GDP

shrinks to more sustainable level. Alternatively, the dollar should fall dramatically for US competitiveness to improve and close the current account deficit. In practice, however, the current account deficit usually shrinks by a combination of lower growth and dollar depreciation, as with the US deficit in the 1980s, since the one reinforces the other. The combination of lower growth and dollar depreciation would enable the US to buy back its assets from foreign residents at much lower prices without having to pay for its debts. Unfortunately for the US, despite the recession and the low growth of the last three years, the US fared better than its main competitors, so the current account deficit widened instead of narrowing. This means that the dollar-fall, so far, is not enough. The dollar should fall much more if the current account deficit is to shrink to a sustainable level. We turn our attention next to examine this particular proposition.

4 The dollar and the external imbalance

Although the dollar fall would help to correct the current account deficit there is no presumption that the ballooning current account deficit should lead to further dollar falls. If this were the case, then the dollar should have fallen anytime in the previous thirteen years. Unfortunately, and in spite of such a popular belief, the current account is not a dollar determinant. Neither is, for that matter, the capital account. Most dollar forecasts are systematically wrong because they are based on variables that are not determinants of the dollar as they purport to be. Neither the small open economy paradigm nor the two-country model (see, e.g. Mundell, 1960, 1963; Fleming, 1962; Dornbusch, 1976; Dornbusch and Fisher, 1980), have had much success in explaining dollar movements. To answer this question we examine the theoretical framework embedded in the K-Model (based on Frowen and Karakitsos, 1998).

4.1 A game theoretic approach to currency determination

The value of a currency depends on the policy actions of the two countries involved, which affect other economic fundamentals. This entails that a game theoretic framework is appropriate in which the equilibrium outcome depends on the policy decisions of both players and where the interactions of such decisions are explicitly modelled. However, in game theory there are four relevant equilibrium outcomes. Three of them characterise a non-cooperative environment, in which each player pursues its own objectives without caring for the objectives of the other, but where the decision of one player adversely affects the other. The fourth equilibrium is relevant when the players agree to compromise and in the pursuit of their objectives take into account the objectives of the other player (cooperative game) also.

Such a framework is appropriate for exchange rate analysis. This is so since policymakers of each country pursue policies that attempt to bring the best possible outcome (optimum) in terms of such target variables as inflation, growth and unemployment, through manipulating the level of interest rates, tax rates or discretionary government spending (in other words, monetary and fiscal policy). The exchange rate is a very important variable in the transmission of these policy actions on the target variables. For example, tight monetary policy with the objective of curbing inflation would be more effective if the currency appreciates, since it is expected to reduce imported inflation. On the other hand, easy monetary policy with the objective of promoting growth would be more effective if the currency depreciates because gains in competitiveness would boost exports and reduce imports. However, such policy decisions, to the extent that they are successful in affecting the value of the currency, would affect economic magnitudes in the other country involved. The policy decisions of one country may favourably or adversely affect economic magnitudes in the other country, where the outcome depends on the state of each economy in the business cycle. If the business cycles are synchronised then the policy decisions of one country will adversely affect the targets of the other. On the other hand, if the business cycles are not synchronised, then the policy decisions of one country will favourably affect the other country.

These considerations imply that a game theoretic framework is appropriate for foreign exchange rate analysis, where the interactions of the two players are explicitly modelled. Most of the time the game is played non-cooperatively because each policymaker decides on monetary policy and fiscal policy with the objective of achieving the targets of its own country without consideration for the effect on the growth or inflation of the other country. When the business cycles of the two countries are not synchronised it does not really matter whether the game is played cooperatively or not. But it does matter, when the business cycles are synchronised, because in such a case both countries need a strong currency if they wish to beat inflation or a weak currency if they opt to promote growth. If both players are of equal weight (symmetric game) and they do not cooperate, in the sense that each country pursues policies that maximise its own targets without due consideration for the targets of the other country, then the relevant equilibrium is Nash. The Nash-equilibrium is always worse than a cooperative equilibrium, which is called Pareto, but it is stable, whereas the latter is unstable. Stability in this context means that once the equilibrium is achieved there is no incentive by either player to deviate from it. A simple example makes the difference between Nash and Pareto obvious. In a stadium with seats for all spectators, they prefer to stand up so that they can see better (Nash-equilibrium). Once one person stands up to see better, there is an incentive for everyone to stand up. In the Nash-equilibrium all spectators stand up, whereas in Pareto-equilibrium they all sit down. Clearly, the Nash-equilibrium is worse than Pareto because all spectators are better off sitting than standing and, collectively, they see equally well whether sitting or standing.

The Pareto equilibrium though is unstable, because a single (short) spectator has the incentive to stand up to see better, but his actions would trigger a process that would result in all spectators standing up. In the currency market there are few instances when the game is played cooperatively, such as the Plaza Accord of 1985 and the Louvre Accord of 1987. But most of the time the game is played non-cooperatively.

If one of the players is more powerful than the other (asymmetric game) then the relevant non-cooperative equilibrium is Stackelberg, whereas the Nash-equilibrium is relevant if both players carry equal weight. The strong player is called the 'leader', while the other the 'follower'. In the context of the euro–dollar rate two characteristics suggest the asymmetric nature of the game and the prevalence of the Stackelberg-equilibrium. The effect of US monetary and fiscal policy on the euro area is bigger than the effect of the euro-area policies on the US. Second, the euro area is more vulnerable than the US to supply shocks, such as the price of oil. Hence, the US can be considered as the leader, while the euro area as the follower.

The leader can exploit its advantage over the follower to achieve an even better outcome. This is accomplished by taking into account the possible reaction of the follower in deciding about its own strategy. In this asymmetric game there are two possible equilibria: Stackelberg-leader and Stackelberg-follower. The first is achieved when the leader exercises its leadership role, while the second is achieved when the 'leader' deliberately lets the 'follower' lead the game. In what follows we show that the US has a clear preference for the Stackelberg-leader equilibrium, when the economy is either overheated or cools down, but inflation continues to rise because of inertia. On the other hand, the US has a clear preference for the Stackelberg-follower equilibrium when the economy is either in the recession or recovery phase of the business cycle, when there is spare capacity. We also provide reasons why investors have an incentive to enforce either the one or the other equilibrium on behalf of the US.

4.2 A policy choice model

This framework is a Stackelberg game with the US as the leader and the euro area as the follower. Such a framework is more appropriate because what is good for the US is good for the rest of the world, given its dominance in the world economy. Especially so since, as it is shown below, the best outcome for the US is a stable equilibrium. The implication of this Stackelberg game is that what matters for the dollar is the US and not its relative position against its main trading partners. Hence, popular variables, like (short or long) interest rate differentials, growth differentials, money supply differentials, inflation differentials, which emanate from the small open economy or the two-country model, may lead to erroneous conclusions about dollar movements, as the models that involve such variables are usually unstable. The models are unstable in the sense that the impact of these variables on the euro–dollar exchange rate changes through time from, statistically significant, positive to negative and finally to zero. The model instability is due to a shift in the equilibrium from Stackelberg-leader to Stackelberg-follower. Once account is taken of this game framework and the shift of the equilibrium between Stackelberg-leader to Stackelberg-follower the resulting euro–dollar is stable. Moreover, the Stackelberg game framework does not imply that the traditional variables should be used for the US only. Instead, what is important is that the dollar should move in such a way so that the US economy can benefit under all circumstances. If this is not so, then not only the US, but also the rest of the world is at risk, as the economic and financial system would then be unstable. Within this framework, the value of the currency is an equilibrium outcome within a policy game. In this game theoretic framework there are two equilibria, but only one of them is stable and most of the time investors enforce the stable equilibrium. The stable equilibrium reflects the best possible outcome from the US point of view, given the state of the economy in the business cycle and the time varying priorities of the US policymakers, among the main targets of economic policy.[2] We explore this theoretical premise in what follows.

We begin by assuming that each policymaker chooses its monetary policy by optimising an objective function that is penalising deviations of actual inflation from its desired level and deviations of actual growth from its desired level. That is, for each country i the utility function U is specified as follows:

$$U_i = \frac{1}{2} \left[q_{ip}(p_i - p_i^d)^2 + q_{iy}(y_i - y_i^d)^2 \right] \tag{1}$$

where q_{ip} is the penalty weight that the policymakers in country $i = 1,2$ are attaching to inflation and q_{iy} is the penalty weight on growth; p_i and y_i are actual inflation and growth respectively, and p_i^d and y_i^d are desired inflation and growth respectively. Country 1 is the US and country 2 is the euro area. The bliss point is taken as the rate of growth of desired output and as inflation the rate that corresponds to desired output, taken as the desired rate of inflation. We may, thus, write:

$$(p_i^d, y_i^d) \tag{2}$$

The US central bank is assumed to pursue a 'balanced' approach to monetary policy between the two conflicting targets of inflation and growth; that is, the Fed is supposed to attach equal weights to the achievement of the inflation and output targets. On the other hand, the ECB is assumed to attach greater weight on inflation than on growth. This implies that while for the US it is assumed that $q_{1p} = q_{1y}$, for the euro area it is assumed that $q_{2p} > q_{2y}$. Each policymaker optimises its own objective function subject to the economic model that defines the feasible combinations of inflation and growth, given the choice of the monetary policy instrument. The model allows for the spill over effects of monetary policy from one country to the other. Thus, growth in each country is affected by the monetary policy of the two countries. Domestic monetary policy has a bigger effect on domestic growth than the foreign one. Inflation depends on the output gap and imported inflation. The latter is influenced by monetary policy as a rise in the domestic interest rate appreciates the domestic currency and depreciates the foreign currency.

Four characteristics are embedded in the model, which differentiates the US from the euro area. First, the euro area relies much more than the US on imported raw materials. Second, the spill over effect of US monetary policy on the euro area is bigger than the spill over effect of the euro area on the US. Thus, the euro area is both more susceptible to imported inflation and it is also more vulnerable to 'a beggar-thy-neighbour policy' than the US. Third, and as already stated, the US central bank is assumed to pursue monetary policy in a more 'symmetrical' manner than the ECB, and attach equal degree of importance to the two conflicting targets of inflation and growth. The ECB is assumed to focus heavily on inflation. This implies that while for the US it is assumed that the Fed degree of priority on growth is equal to that on inflation, for the euro area it is assumed that the priority on inflation exceeds that on growth. Fourth, the US is 'stronger' than the euro area in the sense elaborated above. Therefore, in a game framework the US can be considered as the leader, while the euro area as the follower. The indifference curves drawn in Figures 9.11a and 9.11b reflect these assumptions.

With these assumptions we draw in Figure 9.11a the indifference curves for both the US and the euro area, which take the form of ellipses. Ellipses further away from the bliss point represent lower utility and are therefore less desirable. The US indifference curves have as their centre the bliss point A^u. The US ellipses are very flat. The indifference curves for the euro area, on the other hand, are very steep. The US bliss point lies in the second quadrant of Figure 9.11a. On the other hand, the bliss-point for the euro area, denoted by A^e, lies in the fourth quadrant in the same figure. The optimal policy for each country is obtained by minimising the objective function (1) above, subject to the economic model. Each central bank is choosing its monetary policy by taking as given the monetary policy of the other. The optimal monetary policy for each country is described by its reaction function. In Figure 9.11a the US reaction function is denoted by U, while that of the euro area is denoted by E.

With the assumptions that the euro area is more vulnerable to imported inflation and to beggar-thy-neighbour policies than the US and that it also cares more about inflation than the US, the reaction functions of the US and the euro area look like those in Figure 9.11a. The US reaction function is almost flat and the reaction function of the euro area is very steep. The intersection of the two reaction functions determines the Nash-equilibrium,

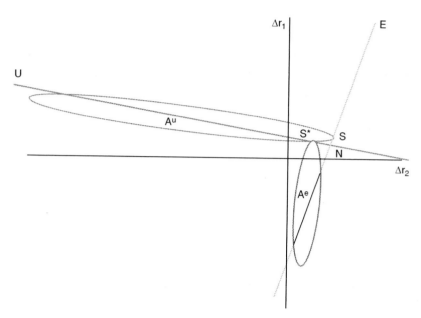

Figure 9.11a   Three possible equilibria in a non-cooperative game

Notes
N – Nash-equilibrium;
S* – Stackelberg-follower;
S – Stackleberg-leader;
E – euro-area's reaction function;
U – US's reaction function A^u and A^e: refer to the US and the euro-area A points, respectively;
r_1 – US interest rate;
r_2 – euro-area interest rate.

denoted by N, which is attained in quadrant 1 under the assumptions made earlier. This implies that as a result of a surge, say, in imported raw material prices the euro area is forced into tighter monetary policy than the US. This appreciates the euro against the dollar and introduces a deflationary effect in euro area with higher unemployment than the US. The Stackelberg-leader equilibrium with the US as leader is defined as a point on the reaction function of the euro area that is tangential on the US indifference curves. In Figure 9.11a the Stackelberg-equilibrium is attained at point S. Clearly, this is a better solution for the US because it lies on a lower indifference curve than the one that passes through point-N. This implies that the Stackelberg-equilibrium with the US as a leader is Pareto-efficient for the US, but not the euro area, since its equilibrium lies on a higher indifference curve for the euro-area. The Stackelberg-follower equilibrium in which the US lets the euro

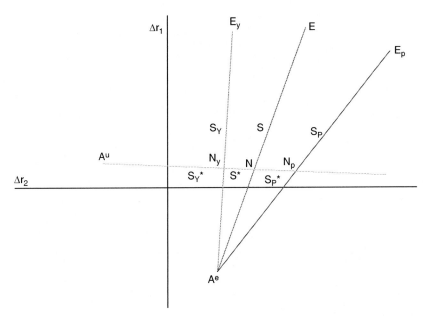

Figure 9.11b Equilibrium sensitivity with respect to ECB inflation and growth priorities

Notes
See *Notes* under *Figure 9.11a;*
E_y – Priority on growth;
E_p – Priority on inflation;
no subscript-neutral position.

area act as a leader is defined as a point on the US reaction function that is tangential to the euro area's indifference curves. In Figure 9.11a the Stackelberg-equilibrium with the euro area as the leader is attained at point-S^*. This is a better outcome for the euro area, since it lies on a lower indifference curve. But it is also optimal for the US. Hence, the Stackelberg-follower equilibrium is Pareto-efficient for both the US and the euro area.

4.3 The choice of equilibrium

This sub-section deals with the issue of which equilibrium is preferable from the US point of view. It turns out that the best possible outcome from the US point of view depends on the business cycle. Figure 9.11c illustrates the way in which the objective function of a central bank changes in the course of the business cycle. Point A represents the bliss point, defined as the rate of growth of potential output. The inflation rate that corresponds to the rate of growth of potential output is the steady state rate of inflation. Points B

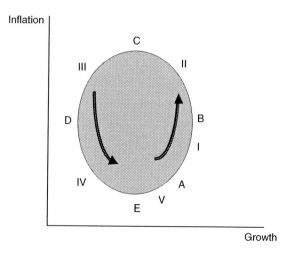

Inflation

Growth

Figure 9.11c   Central bank behaviour in the business cycle

and D represent the peak and the trough of the business cycle in terms of the rate of growth, while points C and E the maximum and minimum rate of inflation, respectively, in the business cycle. These points divide the business cycle into five phases.

In phase I growth is rising above potential, the economy becomes overheated and inflation rises, usually with a lag. The correlation between inflation and growth is positive. In phase II the economy decelerates, but inflation rises, thereby giving rise to negative correlation between the two variables. Inflation increases in phase II, as unit labour cost continues to rise. There are two reasons why unit labour cost rises in this phase, albeit at a decreasing rate as the economy moves from B to C. First, wage inflation is rising and, second, labour productivity growth falls. Both factors contribute to the rise in unit labour cost. In the initial part of phase II wages are increasing as fast as inflation as employees are trying to protect the purchasing power of their wages. Immediately after point-B, near the peak of the business cycle, employees are in a position to protect their real wages since their bargaining power is strong, as unemployment is low and few jobs are lost per month. However, as the economy moves towards point-C the bargaining power of employees weakens, as unemployment is rising and the number of jobs lost per month is increased. Consequently, employees find it more and more difficult to protect the purchasing power of their wages. The real wage rate declines as the economy approaches point-C and the wage-price spiral is finally broken. Near the peak of the business cycle (around point-B) labour productivity declines as firms lag behind in adjusting their labour force to declining demand for their products. Two reasons force firms to adjust sluggishly their labour force. First, uncertainty as to whether the drop in the demand for goods would be temporary or permanent. Second, costs of adjustment in hiring and firing and training costs are forcing firms to see whether they can cope with reduced working hours and smaller temporary staff before they start sacking their permanent staff. However, as the fall in demand gathers pace (i.e. as the economy approaches point-C) falling profitability is forcing firms to absorb into their profit margins the higher cost and decrease their labour force. Consequently, the fall in labour productivity diminishes as the economy approaches point-C. In phase III the economy goes into recession and inflation falls fast, as unit labour cost declines rapidly. Wage inflation abates as unemployment keeps rising and the number of jobs lost per month is increasing. Productivity rises as firms shed their labour force faster than the drop in demand. Profit margins are squeezed further as demand is extremely weak in the recession. The correlation of inflation and growth in phase III is positive. In phase IV the economy recovers, but inflation continues to fall, as unit labour cost rises, albeit at a decreasing rate. This is the inverse of phase II and correlation is negative.

With this information as a background it is easy to see how a central bank would change its priorities in the course of the business cycle. In phases I and II the priority on inflation increases, and the central bank follows tight monetary policy. In phases III and IV the central bank follows easy monetary policy, as the priority on beating inflation is reduced or the priority on growth is increased. Hence, in general, interest rates rise from E to C and fall from C to E. A central bank can be characterised as balanced, 'wet' (or 'dove') and 'tough' (or 'anti-inflation hawk') depending on the values it attaches to the penalty weights on inflation and growth at point-A, that is, when the economy is in steady state. The comparison has to be made at point-A so that one is comparing like with like. This follows from the fact that the penalty weights vary in the course of the business cycle irrespective of the characterisation of the central bank as balanced, wet or tough. The central bank is balanced when the penalty weight on inflation is equal to the penalty weight on growth. The central bank is wet (or dove) when the penalty weight on growth exceeds that on inflation. The central bank is tough (or anti-inflation hawk) when the penalty weight on inflation exceeds that on growth. If the central bank is balanced, then interest rates would start falling at point-C and would start rising at point-E. If the central bank is wet or dove, then interest rates would start falling just before point-C and would start rising after point-E. If the central bank is tough or anti-inflation hawk, then interest rates would start falling after point-C and would start rising before point-E.

Figure 9.11b portrays what happens when central banks change their priorities in terms of the their targets. The US reaction function rotates anticlockwise when the priority on inflation increases, that is, when the economy is in phase I or II. When the priority on growth increases, that is, when the economy is in phase III or IV, the US reaction function rotates clockwise. Nonetheless, the rotation of the US reaction function in the course of the business cycle is small. The US reaction function remains effectively flat. The reaction function of the euro area, on the other hand, rotates clockwise when the priority on inflation increases, that is, when the economy is in phase I or II. The reaction function rotates anti-clockwise when the priority on growth increases, that is, when the economy is in phase III or IV. The euro-area reaction function is much more sensitive than the US in the course of the business cycle.

For the sake of simplicity it is assumed that the US reaction function is fixed in the course of the business cycle, while the euro-area's reaction function takes three positions. It is neutral when the economy is growing at the rate of potential output (i.e. in the steady state), steeper when the economy is in recession or in recovery (i.e. in phase III or IV) and flatter when inflation is rising (i.e. in phase I or II). In Figure 9.11b, E denotes the euro-area's reaction function in the neutral position; E_y denotes the euro-area's reaction function when the ECB attaches high priority in promoting growth. E_p denotes the euro-area's reaction function when the ECB attaches high priority in beating inflation. In each reaction function there are three equilibria if the policy game is played non-cooperatively, Nash, Stackelberg-leader and Stackelberg-follower. The assumption that the US reaction function is fixed restricts the choice of equilibrium in the policy game to just nine instead of twenty-seven and makes the conclusions crispier by eliminating unnecessary detail.

With this background analysis it is easy to see which equilibrium would be preferable from the US point of view in the course of the business cycle. When the US is either in the overheating or the cooling down phase (i.e. in phase I or II) of its business cycle, the best outcome is described by the Stackelberg-leader equilibrium, denoted by point-S. The Stackelberg-leader equilibrium is Pareto-efficient (i.e. welfare improving) for the US, but not for the euro area. But such an equilibrium is stable. This equilibrium implies higher interest rates both for the US and the euro area. The US would choose higher interest rates in order to reduce inflation, which is its primary objective in phase I or II. This would appreciate the dollar against the euro and would raise imported inflation in the euro area. However, given the anti-inflation bias of the ECB, interest rates would rise in the euro area in order to safeguard the value of the currency against imported inflation. But this would engulf the euro area into a deflationary gap, in which either unemployment would rise if the economy were in recession or unemployment would not fall if the economy were in recovery. Therefore, the Stackelberg-leader equilibrium is welfare improving for the US, but not for the euro area.

If both the US and the euro area are in phase I or II, then the reaction function of the euro area would be flatter and point-N would be further to the right to N_p in Figure 9.11b. The US can still improve its welfare by choosing the Stackelberg-leader equilibrium, but its overall welfare is lower because the improvement is from a lower base (i.e. compared to N). Overall the euro-area welfare is smaller in the new Nash-equilibrium N_{p}, relative to N. It becomes even worse as the US chooses the Stackelberg-leader equilibrium S_p. The US choice of the Stackelberg-leader equilibrium is self-enforceable. The euro area would be forced to choose this equilibrium as it enters into an interest rate war with the US because of the anti-inflation bias of the ECB. This is what happened in the first half of the 1980s and it is probably what is happening since the end of 1999. If, on the other hand, the euro area is in phase III or IV when the US is in phase I or II, that is, when the business cycles are desynchronised, then its reaction function is steeper at E_y, and point-N would lie further to the left to N_y. The US can still improve its welfare by choosing the Stackelberg-leader equilibrium, but now its overall welfare is higher because the improvement is from a higher base (i.e. compared to N). Overall the euro-area welfare is higher, but it is somewhat reduced as the US chooses the Stackelberg-leader equilibrium. An improvement in the euro-area welfare is possible only if the ECB is prepared to accept both a weaker euro and higher inflation. If the ECB is unwilling to submit to higher inflation and weaker currency, then its reaction function will rotate clockwise (i.e. it would become flatter) as the US attempts to choose the Stackelberg-leader equilibrium. Inflation would still rise and the currency would become weaker, but by less than the original equilibrium. Both from the US and the euro area's point of view de-synchronisation of the business cycles is preferable than synchronisation.

In the recession or the recovery phase (i.e. in phases III or IV) the Stackelberg-follower equilibrium in which the euro area acts as a leader, namely point-S*, is by far a better outcome for the US irrespective of the position of the euro area in the business cycle. In this case the US is exploiting the flatness of its reaction function and the steepness of the euro-area reaction function. Given the flatness of the US reaction function, US interest rates would rise by almost the same amount as in the Nash-equilibrium. However, the euro area would adopt a less tight policy than at N and therefore the dollar would appreciate compared to Nash. This would allow the US to soothe the recessionary effects of the surge in raw material prices, which is its primary objective in phase III or IV, while minimising the inflationary consequences. Since the US is adopting almost the same degree of tightening, the recessionary effects of the raw material price increase are the same in N and S*. However, by letting the euro area lead the US is benefiting both in terms of inflation and growth. Inflation at S* is lower than N, because the dollar is stronger and hence imported inflation is lower. Growth is higher because domestic demand in the euro area is more buoyant thereby stimulating US exports. The rise in dollar results in a loss in US competitiveness. US exports still increase, though, as the effect of the stronger domestic demand in the euro area more than offsets the loss in competitiveness. Thus, the Stackelberg-follower equilibrium is Pareto-efficient (i.e. welfare improving) for the US. Such equilibrium is also Pareto-efficient for the euro area, as it lies on a lower indifference curve than the one that passes through point-N, the Nash-equilibrium. If euro area lags behind the US in the business cycle, as it happened in the 1980s and the 1990s, and it is in phase I or II, while the US is in phase III or IV, then the euro area's reaction function would be even flatter. The choice of equilibrium now lies on E_p and therefore point-N would lie, almost horizontally, further to the right to N_p in Figure 11b. In this case there is still room for welfare improvement for both the US and the euro area. The US would still choose the Stackelberg-follower equilibrium at S_p^*. However, overall welfare for the US diminishes because the improvement is from a lower base. The euro area welfare is lower compared to N, but this is desirable since euro area attaches a high priority in reducing inflation. The dollar would still appreciate compared to the new Nash-equilibrium N_p, but it would be weaker compared to the original Nash-equilibrium, N, that is, the equilibrium when euro area is growing at potential output. European welfare improves at S_p^* compared to N_p because the Fed is not competing with the ECB over the currency. The Fed does not lift interest rates to defend the dollar and hence the ECB tightens less than otherwise. Thus, although the dollar depreciates compared to N, it is till stronger compared to N_p. The euro area welfare improvement therefore reflects the smaller degree of tightening by the ECB. Such an outcome is optimal for euro area because the Fed tolerance over the dollar arises as a result of the US being in recession or in recovery and therefore the smaller the dollar appreciation the better. Hence, desynchronisation of business cycles is preferable from Europe's point of view, but not from the US, as S_p^* is further away from the bliss point than S^*.

If, on the other hand, the business cycle of the euro area is synchronised with the US and both regions are in phase III or IV, then the euro area reaction function will be even steeper and the Nash equilibrium would lie, almost horizontally, further to the left to N_y in Figure 9.11b. Again there is room for welfare improvement for both the US and euro area compared with the new Nash-equilibrium N_y. The US will still choose the Stackelberg-follower equilibrium. But now, overall welfare for the US is enhanced since the improvement is from a higher base. Hence, synchronisation of business cycles is preferable to non-synchronisation from the US point of view. The dollar would appreciate compared to the new Nash-equilibrium at N_y, as the euro-area interest rates do not rise a lot. The dollar would be even stronger compared to the original Nash-equilibrium N. Synchronisation is preferable from the US point of view because the euro-area growth is higher at S_y^* than at N_y and hence US exports are more buoyant, in spite of the stronger dollar. The choice of Stackelberg-follower equilibrium is Pareto-efficient also for the euro area as the stronger dollar results in smaller degree of tightening by the ECB.

In summary, the Stackelberg-leader equilibrium is a better outcome for the US when the economy is either overheating or is cooling down (i.e. in phases I and II). The Stackelberg-follower equilibrium is a better outcome for the US when the economy is either in recession or in the recovery phase (i.e. in phases III and IV). The next issue is how the US enforces its choice of equilibrium, whether this is a Stackelberg-leader or a Stackelberg-follower outcome. In each case markets impose such equilibrium because, usually, this is the only stable equilibrium in the absence of foreign exchange intervention. A market economy relies upon market discipline for the stability of the system. Investors, in trying to protect the value of their portfolios usually enforce a stable equilibrium. Whenever the US business cycle is not synchronised with that of the euro area, the resulting equilibrium is stable, simply because there is no conflict – one player's interest dictates a strong currency, while the other's dictates a weak currency. By contrast, whenever there is synchronisation of the business cycles, there is a conflict in that it is in both players, interest to have either a weak or strong currency. In the latter case, investors impose the equilibrium that enhances US welfare even if that is detrimental to the euro area in the short run, since it is stable. Thus, in phases I and II when the Stackelberg-leader equilibrium is prevalent and the US budget deficit is shrinking, investors buy dollars, as this helps the US to fight inflation and provide finance to a widening current account deficit. The alternative would imply instability for the US and, consequently, for the world economy and its financial system. In phases III and IV, when the Stackelberg-follower equilibrium is prevalent and the US budget deficit is widening, investors sell dollars, as this helps the US economy to recover, which in time will revive the rest of the world, and helps to close the current account deficit. The alternative would again imply instability for the US and the world financial system. One important qualification to this thesis is the possibility of 'irrational exuberance'. Investors in their monolithic pursuit of profit can choose an unstable equilibrium.

The stability issue clarifies why the ECB in some periods is unable either to stem the euro plight or the euro rise. In the post-bubble environment a rate cut by the ECB does not have the desired effect of restraining the euro rise, as its business cycle is synchronised with that of the US. Since the burst of the bubble in 2000 both the US and the euro area are struggling to recover and a weak currency is desirable by both. In the absence of intervention the only stable equilibrium is the one that favours dollar weakness, and this is the one that markets impose. The equilibrium with weak dollar is stable because it would lead to a US-led world recovery, whereas a dollar rise (and consequently a euro fall) would not help the rest of the world to recover and, perhaps, not even the euro area itself. In this respect, the experience of France in the early 1980s is pertinent. At the time, the rest of G-7 pursued deflationary policies to fend the inflation effect of the second oil shock, while the socialist French government pursued expansionary policies to fight the recession. In the event, France was forced, within a short period, to reverse its policies, as it led to instability through a currency crisis. In the period between the end of the Asian-Russian crisis (1998) and the burst of the equity bubble (2000) the ECB, and prior to it the Bundesbank, was again unable to stem the euro plight, in spite of tight monetary policy because its business cycle was again synchronised with that of the US. By contrast, whenever the US business cycle is not synchronised with that of the euro area, the resulting equilibrium is stable, simply because there is no conflict – one player's interest dictates a strong currency, while the other's dictates a weak currency. This was the case between 1994–98, when the US was overheated, but the euro area was operating with spare capacity.

4.4   The recent behaviour of the dollar

It follows from the analysis so far in this chapter that the dollar is strong when the US wants to cap inflationary pressures and it is weak when the US wants to promote growth through exports. In the last three years the dollar has been weak because the US wants to have an export-led recovery. In the second half of the 1990s the dollar was strong because the US was growing faster than its potential, thereby creating inflationary pressures. The strong economy helped to reduce the budget deficit and general government debt and bond yields fell, while monetary and fiscal policy was tight. In the last three years the economy has been weak, monetary policy is easy, fiscal policy is also easy and both the budget deficit and general government debt are soaring. The overall effect of these factors has contributed to the dollar fall and would continue to cause a fall in the future.

Figure 9.11d shows the dollar real effective exchange rate, based on a trade weighted wide basket of currencies. It is a wide measure of US competitiveness, which is stationary, unlike the nominal exchange rate, which is non-stationary.[3] During June of 2003 the dollar became seriously oversold and the rally during the summer brought it back to equilibrium. However, for the aforementioned reasons, the dollar would continue its decline with a target of 94.2 on its broad trade weighted index by December 2004, from its current value of 105.4 in August 2003. This implies another 11% depreciation in the real value of the dollar against all currencies. The K-Model conforms to all principles of the Stackelberg game and explains dollar movements in the last seventeen years with just 1% forecast error. This means that with an error of 2% the model can explain 95% of all past dollar volatility. Indeed, in the last 210 months there have been only five instances where the dollar error has exceeded 2% (see Figure 9.12). On that basis the forecasting ability of the model is such as to claim that with 95% probability the dollar in the future will lie within the interval of the central projection plus or minus 2%. This assumes that the behaviour of the dollar will continue to be governed by the same structure that is encapsulated in the K-Model. The critical assumption here is that the leadership role of the US would not be challenged in the forecast period, an assumption that will probably be easily satisfied for a period of one year. Hence, there is no reason to assume that the structure of the K-Model will be invalidated in the short-term future.

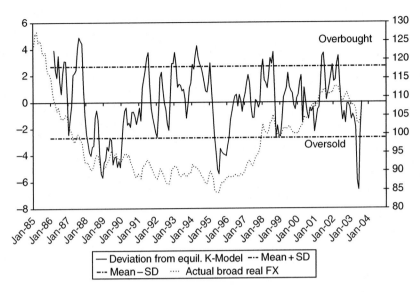

Figure 9.11d Real dollar exchange rate – long-run valuation

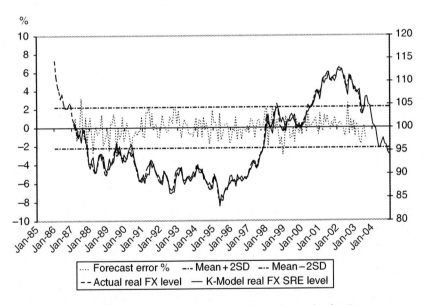

Figure 9.12 Real dollar exchange rate – short-run fair value and valuation

To gain further insight into the effect of the dollar depreciation on the euro we employ the K-Model of the German real effective exchange rate (a measure of German competitiveness). Figure 9.13 shows that during May 2003 the German real effective exchange rate had become just 4.4%

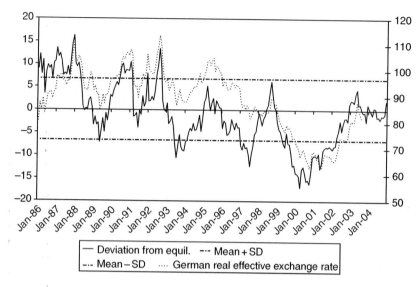

Figure 9.13   German real effective exchange rate – long-run valuation

overvalued. The dollar rally during the summer brought the German real effective exchange rate back to equilibrium. Figure 9.14 shows that the German real effective exchange rate will appreciate to 94.4 by December 2004 from 81.2 in August 2003. This implies a further appreciation of 16% for the real euro in just over a year. Figure 9.15 shows the actual and projected nominal and real effective rate for the dollar and the euro. The euro will appreciate to 1.28 by December 2004. Figure 9.16 shows the dollar effective exchange rate against a broad basket of currencies and against the major currencies. A cursory look shows that whereas the dollar has depreciated 15.5% against the major currencies since March 2002, it has only depreciated 7.5% against all currencies. This explains why the US is putting pressure on countries such as China to revalue their currencies against the dollar, if it is to succeed in engineering an export-led recovery. Given its Stackelberg leadership role the dollar should depreciate against all currencies during the foreseeable future.

5   Summary and conclusions

The huge US current account deficit (the external imbalance) has persisted for far too long, although, so far, it has been financed very easily. The accumulation of those deficits has turned the US into a net debtor to the ROW of the order of 23% of its GDP. This external debt has been used, for a long time, mainly to sustain the US excess expenditure over its income, but also

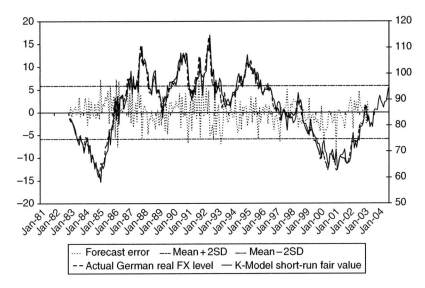

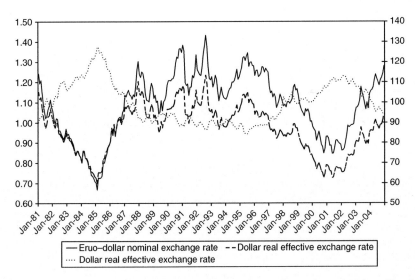

Figure 9.14   German real effective exchange rate – short-run valuation

Figure 9.15   Nominal and real exchange rates – dollar and euro (actual and predicted since Sep. 03)

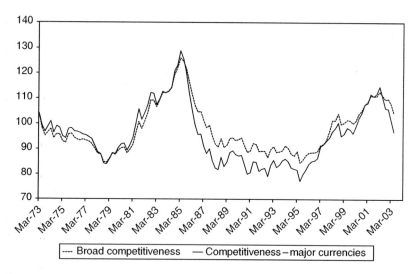

Figure 9.16   US competitiveness

to buy ROW companies. Compared to other countries the external debt of the US is large, but it is in US dollars. Hence, traditional insolvency problems that are created by debt to ROW in ROW currency do not arise in the case of the US. Although foreign residents hold more than half of US government debt, the debt is smaller than any other G7 country. Moreover, although US corporate debt is 46% of GDP, foreign residents hold only one quarter. Hence, there is no compelling reason why foreign residents should lose confidence in the ability of the US to service its debt.

However, foreign residents may lose their appetite to lend the US, if they continuously suffer losses from their holdings of US assets. Foreign residents have not only missed the major US bull equity market in the 1990s, but they have also suffered losses during the bear equity market of 2000–03. Moreover, foreign residents have recently suffered heavy losses on their holdings of US bonds. The dollar has plunged in the last three years, which may have aggravated such losses. From this point of view the external imbalance is one of the problems that face the US economy. Unless the current account deficit is balanced in the long run or at least narrowed down, the US lacks the foundations for a sustainable new business cycle, since the current account deficit is bound to grow even bigger in the case of a recovery.

The US will be able to get rid of its debt not by paying it back, but by buying it back at lower prices once foreign residents have suffered huge losses on their holdings of US assets. During the bear market of the last three years the US sold its stock holdings to the ROW. Slower growth and sharp dollar depreciation would enable the US to buy back its assets from the ROW. Unfortunately for the US, despite the recession and the low growth of the last three years, the US fared better than its main competitors, so the current account deficit widened instead of narrowing. This means that the dollar fall, so far, is not enough. The dollar should fall much more if the current account deficit is to shrink to a sustainable level. But even a bigger current account deficit will not cause a dollar fall, since, despite popular belief, it does not affect it. The opposite is true. The current account deficit is affected by the real value of the dollar.

Our game theoretic approach to dollar determination reveals that the currency is strong when the economy is growing faster than its potential, fiscal policy is easy and monetary policy is tight, the government debt is falling and bond yields are declining.[4] All of these factors account for one per cent error in dollar movements and, with the exception of bond yields, are pointing to a weaker dollar in the future. In essence, the dollar would continue falling because the US economy is operating with spare capacity and wants to boost its exports in strengthening the recovery. The K-Model suggests that the real value of the dollar will further depreciate 11% against all currencies and 16% against the major currencies by the end of 2004. The nominal value of the euro will climb to 1.28 against the dollar during this forecast period. The dollar will continue to depreciate even beyond the forecast period, if the US recovery turned out to be cyclical and lost its steam after the November 2004 presidential election.

10
The Long-term Risks to US Financial Markets

1 Introduction

Bond yields are likely to rise gently this year, thereby causing a threat neither to equities nor to an overvalued housing market, as inflation is likely to dissipate for most part of 2004 and the Fed might delay its monetary tightening. In spite of market worries, both bonds and equities are near their respective equilibrium. However, there are serious risks to financial markets and the economy as a whole from fiscal policy turning once more easy in 2004. The Fed, then, would have a difficult job in keeping the economy on a sustained path to recovery. With strong growth, above potential, the Fed can afford to wait before tightening, as growth is likely to decelerate in 2005 and inflation is likely to remain muted. But the Fed would be forced to tighten more aggressively after the presidential election. Bond yields will rise in 2005 but not to levels that would undermine the housing market. The victim might be the equity market with prices falling precipitously revisiting the March 2003 levels, if the slowdown of the economy were sharp.

With growth at potential in 2004 the Fed should tighten moderately and pre-emptively towards the end of the first half of 2004, but a bit more aggressively thereafter. Bond yields will rise gently in 2004, but even more sharply in 2005, as inflation accelerates with growth continuing at around potential. The housing market would be the victim of rising interest rates, but equities might be spared. We investigate these possibilities in the final chapter of this book. We begin in section 2 by looking into bond market valuation before we examine the theoretical aspects of the issue in hand. This covers both the bond and equity markets separately (sections 3 and 4 respectively). We provide relevant empirical investigation in section 5, before we summarise and conclude in section 6.

2 Bond market valuation

The bond market holds the key not only to the equity market, but also to the economy as a whole. The imbalances in the private sector are dormant at the moment, as the economy is recovering. However, if long-term interest rates were to rise to critical levels, then these imbalances would reawaken and threaten not only the sustainability of the recovery, but may also trigger another recession. The really interesting question then is the extent to which, and how fast, bond yields rise in the next two years.

The ten-year bond yield peaked at the beginning of 2000 at 6.75% and fell for the following three and a half years hitting a low of 3.12% in mid-2003. The bond market rally was caused by the burst of the new economy bubble and the ensued recession for the economy as a whole and double-dip recession for the industrial sector that lasted until the spring of 2003. Hence, the bond market correctly discounted the recent downturn and the false dawns in the last three and a half years. However, bond yields rose relentlessly in the three months to September 2003 with the ten-year climbing some 150 basis points (bps) to 4.6%, as evidence of an emerging sustained US recovery mounted. Since then bond yields have abated somewhat with the ten-year hovering just above 4.0%. There are currently two polar views on the bond market. According to the first view the bond market is undervalued, as long-term interest rates are still too high, given that the Fed funds rate is only 1%. In other words, the yield curve is too steep and is unlikely to become steeper in the course of 2004. Figure 10.1 provides support for this hypothesis. The spread between the ten-year yield and three-month Treasury bill rate has always reached 3.0%–3.75% at the beginning of a typical recovery, with the exception of 1982, when it hit 4.5%. At the beginning of the current recovery the spread hit 3.5% in August 2003, in line with other

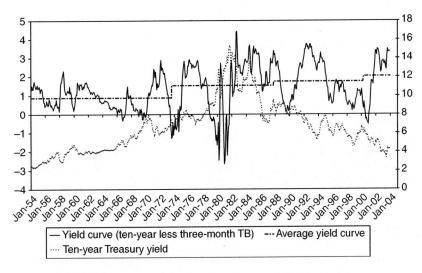

Figure 10.1 Yield curve (ten-year Treasury less three-month TB)

business cycles. In a typical cycle, once the recovery is under way the yield curve flattens, but this may be caused either by short-term interest rates rising faster than long-term ones, or by a rise of short-term rates and a fall in long-term ones, if the bond market had overestimated the forthcoming degree of monetary tightening. If the Fed tightening in the course of 2004 were modest, as Fed officials have repeatedly stressed, then the ten-year yield would not rise noticeably in the course of 2004 and may even fall, as it has already discounted the forthcoming monetary tightening – in fact, this is the reason for being undervalued, according to this view.

According to the second view, the bond market is currently extremely overvalued, as long-term interest rates are very low, given the large swing in the budget deficit in the last three years and the strength of the recovery. Advocates of this view, point to the dual system of fixed and flexible exchange rates of the US with its main trading partners. With those partners that the US has a freely floating exchange rate, like the euro area, the US benefits from the depreciation of the dollar, as it helps the economy to recover through exports. With those partners that the US has a fixed exchange rate system, like China, or dirty floating, meaning a lot of foreign exchange intervention, like Japan, the US benefits as these partners help the US to finance its budget deficit. This makes fiscal policy more effective in stimulating domestic demand in the US. Hence, the dual foreign exchange rate system is the best of all possible worlds for the US.

Table 10.1 shows the arithmetic of this argument. The Federal debt hit bottom in the middle of the recession in the second quarter of 2001. Since then it increased by nearly $800 billion, partly because of the weakness of the economy that swells the budget deficit due to the operation of automatic stabilisers, and partly because of discretionary easy fiscal policy in the form of tax cuts, depreciation incentives to the corporate sector and increased defence spending because of the war on terror. The overseas sector absorbed two thirds of this extra supply of Treasuries. Japan was the single most important buyer of the new issues of Treasuries, accounting for one-third of the total, while China absorbed only one-tenth. Japan and China together absorbed 38% of the new supply of Treasuries, but half of the foreign demand.

For some time now the Bank of Japan is printing money, as it buys directly government bonds. A proportion of this money ultimately ends up in buying US Treasuries. Hence, US long-term interest rates are artificially low. Had it not been for the policies of the Bank of Japan, long-term interest rates in the US would have been higher, either by accident or by design. Therefore the bond market is overvalued. This shows the vulnerability of the US bond market, as it depends on overseas demand and particularly that of Japan and China, which may dry out at some point in time. The appetite of non-USA residents to absorb US paper and, therefore, the willingness to finance the US budget deficit depends partly on the dollar, as a large depreciation may

Table 10.1 Federal debt and its finance

	Federal govt. debt in billion dollars	Foreign holdings of US Treasuries		Japan: holdings of US Treasuries		China: holdings of US Treasuries		Japan and China Holdings of US Treasuries		
		billion dollars	% of total	billion dollars	% of foreign total	billion dollars	% of foreign total	billion dollars	% of foreign total	as % of Fed debt
Minimum govt debt (Jun. 2001)	3251	983	31	301	31	73	7	374	38	11
Latest months (Nov. 2003)	4 030	1 504	37	526	35	144	100	669	44	17
Difference	779	521	6	225	4	71	2	296	7	5

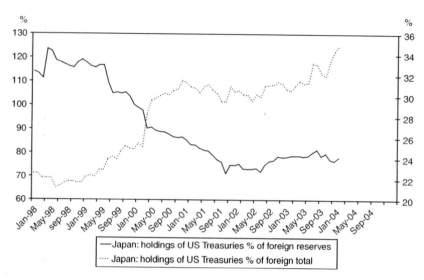

Figure 10.2   Japan – holdings of US Treasuries

more than offset the benefits of holding these assets in the case of Japan or make them less attractive to rival bonds, such as euro area, in the case of China. However, there are loopholes in this argument. Overseas holdings of US Treasuries increased by only 6% in this time period from 31% of the total in June 2001 to 37% in November 2003. Japan may have been the single most important buyer of US Treasuries, but the net increase as a proportion of overseas demand was only 4% from 31% in June 2001 to 35% in November 2003 (see Figure 10.2 and Table 10.1). China's holdings of US Treasuries increased by only 2% of foreign demand to 10% in the same time period (see Figure 10.3). Moreover, Japan's holdings of US Treasuries as proportion of its foreign reserves has remained unchanged in the period of ballooning US budget deficit (see Figure 10.2). Therefore, Japan's appetite has neither increased nor decreased. China's appetite for US Treasuries has also not changed, as its holdings as proportion of its reserves has also remained unchanged (see Figure 10.3). Hence, the extra absorption by Japan and China reflects the same proportionate allocation of foreign reserves. Foreign reserves have increased and this allowed the two countries to increase their holdings of US Treasuries. There is no reason to doubt that this may drastically change in the future.

These arguments, though, neither support nor reject the hypothesis that the US bond market is overvalued. Japan and China's holdings of US Treasuries as per cent of the Federal debt has only increased by 5% in this time period to 17% in November 2003 (see Table 10.1 and Figure 10.4). Had

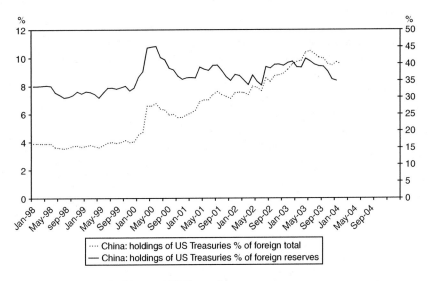

Figure 10.3 China – holdings of US Treasuries

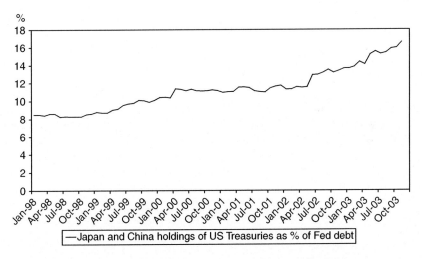

Figure 10.4 Japan and China holdings of US Treasuries as % of Fed debt

the 5% increase not been met by Japan and China, the US long-term interest rates may have been higher. If they were, then the US bond market should be declared overvalued. We have tested this hypothesis by including in the K-Model of the US bond market the proportion of US Treasuries held by Japan and China together. The coefficient is negative, implying that the larger these holdings are, the lower the US ten-year Treasury yield. But the coefficient is not statistically significant! Therefore, there is some truth in the argument that buying of US Treasuries by these two countries helps keep US bond yields lower than otherwise, but the effect, so far, is insignificant. This may, of course, change in the future if these trends persist.[1]

To shed light on the issue of whether the bond market is overvalued or undervalued we have used the K-Model that incorporates the steepness of the yield curve as one of its determinants, in line with the first view. However, in this test and in the simulations reported later on, Japan and China's holdings of US Treasuries, which is advocated by the second view, are excluded. The rationale for excluding this variable is that it is statistically insignificant. Table 10.2 shows that the US bond market is only 14 basis points overvalued with a fair value of 4.3%. Hence, the rally since last September that has brought the market down to 4.0% is slightly overdone. Nonetheless, bond yields can either rise or fall irrespective of whether they are overvalued or not. To shed light on the likely course of bond yields we have conducted some simulations, but in order to appreciate the significance of the above two tests and the risks to the bond market over the next two years, we first highlight the structure of the K-Model on this aspect.

3 Theoretical underpinnings of the bond market

The K-Model of the bond market is based on the premise that government bonds of different maturities are very close substitutes in the investor's portfolio. As a result of this premise an arbitrage relationship holds between government bond yields of different maturities. This arbitrage relationship entails that the yields (taking into account the relative risk premium) of two different maturities are brought into equality, instantaneously, by corresponding changes in their relative demands. If the yield on a long maturity (say ten year) is higher than the yield on a short maturity (say three-month) by an amount not justified by economic fundamentals then investors will buy the long bond and sell the short bond to exploit the yield differential. By doing so, the price of the long bond will rise pushing the yield down, while the price of the short bond will fall pushing the yield up. The process will continue until the yield spread between long and short maturities is equal to the investors' expected risk premium.

If we denote by R the current yield of the long maturity (i.e. the coupon divided by the price of the bond), g^e the expected capital gains (losses) on the long maturity, r, r^e the expected, which is equal to the actual, short-term interest rate, α the preferred habitat premium; and p^e the expected inflation premium, then the arbitrage relationship can be written in the following form:

$$(R + g^e) = r^e + (p^e + \alpha) \tag{1}$$

271

Table 10.2 The effect of growth on financial markets

	Current values Sep. 03–Jan. 04	Real gross private domestic investment %	Corporate profits %	CPI-inflation %	US ten-year Treasury yield	S&P 500
			Scenario I (weak recovery)		Scenario II (strong recovery)	
Assumptions						
Industrial production %						
1st year	2.4		3.0		4.6	
2nd year			3.0		1.4	
Trade weighted exchange rate index						
1st year	84.4		80		80	
2nd year			80		80	
Fed funds rate %						
1st year	1		1.25		1.25	
2nd year			1.5		1.5	
Federal budget deficit as % of GDP						
1st year	4.9		5.5		5.5	
2nd year			5.5		5.5	

Table 10.2 Continued

	Current values Sep. 03–Jan. 04	Real gross private domestic investment %	Corporate profits % Scenario I (weak recovery)	CPI-inflation %	US ten-year Treasury yield Scenario II (strong recovery)	S&P 500
Effects on financial markets						
Current level		3.6	33.1	1.9	4.14	1132
Deviation from Long-run Equilibrium (LRE)		0.6	22.0	6.9	-0.14	-1.7%
Scenario I (weak recovery)						
12-M SRE (future short-run equilibrium)		1.1	-4.0	1.2	4.32	1200
24-M SRE (future short-run equilibrium)		0.8	-6.2	2.6	6.40	1074
12-M SRE and current level (difference)		-2.4	-37.1	-0.8	0.18	6%
24-M SRE and current level (difference)		-2.8	-39.3	0.5	2.26	-5%
Scenario II (strong recovery)						
12-M SRE (future short-run equilibrium)		4.2	0.5	2.1	4.73	940
24-M SRE (future short-run equilibrium)		-2.2	-13.2	1.6	5.21	883
12-M SRE and current level (difference)		0.6	-32.6	0.1	0.6	-17%
24-M SRE and current level (difference)		-5.8	-46.3	-0.4	1.1	-22%

Since the arbitrage equation holds for expected rather than actual yields it is better described as an equilibrium relationship, for any given holding period. The left-hand side of (1) represents the total holding period return (i.e. current yield plus expected capital gains), of the long maturity, say ten-year. The first term on the right hand side of (1) is the yield on the short maturity, say three-month, and the last two terms, in parenthesis, represent the risk premium between the yields of the two maturities. The risk premium consists of two components, the inflation premium and the preferred habitat premium (see below). Although the arbitrage relationship holds between any two maturities, it is convenient to think of the short-term interest rate, r, as the instrument of monetary policy, which acts as an anchor to the yields of all maturities.

Equation (1) can be written in a number of different ways, such as:

$$(R - r^e) = -g^e + p^e + a \tag{1a}$$

In this form it asserts that the spread between the long and the short yield reflects investors' expected capital gains (or losses) from holding the ten-year bond (g^e) plus a risk premium for convincing investors to deviate from their preferred habitat (α), plus an inflation premium based on expected inflation over the holding period (p^e). The preferred habitat premium arises from the fact that in minimising risk investors will try to match the maturities of their assets and liabilities (preferred habitat). Hence, if they are to take some risk and deviate from their preferred habitat they should be compensated by receiving a corresponding premium. For example, if investors have funds available for investment for only six months then without any risk they can invest in a six-month bond. However, if they were to invest in a longer bond they would do so only if they were sufficiently compensated for the risk they will assume. The preferred habitat premium therefore will be positive for investors who invest for a holding period longer than their preferred habitat and negative for investors with a shorter holding period. On average, however, the more plausible value for α is positive, as most lenders will have a bias towards short maturities to minimise the risk of departing from their money, while most borrowers would prefer long maturities to enable the investment to work out. The inflation premium p^e arises from the fact that at the end of the holding period inflation may have eroded the value of the principal.

Investors' expected capital gains from holding a long bond depend on the current yield (R) and the expected yield (R^e) over a given holding period (t to $t+1$). If rates are expected to rise, there will be capital losses, and vice-versa. The arbitrage relationship requires that with unchanged monetary policy (i.e. fixed r), the bond yield will rise to offset the capital losses; we may, thus, write:

$$g^e = g(R, R^e) \tag{2}$$

In calculating the expected capital gains investors must have an estimate of the yield at the end of the holding period, R^e. It is assumed that investors are basing such a forecast on fiscal and monetary policy. The size of the budget deficit determines the new supply of bonds (ΔB). If investors expect the budget deficit to widen then the supply of bonds will increase and the expected long yield at the end of the holding period will rise, too, as investors will demand a higher yield to carry the extra paper in their portfolios. The expected conduct of monetary policy will also determine the expected long yield at the end of the holding period, as the instrument of monetary policy, the fed funds rate, will determine the cost of carry. If investors expect the central bank to tighten monetary policy then the expected long yield will rise, too. We can therefore write:

$$R^e = R\ (\Delta B,\ r^e) \tag{3}$$

Investors form expectations of the short-term interest rate by assuming that the central bank is rational and its decision on monetary policy is optimal, given the information about the current state of the economy and the central bank's policy brief. It is, therefore, assumed that the central bank decides on the future course of interest rates by optimising an objective function, which is specified to varying degree of detail by law, subject to the way monetary policy affects its targets. Such an optimisation results in a relationship between the instrument of monetary policy, r, and the targets of economic policy. The assumption of rationality implies optimality, but that does not necessarily mean that no mistakes are made in the conduct of monetary policy. If the objective function were wrongly specified, then the optimal policy would be inappropriate.

A general objective function includes the ultimate targets of inflation (p), growth (Y), or unemployment, and the current account of the balance of payments (CB), in deviation from their target values; the intermediate targets of the money supply (broad or narrow, M), and the exchange rate (e); and the long term constraints of budget deficit, which determines the new supply of bonds (ΔB), and government debt as a per cent of GDP (D). The target value of growth is usually assumed to be the rate of growth of potential output ($\bar{Y}$), as it is generally regarded that monetary policy cannot affect that rate, but fluctuations around it. We can therefore write:

$$r^e = r[(Y - \bar{Y}),\ p,\ CB,\ e,\ M,\ \Delta B,\ D] \tag{4}$$

If the economy grows faster than potential output, or inflation is higher than its target, or the current account deficit widens, or the money supply growth exceeds its target, or the exchange rate falls short of its target, or the budget deficit widens, or, finally, the size of government debt as per cent of nominal GDP exceeds its target, then investors expect the central bank to tighten monetary policy. It is obvious that if any of these variables is not a central bank target, then changes in this variable do not alter investors' expectations on the likely conduct of monetary policy. Equation (4) is the investors' perception of the central bank's future actions. Clearly, therefore, each investor would have different expectations of what the central bank would do because, first, they are not sure of the information set that the central bank takes into account in formulating its policy; second, of the precise form of the central bank objective function; and third, of the bank's model that describes the way monetary policy affects its targets. This diversity of expectations is the single most important factor behind the volatility of the bond market.

Investors must look at the entire wage–price nexus in order to form expectations of inflation. It is, therefore, assumed that the relationships described in Chapter 3, form the basis of expected inflation. Although this is a set of eleven equations, it can be written in a succinct way as follows:

$$p^e = p[(Y - \bar{Y}), p_{t-i}, COM, e, SMP, SFP] \tag{5}$$

The implicit assumption made here is that investors' expectations of inflation are rational. Expected inflation depends on the extent of the slack or overheating in the economy, $Y - \bar{Y}$, which affects profit margins; past inflation, p_{t-i}, which serves as an indication of future inflation in some phases of the business cycle; commodity prices, COM; and the exchange rate, e, which are both indicators of imported inflation; and, finally, the stance of monetary and fiscal policy, SMP and SFP, respectively. The stance of monetary policy reflects the central bank's vigilance in ensuring that future inflation will remain tamed. The significance of this term can be seen as follows. Assume that a central bank is 'wet' with respect to inflation targeting, assigning a low priority to it and a large priority in promoting growth and reducing unemployment. This means that the central bank is prepared to accommodate some inflation by not raising interest rates. Assume that investors correctly anticipate through equation (5) such a central bank action on r^e. However, the bond yield will still rise in spite of no expectations of monetary tightening because the accommodating stance of monetary policy will raise the inflation premium, p^e.

It does not necessarily follow that investors need to concentrate on all these indicators, at any point in time, in forming expectations of inflation. For example, once the economy exceeds potential output growth and any previous slack in capacity has been eliminated, actual inflation is not a reliable indicator of future inflation. Forward-looking investors form expectations of inflation through the output gap (i.e. the difference between actual and potential growth). Once the economy cools down, because of monetary tightening, investors form expectations of inflation by observing actual inflation, since inflation will continue to rise for some time after the economy peaked, due to inertia. Actual inflation usually peaks in the neighbourhood of the recession. Hence, once the economy is in recession, actual inflation is not a good gauge of expected inflation. The output gap is again a forward-looking measure of expected inflation. Finally, during the recovery phase actual inflation is a better proxy for expected inflation. If the economy is in recession a rise in imported inflation either through an increase in commodity prices or a depreciation of the exchange rate is unlikely to lead to higher inflation, as such cost increases are likely to be absorbed into profit margins. Thus in recessions commodity prices and the exchange rate are not important indicators of expected inflation. However, these factors become important once the economy returns or exceeds potential output.

Investors judge the stance of monetary policy by looking at a number of factors. A high or rising real interest rate, $r - p^e$, is an indication of tight monetary policy. Comparing the current real interest rate with its average value over similar business cycles can make a crude judgment. The qualification is important because comparing the behaviour of say the 1970s and the 1980s that were dominated by the oil shocks is of no use in forecasting what the neutral stance of monetary policy ought to be in the 1990s or in the twenty-first century. A more accurate judgement of the stance of monetary policy involves a comparison of the current real interest rate with the level that is consistent with optimising the central bank's objective function. The second indicator of the stance of monetary policy is the shape of the yield curve. This actually reflects investors' perceptions of the stance of monetary policy, but is a good measure because central bankers decide on their own policy actions by looking at their impact on the markets. A steep yield curve is a reflection that monetary policy is easy and that a recovery is on the way, while a flat or inverted yield curve means that monetary policy is tight and that the economy would decelerate.

The money supply used to be an indicator of the stance of monetary policy, but its importance has diminished nowadays in many countries, as it has become an unreliable indicator at the turning points of the economy since it involves large portfolio shifts. Finally, rising commodity prices and a falling exchange rate are an indication that monetary policy is easy and vice-versa. We can therefore summarise the stance of monetary policy as:

$$SMP = m[(r - p^e), R - r, COM, M, e] \tag{6}$$

Finally, investors form expectations of the stance of fiscal policy by observing changes in the structural or cyclically adjusted budget deficit, ΔBS^s. That is,

$$SFP = f(\Delta BS^s) \tag{7}$$

The set of equations (1)–(7) forms the basis of the bond market model. This model is next used to value equities and infer the long-term risks to financial markets.

4   Theoretical underpinnings of the equity market and valuation

It can be shown (Campbell, 1991) that the (log) stock price, P_t, can be expressed as the product of a constant, C, times the discounted present value of all future stock dividends [$DPV(d)$], less the discounted present value of all future risk premia [$DPV(pr)$]. This is simply a generalisation of Gordon's (1962) static growth model, but in a dynamic context.

$$P_t = C + DPV(d) - DPV(pr) \tag{8}$$

Equation (8) is not a theory of equity pricing, but an identity. In the K-Model it is turned into a theory by specifying how expectations of the future stream of dividends and risk premia are formed. Equities are assumed to be close substitutes to both bonds and money. The gross substitutability assumption implies that the demand for equities is a positive function of their own return, but a negative function of the return of the gross substitutes (Brainard and Tobin, 1968). Equities are regarded as the riskiest of the three assets, as they have the highest volatility. Despite this drawback they are still included in the investor's portfolio as they offer the highest return. The risk premium is the excess of the equity return over the return of the gross substitutes, as it reflects the amount by which an investor would have to be compensated to assume the risk of equities and include them in the portfolio. The equity risk premium is assumed to be a function of four variables. First, the excess equity return, *EER*, which is defined as the inverse of the *P/E*-ratio less the real bond yield on sovereign debt, $R - p^e$. An increase in corporate earnings raises the excess equity return, lowers the equity risk premium and, therefore, raises the price of equities, other things being equal. An increase in the *P/E*-ratio lowers the excess equity return, raises the equity risk premium and, therefore, lowers equity prices. Second, the equity risk premium depends on the yield gap, which is defined as the bond yield on sovereign debt less the dividend yield, $R - d$. An increase in the dividend yield, d, lowers the yield gap and the equity risk premium and, therefore, raises equity prices, *ceteris paribus*. Third, the equity risk premium depends on credit risk, which is defined as the excess of corporate bond yields over corresponding sovereign debt, $R_c - R$. A widening of the spread between corporate and sovereign bond yields (i.e. an increase in credit risk) raises the equity risk premium and, therefore, lowers equity prices, *ceteris paribus*. Fourth, the equity risk premium depends on the short-term real interest rate, $r - p^e$. A higher real interest rate increases the equity risk premium and, therefore, lowers equity prices, *ceteris paribus*. We can therefore summarise the relationship of the equity risk premium as follows:

$$DPV(pr) = p[(EER, (R - d), (R_c - R), (r - p^e)] \tag{9}$$

The relationship of the equity to the bond market is obvious since the bond yield affects the equity risk premium. An increase in bond yield, first, lowers the excess equity return, raises the equity risk premium and, therefore, lowers equity prices. It also increases the yield gap, raises the equity risk premium and lowers equity prices. However, the impact effect of an increase in the bond yield of sovereign debt is to reduce credit risk, which lowers the equity risk premium and, therefore, raises equity prices. This perverse effect is more than offset by the other two channels, but, moreover, it lasts only for a while. As yields on sovereign debt rise, risk averse investors replace corporate bonds with government bonds, thereby raising again credit risk and intensifying the effect of the other two channels. Since the bond market plays such a crucial role in determining the equity risk premium it is endogenous to the equity model. Investors form expectations about future corporate earnings (or dividends) by extrapolating the effects of currently available economic fundamentals on the future course of earnings. Most of these economic fundamentals refer to macro developments and their impact on either costs or profits. Obviously, any variable that increases the discounted present value of future earnings raises equity prices.

The most important variable is the growth rate of the economy, or more precisely its deviation from potential output $(Y-\bar{Y})$. A positive output gap implies a booming economy that raises corporate profits through higher volume of sales, higher profit margins and increased pricing power. The K-Profits Model analysed in Chapter 4 is crucial in determining the discounted present value of the future stream of corporate earnings and in the analysis that follows is endogenous to the equity market. The second variable that affects the discounted present value of future corporate earnings is the exchange rate, e. A lower dollar affects earnings through two channels. First, it makes US exports more competitive and imports dearer. This increases corporate earnings both from abroad and from the domestic market, as there is a substitution effect between foreign and domestic demand. Secondly, a lower dollar increases the value of consolidated balance sheet profits by boosting those that are generated by US affiliates operating abroad. The third variable that affects the discounted present value of future corporate earnings is wages and prices. The entire wage–price sector of 11 equations analysed in Chapter 3 is endogenous to the equity model, as it affects either the cost of production or the pricing power of companies. The fourth variable is overall liquidity in the economy. An increase in the money supply (broad definition) enhances gearing that pushes equity prices up. Finally, investors look at company specific variables or variables that affect the overall company environment, such as the governance crisis, in determining future corporate profitability, Z. We can, therefore, summarise the relationship of the discounted present value of future earnings as:

$$DPV(d) = d[(Y-\bar{Y}),\ e,\ M,\ C,\ Z] \tag{10}$$

The five variables included in equation (10) comprise the information set of economic fundamentals that investors look at to work out the implications for future earnings. However, what is still missing for a complete theory of equity pricing is the mechanism that investors use in extrapolating the impact of this information on future profits. It is assumed that investors are forward-looking and therefore the mechanism they use is a model of the economy that relates current values of policy and other exogenous variables to future values of economic fundamentals. Four variables are important in the model of the economy: fiscal and monetary policy, developments in the world economy and the market perception for the overall effect of the other three factors. Fiscal policy is measured by changes in the structural or cyclically adjusted budget deficit (ΔBS^e). The effect of monetary policy is measured by the impact of the real short-term interest rate ($r - p^e$) on the main macro variables, like GDP, consumption and investment. World trade (WT), captures developments in the world economy. Finally, the yield curve captures the market perception of the impact of policy and world trade on the economy. We can summarise the model of the economy as:

$$Y = Y\left[(r - p^e), \Delta BS^e, WT, (R - r)\right] \tag{11}$$

Changes in the current stance of fiscal or monetary policy would affect the economy for the next two years. If investors have a longer horizon or they want to compute the effects of policy over a longer period they must form expectations of future policy. In the case of monetary policy, which is subject to more swings than fiscal policy, the investors' mechanism for forming expectations is the one described above in the bond model (see equation 4). Hence, both the bond and the equity markets are influenced by the same mechanism.

Unfortunately, the rationality assumption cannot be invoked for fiscal policy and, therefore, there are no rules that can be used in forecasting it in the short run. The only fiscal rule that can be used is for the long run. Such a rule is based on fiscal rectitude and entails that the budget is balanced in the course of the business cycle. However, as the experience of the euro area shows, where such fiscal rectitude was agreed in the Maastricht Treaty, governments are prepared to renege it. Even worse, the process of abandoning or modifying any fiscal rectitude rule is long and painful and when finally it is applied it might turn out to be pro-cyclical (which means destabilising the cycle) rather than counter-cyclical (which means stabilising it). The experience of the euro area shows that fiscal policy would turn easy in 2004, which coincides with the upswing of the cycle making the policy pro-cyclical. World trade, on the other hand, can be modelled, as developments in the world economy would depend on the policy-mix (fiscal and monetary) of the euro area and Japan and, of course, the US.

The system of equations (8)–(11) forms the basis of the equity model. Monetary policy has a powerful role in equity prices, not only because the short-term interest rate affects the substitution effect between equities and money in the portfolio allocation, but also because it affects the main activity variables, like GDP, consumption and investment, as well as wages and prices. The equity model of the S&P 500 shows that, at the end of January, it was just 1.7% undervalued (see Table 10.2). These tally well with the conclusion that the bond market was slightly overvalued (14 basis points). However, for all intense and purposes both markets can be considered near their respective equilibrium.

5   The long-term risks to financial markets

In order to assess the long-term risks to financial markets we have conducted two simulations using (i) the financial model, (ii) the profits model, (iii) the wage–price model, and (iv) the investment model. The K-Model is simulated under two alternative scenarios. These scenarios are the same as in previous chapters (for example, Chapter 3 that discusses the implications for the wage–price sector; Chapter 4 that delves into the effect on profits, etc.). The reason for that is that we want to examine the implications of these two scenarios for the various sectors of the economy and financial markets. Since the financial model is linked with the profits model, the wage–price model and the investment model, it follows that the assumptions that pertain in the relevant chapters are valid in this chapter, too.

Scenario I (weak recovery in 2004): What would happen to bonds and equities if the current recovery were to falter in 2004 and became once again anaemic?

Scenario II (strong recovery in 2004): What would happen to bonds and equities if the recovery that started after the Iraq war continued to be strong throughout 2004?

5.1   Scenario I (weak US recovery in 2004)

The essence of this scenario lies on the assumption that the strength of the second and third quarters of 2003 was due to one-off factors related to the fiscal package of the current Administration and rising confidence because of lower geopolitical risks after the end of the Iraq war. The stance of fiscal policy turned 1.6% of GDP easier with the 'Jobs and Growth Tax Relief Reconciliation Act of 2003'. The act provided for an additional first-year bonus depreciation write-off, increasing the immediate depreciation write-off from 30% (provided for in the 'Job Creation and Worker Assistance Act of 2002') to 50% for property acquired after 5 May 2003, and placed in service before 1 January 2005. The additional depreciation provided for by the 2003 act increased depreciation expenses in the second quarter by $83.7 billion and in the third quarter by $30.9 billion. In addition, the 2003 act provided for a reduction of $100.9 billion in July in personal tax and non-tax payments. The act reduced withheld federal taxes $45.8 billion as a result of new marginal tax rates, the expansion of the 10% income tax bracket, and acceleration in 'marriage-penalty' relief. Federal non-withheld taxes (payments of estimated taxes plus final settlements less refunds) were reduced by $55.5 billion because of advance payments of the child tax credit that began being mailed out 25 July 2003. The fiscal stimulus provided through the depreciation incentives and tax relief, ignoring the additional measures on dividend income, as they are controversial with respect to their effect on demand in the economy, is estimated to be 1.6% of nominal GDP. In addition, monetary policy was eased once more at the end of June 2003 with the Fed funds rate cut to 1%. The accommodative stance of fiscal and monetary policy will keep the economy going, but the imbalances in all sectors will weigh down on the economy and the recovery will begin to falter during the course of 2004 from the torrid pace of 8% in the third quarter of 2003. Nonetheless, the economy will grow at the rate of potential output in 2004 and 2005 with industrial production growth averaging 3%. It is further assumed that the dollar would depreciate a bit more, while the budget deficit would worsen during the two-year period. Table 10.2 summarises the assumptions underlying Scenario I, along with their current values between September 2003 and January 2004.

With these assumptions CPI-inflation would abate in the course of this year hitting a low of 1.2% in October 2004, as wage- and PPI-inflation dissipate (see, for more details Chapter 3 earlier). However, PPI for finished, intermediate and crude materials prices would bottom sooner, while wage inflation would bottom later (under the assumptions made here in October 2004). In spite of the benign inflation environment, the Fed should tighten at the time that PPI hits bottom, probably in the second quarter of 2004. Unless such pre-emptive tightening takes place, inflation will rise precipitously in 2005 because of the long lags of monetary policy on inflation. As the actions of the Fed may have severe consequences on equities, it is assumed that the tightening would be mild of just 25 basis points with the Fed funds rate climbing to 1.25% at the end of the second quarter of 2004. The Fed would then wait until the presidential election is out of the way before it lifts the Fed funds rate to 1.5%. With these assumptions the ten-year yield will oscillate around 4% for most part of 2004 ending the year at 4.3% (see Table 10.2 and Figure 10.5). Such low rate will not threaten the housing market and equities. Therefore, consumption will remain strong and the economy will grow at potential output (see Chapter 7 for more details).

With the economy assumed to grow at potential output and industrial production at 3% per annum, employment would strengthen with average monthly job creation at 170 thousand (see Chapter 3). Such strong job creation would erode the recent large productivity gains and profit margins would fall from their record levels at the end of 2003 (see Chapter 4 for more details). Investment growth would accordingly dissipate (see Chapter 5 for more

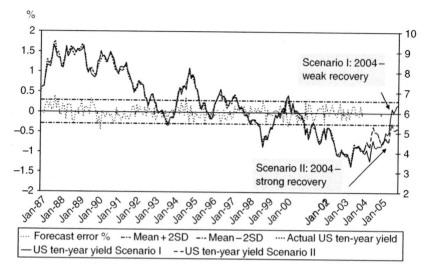

Figure 10.5   US ten-year yield – short-run equilibrium

details). As a consequence of these developments, equity prices would continue to climb higher in the first half of 2004. However, they would fall moderately in the second half of the year with the S&P still ending the year at 1200. Inflation will accelerate in 2005 and the Fed would tighten after the presidential election. Bond yields will climb in the first half of 2005, but rather steeply in the second half hitting the critical levels at which the housing market would collapse. Corporate profits would stabilise in 2005 and investment would begin to recover, but mainly in the second half. As a result of these developments equities would continue falling, but would recover in the second half of 2005 with the S&P ending the year at 1075 (see Figures 10.6 and 10.7).

The conclusion of this simulation is that even without another fiscal stimulus in 2004 and with the economy growing at potential output, financial markets may encounter some risks in the next two years. Even a modest and pre-emptive monetary tightening would keep the bond market out of trouble in 2004, but it would fail to do so in 2005. Bond yields are likely to climb steeply in the second half of 2005 to levels that would seriously undermine the housing market. Equities would advance strongly in the first half of 2004, but they will give back most of the profits in the following twelve months. They will begin to recover though in the second half of 2005. In spite of this volatility, equities will not fuel the erosion of personal sector wealth from falling property prices, thereby sheltering the consumer from dragging the economy into recession. With investment recovering in the second half of 2005 the economy would scrape through the recession and begin to recover yet again.

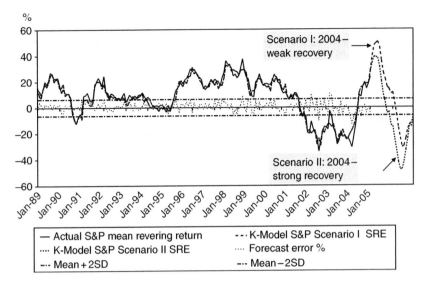

Figure 10.6   S&P mean reverting return

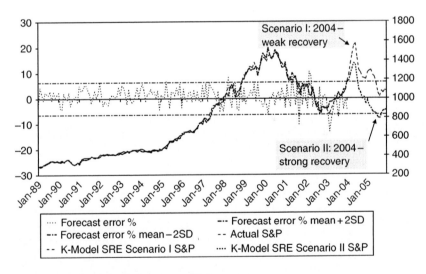

Figure 10.7   S&P 500 – short-run equilibrium

5.2   Scenario II (strong US recovery in 2004)

The essence of Scenario II lies on the premise, which is largely true, that a combined fiscal and monetary stimulus will last for at least a year, and probably eighteen months, before it tapers off. Given that the US fiscal stimulus was introduced between May and July 2003, the US economy should remain strong until the end of 2004. The role of the accommodative stance of monetary policy is to prevent long-term interest rates from rising and therefore prolong the effects of the fiscal stimulus. However, despite forty years low short-term interest rates introduced by the Fed in the last three years, long-term interest rates have risen sharply since June 2003 and the yield curve is extremely steep. If interest rates stay at this high level, or even rise further, which is very likely, the stimulus from fiscal policy will ultimately peter out. This means that growth will diminish in 2005 and beyond, other things being equal.

Given that the average growth for the preceding four quarters before the fiscal stimulus was introduced was 2.6%, that the fiscal stimulus was 1.6% of GDP and that the first year multiplier is about unity, the central projection for average US growth until the second half, or the end, of 2004 should be 4.2%. This is very close to the consensus projection, as of December 2003, for 4.4% growth in 2004. Since the depreciation incentives on new structures will only count if premises are ready for service at the beginning of 2005, companies that would like to take advantage of the scheme should already have started spending. This explains the buoyant recovery of investment in the second quarter of 2003 that was responsible, to some extent, for the unexpectedly strong growth in that quarter. The other major factor that contributed to the unexpectedly strong second quarter was the explosion of defence spending because of the Iraq war. The stunning 8% growth in the third quarter of 2003 was caused by the combination of strong consumption, due to the income tax cuts that were introduced in that quarter, the last-wagon effect for those companies that wanted to take advantage of the depreciation incentives on new structures, which accounted for $30 billion and worldwide improving confidence because of lower geopolitical risks after the end of the Iraq war that boosted US exports in the third quarter. This implies that the stunning third quarter growth was due to one-off factors that are likely to dissipate in the first half of 2004. Nonetheless, the economy should still grow at 4.2% – central projection until the second half of 2004. Industrial production will average 4.6% growth in 2004, but will fall to 1.4% in the course of 2005. The average rate of growth of industrial production over the two-year period will be 3%, the same as in Scenario I of weak recovery. However, in Scenario II growth would be stronger in 2004 and weaker in 2005 than in Scenario I, but with the same average growth for the two-year period (see Table 10.2 for the detailed assumptions of Scenario II).

Paradoxically, the higher growth rate of the economy implies that the Fed can afford to wait longer before it tightens monetary policy (see Chapter 3 for more details). With Scenario I the Fed should tighten in the second quarter of 2004, but with strong growth the Fed should tighten after the presidential election. The explanation of this paradox is that with strong growth inflation would remain muted both in 2004 and 2005, whereas with slow growth inflation will fall more in 2004, but will rise sharply in 2005. Although there is no trade-off between inflation and growth, there is one between the volatility of growth and the volatility of inflation. Scenario I implies low growth volatility and high inflation volatility, which given the lags of monetary policy on inflation entails early tightening. In contrast, Scenario II implies high growth volatility and low inflation volatility. Hence, the Fed can afford to wait before it tightens monetary policy.

With Scenario II the Fed would tighten after the US presidential election with the Fed funds rate climbing to 1.5% in the early part of 2005. However, stronger growth in 2004 would prevent the steep fall in inflation of Scenario I. Hence, bond yields will be higher than Scenario I in 2004. At the end of 2004 the ten-year yield would be 40 basis points higher than Scenario I at 4.7%. Bond yields will rise in 2005, but significantly less than Scenario I, as inflation would remain muted, growth in the economy decelerates rapidly, but short-term interest rates rise (see Table 10.2 and Figure 10.5). At the end of 2005, the ten-year yield would be 120 basis points lower than Scenario I at 5.2%. The housing market, therefore, may just escape a collapse. Job creation would be stronger than Scenario I in 2004, but weaker in 2005, as the economy slows. Therefore, the erosion of productivity gains would be stronger in 2004, but smaller in 2005. Hence, profit margins would fall much more than Scenario I. But stronger growth in 2004 would mitigate the fall in profits. Investment would remain stronger than Scenario I in 2004, but much weaker in 2005, especially in the second half. As a result of these developments, equity prices would not rise as much as Scenario I in 2004. But they would fall more precipitously from the second half of 2004 onwards. During 2005 equities would go into a free fall, as the Fed tightens, bond yields rise, profits and investment fall and the economy slows.

The conclusion of this simulation is that fast growth in 2004 fostered by yet another fiscal package and even with no tightening of monetary policy would spur trouble for financial markets, but the other way round than Scenario I. Bond yields would be higher in 2004 and lower in 2005 than Scenario I. In spite of this volatility the housing market would most likely be spared from a collapse and therefore wealth would not suffer, thus shielding the consumer. However, equity prices would not rise as much as Scenario I in 2004, but would fall steeply in 2005, revisiting the lows reached in March 2003. The fall in equity prices would erode wealth and the personal sector imbalance would re-emerge as a problem.

6   Summary and conclusions

The bond market holds the key not only to the equity market, but also to the economy as a whole. The imbalances in the private sector are dormant at the moment, as the economy is recovering. However, if long-term interest rates were to rise to critical levels, then these imbalances would reawaken and threaten not only the sustainability of the recovery, but may also trigger another recession. The interesting question is, then, how far and how fast can bond yields rise in the next two years. The advocates of the yield curve approach argue that the bond market is undervalued, as the cost of carry is very high. At the other end of the spectrum, there are those who base their analysis on the interdependence of global bond markets. They argue that the US bond market is extremely overvalued, given the large swing in the budget deficit and the strength of the economy. They argue that the overvaluation has resulted from buying of US Treasuries by Japan and China.

The K-Model includes the cost of carry as a determinant of the bond market, as well as the budget deficit and the strength of the economy. Hence, it provides an appropriate framework for testing these two hypotheses. Although we find that there is a negative relationship between Japan and China's holdings of US Treasuries and bond yields, this is still not significant to cause worries to US policymakers. Nonetheless, although the cost of carry is very high, the bond market is not undervalued as the advocates of the yield curve approach argue, but slightly overvalued, as at the end of January 2004 the fair value for the ten-year yield is 4.3%. Despite the relentless rally of equities since the end of the Iraq war, the market is not yet overvalued, as it was seriously undervalued in March 2003, and economic fundamentals have been improving. At the end of January the S&P was still 1.7% undervalued. Hence, both markets are around equilibrium and the probability is that bond yields would not rise noticeably this year to cause trouble to equities, as inflation pressures would abate and the Fed might delay monetary tightening. Hence, there is still some upside for equities this year. Consequently, we continue for the time being to support the investment strategy that places an overweight position on equities and an underweight on bonds. However, there are serious risks to financial markets stemming mainly from fiscal policy. In order to assess these risks we have conducted two simulations using the K-Model. In particular, we have evaluated two alternative scenarios regarding growth. Scenario I assumes steady growth for both 2004 and 2005 at potential output, while in Scenario II growth is fast in 2004, but slow in 2005, with the average for two-year period being the same.

The conclusion of Scenario I is that even without another fiscal stimulus in 2004 and with the economy growing at potential output, financial markets may encounter some trouble in the next two years. Even a modest, but pre-emptive, monetary tightening would keep the bond market out of trouble in 2004, but it would fail to do so in 2005. Bond yields are likely to climb steeply in the second half of 2005 to levels that would seriously undermine the housing market. Equities would advance strongly in the first half of 2004, but they will give back most of the profits in the following twelve months. They will begin to recover though in the second half of 2005. In spite of this volatility, equities will not fuel the erosion of personal sector wealth from falling property prices, thereby sheltering the consumer from dragging the economy into recession. With investment recovering in the second half of 2005 the economy would scrape through the recession and begin to recover yet again.

The conclusion of Scenario II is that fast growth in 2004, fostered by yet another fiscal package and even with monetary tightening delayed until after the presidential election, would spur trouble for financial markets, but the other way round than Scenario I. Bond yields would be higher in 2004 and lower in 2005 than Scenario I. In spite of this volatility the housing market would most likely be spared from a collapse and therefore wealth would not suffer, thus shielding the consumer. But equity prices would not rise as much as Scenario I in 2004. They would fall, nonetheless, steeply in 2005, revisiting the lows reached in March 2003. The fall in equity prices would erode wealth and the personal sector imbalance would re-emerge as a problem.

These simulations are not supposed to highlight the most likely course of the economy over the next two years, but the long-term risks to financial markets and the economy as a whole from yet another fiscal package in 2004, which may be triggered by electioneering. Companies may, in fact, act in such a way that the risks illustrated in these simulations may be avoided. The pace of job creation is the key to the US economy. Strong job creation of the order of 200 thousand per month may be good for robust consumption growth. However, such job creation is likely to erode the recent record levels of productivity growth and lead to falling profits that would curtail investment. It may, therefore, be that companies would not hire as many people as assumed in the simulations and investment and profits would remain strong. Growth in 2004 would then be investment-led, with consumption taking a second seat because of anaemic job creation. Equity prices would then be spared from another collapse. The message, therefore, for policy may be very simple. If the price of fast growth in 2004, spurred by yet another fiscal package, is slow growth in 2005, then this is undesirable, as it would spur problems for financial markets and the economy as a whole.

Notes

1 Introduction

1. Neutral level of a variable is defined as the level that corresponds to the rate of growth of potential output.

2 The Causes and Consequences of the Post-'New Economy' Bubble

1. For example, the US Federal Reserve System reduced its 'funds' interest rate no less than thirteen times between early 2001 and at the time of writing (March 2004). This rate now stands at 1%, a record low level. This is not confined to the US only. In the Economic and Monetary Union (EMU), the European Central Bank (ECB), although rather slow in reducing its 'repo' interest rate, is now holding this rate at 2%. These are only two, but representative examples, of what the situation has been worldwide.
2. Greenspan (2000) defines wealth effects as follows: 'Historical evidence suggests that perhaps three to four cents out of every additional dollar of stock market wealth eventually is reflected in increased consumer purchases. The sharp rise in the amount of consumer outlays relative to disposable incomes in recent years, and the corresponding fall in the saving rate, has been consistent with this so-called wealth effect on household purchases. Moreover, higher stock prices, by lowering the cost of equity capital, have helped to support the boom in capital spending' (p. 2).
3. There were many recessions caused by asset and debt deflation throughout the seventeen and eighteen centuries. Most important of which were the tulip-mania in the middle of the seventeenth century, and the Mississippi, and South Seas bubble of the early eighteenth century (see, e.g., Garber, 2000).
4. It should be noted that the statement in the text about the savings deficiency, is only correct by the specific definition of national savings, namely equal to the trade gap. This measure of savings has no operational function apart from restating the trade gap. This is how it is meant to be used here.
5. Interestingly enough, the dollar reached a three-year low with respect to the euro (0.779), and an 11-year low with respect to pound sterling (0.53), after the chairman of the Fed delivered his semi-annual report on monetary policy to the Congress on 11/12 of February, 2004. He made the comment that a gradual weakening of the dollar would help narrow the US external deficit, and would have no adverse effect on US capital markets. The market somehow interpreted that unusual remark on currencies by the Fed chairman, as a clear sign of the Fed's tacit acceptance of the dollar's slide.
6. An interesting proposal is contained in the study by Bordo and Jeanne (2002). Using a stylised model they examine the possibility of pre-emptive monetary policy to conclude that 'optimal policy depends on the economic conditions in a complex, non-linear way and cannot be summarized by a simple policy rule of the type considered in the inflation-targeting literature' (p. 1).
7. Net wealth reverts back to its mean, albeit at long intervals of 5–10 years. This is a direct consequence of the fact that net wealth as percent of disposable income is a

stationary variable, that is, its mean and standard deviation are not time varying. Technically, it is integrated of order zero. The stationarity property follows from the fact that the constituent components of net wealth, namely assets and liabilities, are each one a non-stationary variable integrated of order one. Hence their difference (assets less liabilities) is stationary, that is, integrated of order zero. The mean reverting property of net wealth implies that bubbles, and in general imbalances, can be identified and their consequences can be quantified.

8. This does not mean that we support inflation targeting, which has its own problems and peculiarities, as argued in Arestis and Sawyer (2003).

3 Wages and Prices and the Proper Conduct of Monetary Policy

1. The difference between Headline and Core inflation is that the latter excludes volatile items, namely food and energy.
2. For a New-Keynesian view on the inflation/unemployment trade-off see, for example, Mankiw (2001a).

4 Corporate Profits and Relationship to Investment

1. The corporate profits discussed here are not shareholder reported earnings. They are the profits that are based on National Income and Product Accounts (NIPA). This measure of profits is designed to gauge the economic profitability of current operations. It excludes a number of one-time charges that appear in shareholder reports and, importantly, records options as an expense, albeit at the time of the exercise. Although this treatment of options is not ideal, it is arguably superior to their treatment in shareholder reports, where options are generally not expensed at all. NIPA profits closely approximate those obtained from reports submitted for tax purposes, and, for obvious reasons, corporations tend not to inflate taxable earnings.
2. The profits of non-financial corporations account for 60% of the total, while profits from the rest of the world account for only 14% of the total.
3. The non-financial corporate sector consists of manufacturing, transportation and public utilities, wholesale and retail trade and other.
4. In other words, a company may be geared to maximising profits at, say, 1 billion dollars in sales, when sales are at 600 million, given growth anticipations. If and when it becomes clear that sales are not as high as predicted, the company reorganises to maximising profits at the 600 million dollar sales level. Productivity goes up and unit labour costs down, because now they are operating exactly at the scaled level of 600 million, whereas before they may have been able to achieve the same unit labour costs at 1 billion dollar in sales. But as they fell short of the 1 billion level, unit costs jumped higher.

5 Long-term Risks to Investment Recovery

1. This definition of debt includes commercial paper, corporate bonds, bank loans, other loans and advances and mortgages.

2. The relationship between the rate of interest and investment is particularly important in the neo-classical investment theory (Jorgenson, 1971) and in Keynesian economics (Keynes, 1936). There are, of course, important differences between the two approaches: perhaps the most important is that whilst in neoclassical economics the relationship emanates from the attempt to determine the optimal capital stock, in Keynesian economics the relationship does not rely on invoking the optimal capital stock notion; uncertain expectations are by far the most important element in this approach (see, e.g., Binswanger, 1999, where more details on this and other differences are offered). One other aspect refers to the relative importance between cost-of-capital and activity economic variables. It is generally recognized that activity variables, especially output, have 'a more substantial impact on investment' (Chirinko, 1993, p. 1881).

3. We include in this category the q theory of investment, introduced by Keynes (1936) and further developed by Brainard and Tobin (1968) and Tobin (1969, 1978).

6   The Housing Market and Residential Investment

1. Another OECD study argues that since owner-occupation rates exceed 50% in most OECD countries, a significant number of households are bound to be affected by changes in property prices (OECD, 2000a).

2. GSE stands for Government Sponsored Enterprises and refers specifically to Fannie Mae and Freddie Mac.

3. A trendless variable is one that has neither an upward nor downward trend. It is more rigorously defined as a stationary variable, which means that its mean and standard deviation are not time varying. A stationary variable has the property that it reverts to its mean.

4. In terms of textbook economics, in the short run we are moving up along the supply curve in response to a shift in the demand curve, while in the long run the supply curve shifts to the right because of higher residential investment.

5. The impact of HP on RRI has received renewed interest recently, where the relationship emanates through the impact of house prices on profitability; see, for example, OECD, 2000b.

6. An interesting study that compares the US and the UK housing markets is Banks *et al.* (2003). This study compares households' decisions in buying houses at various stages of their lives in the two countries. The smaller volatility in the US in relation to the UK market is explained by resorting to the absence of hedging possibilities in the UK. This means that since no hedging against further increases in house prices exists, except of course to buy housing itself, it forces people to buy houses sooner in their lives.

7   Long-term Risks of Robust Consumer Behaviour

1. The sample in Jappelli and Pagano (1989) contains countries with capital markets that have reached different degrees of development: Sweden (12), US (21), Japan (34), UK (40), Spain (52), Greece (54), Italy (58), where in brackets the percentage of households that are liquidity-constrained is shown, comprise the sample of countries. Three groupings are identified. Sweden and US have a low percentage of households that are liquidity-constrained; UK and Japan then follow, while for Spain, Greece and Italy the opposite to Sweden and US is true.

2. The result for the UK is sensitive to the seasonal adjustment procedure: the 35% quoted in the text is for seasonally adjusted quarterly data; it is 65% when annual differences of seasonal unadjusted data are used. For Japan no relevant percentage was identified (Campbell and Mankiw, 1991, pp. 737–8).

3. While it is true that liquidity constraints have received a great deal of attention in the literature, 'much work needs to be done to incorporate them in a consistent fashion' (Attanasio and Blank, 2001, p. 6). In this context the difference of consumer behaviour in developed and developing economies becomes paramount (for a recent study that concentrates on low-income countries, see Rosenzweig, 2001).

4. See Carroll and Kimball (2001) for a discussion of the tight relationship between liquidity constraints and precautionary behaviour. In fact, 'The precautionary saving motive can generate behaviour that is virtually indistinguishable from that generated by a liquidity constraint, because the precautionary saving motive essentially induces self-imposed reluctance to borrow (or to borrow too much)' (Carroll, 2001, p. 32).

5. Two further dimensions of the analysis in the text are worth mentioning: the first is the possibility of discounting of the future changing over time, the hyber-bolic discounting approach (Angeletos *et al.*, 2001); and the second that refers to cross-national differences in savings rates (Deaton, 1992).

6. Carroll and Samwick (1997), using the Panel Study of Income Dynamics, provide evidence that supports the proposition that consumers who face greater uncertainty hold more wealth, and that they engage in 'buffer-stock' saving behaviour.

8 Foreign Demand

1. The euro area comprises 12 members at this juncture. The 12 members are: Austria, Belgium, Finland, France, Germany, Greece, Ireland, Italy, Luxembourg, the Netherlands, Portugal and Spain.

2. The importance of foreign trade for growth has been demonstrated by a number of studies; see, for example, OECD (2000c, pp. 143–144).

3. For full details on the ISM, visit www.ism.ws.

9 The US External Imbalance and the Dollar: A Long-term View

1. This chapter was written when the dollar/euro exchange rate was 1.09. We have consciously not updated the data so that predictions can be compared to outcomes on this very difficult variable to model.

2. Game theory has been used extensively in micro-economics, but not to the same extent in macro-economics. In the latter case, applications in the area of macro policies in an interdependent world is probably one exception. The contributions by Cooper (1985) and Hamada (1974), (1976), (1979) and applications by Canzoneri and Gray (1983), and Sachs (1983) utilise game theory deal with the behaviour of the exchange rate.

3. A variable is stationary if its mean and standard deviation are not time varying. As it is well known, modelling of non-stationary variables produces nonsense correlations, unless the variables are co-integrated.

4. There seems to be a contradiction between the effects of fiscal policy and government debt, but this is not so. In the short run easy fiscal policy (widening budget

deficit) boosts the dollar, but in the long run the higher government debt that results from such policy, weakens the currency.

10   The Long-term Risks to US Financial Markets

1. The estimated equation turned out to be as follows:

$$BY = 0.707 + 0.716SY + 0.097CPI + 0.945TB3M - 0.038GS$$
$$(5.9) \quad (27.5) \quad (4.1) \quad\quad (38.3) \quad\quad (2.8)$$
$$- 0.011AFX - 0.003JPCH$$
$$(4.1) \quad\quad (0.6)$$

$R^2 = 0.97$, F-statistic = 1186.7, No. of Observations = 216 (monthly data, January 1986 to December 2003); where BY = 10-year bond yield; SY = steepness of the yield curve; CPI = inflation (consumer price index definition); $TB3M$ = 3-month treasury bills; GS = government surplus; AFX = degree of currency appreciation; and $JPCH$ = Japan's and China's holdings of US Treasuries.

Bibliography

Alchian, A.A. and Klein, B. (1973), 'On a Correct Measure of Inflation', *Journal of Money, Credit and Banking*, 5(1), 173–91.

Ando, A. and Modigliani, F. (1963), 'The "Life Cycle" Hypothesis of Saving: Aggregate Implications and Tests', *American Economic Review*, 53, 55–84.

Angeletos, G.M., Laibson, D., Repetto, A., Tobacman, J. and Weinberg, S. (2001), 'Hyperbolic Consumption Model: Calibration, Simulation, and Empirical Evaluation', *Journal of Economic Perspectives*, 15(3), 47–68.

Arestis, P. (1986), 'Wages and Prices in the UK: The Post Keynesian View', *Journal of Post Keynesian Economics*, 8(3), 339–58. Reprinted in M.C. Sawyer (ed.), Post-Keynesian Economics, Aldershot: Edward Elgar Publishing Limited, 1988, 456–75.

Arestis, P. and Karakitsos, E. (2002), 'How Far Can Equity Prices Fall Under Asset and Debt Deflation?', *Working Paper No. 368*, Levy Economics Institute of Bard College, December.

Arestis, P. and Sawyer, M.C. (2003), 'Inflation Targeting: A Critical Appraisal', *Levy Economics Institute Working Papers Series*, No. 388, September.

Arestis, P., Cipollini, A. and Fattouh, B. (2004), 'Threshold Effects in the U.S. Budget Deficit', *Economic Inquiry*, 42(2), 214–22.

Attanasio, O.P. and Blank, J. (2001), 'The Assessment: Household Saving – Issues in Theory and Policy', *Oxford Review of Economic Policy*, 17(1), 1–19.

Baddeley, M.C. (2003), *Investment: Theories and Analysis*, Basingstoke: Palgrave Macmillan.

Banks, J., Blundell, R., Smith, J.P. and Smith, Z. (2003), *Housing Wealth over the Life-Cycle in the Presence of Housing Price Volatility*, London: Institute of Fiscal Studies and University College.

Bernanke, B.S. and A.S. Blinder (1988), 'Credit, money and aggregate demand', *American Economic Review*, 78(2), 435–9.

Bernanke, B.S. and M. Gertler (1989), 'Agency costs, net worth, and business fluctuations', *American Economic Review*, 79(1), 14–31.

Bernanke, B.S. and M. Gertler (1999), 'Monetary policy and asset price volatility', in *New Challenges for Monetary Policy*, proceedings of the Symposium sponsored by the Federal Reserve Bank of Kansas City, Jackson Hole, Wyoming, 77–128.

Bernanke, B. and Gertler, M. (2000), 'Monetary Policy and Asset Price Volatility', *NBER Working Paper No. 7559*, Cambridge, MA: National Bureau of Economic Research.

Binswanger, M. (1999), *Stock Markets, Speculative Bubbles and Economic Growth: New Dimensions in the Co-evolution of Real and Financial Markets*, Cheltenham, UK: Edward Elgar Publishing.

Bordo, M.D. and Jeanne, O. (2002), 'Monetary Policy and Asset Prices: Does "Benign Neglect" Make Sense?', *IMF Working Paper, WP/02/225*, Washington, DC: International Monetary Fund.

Brainard, W.C. and Tobin, J. (1968), 'Pitfalls in Financial Model Building', *American Economic Review*, 58(2), 99–122.

Browning, M. and Crossley, T.F. (2001), 'The Life-Cycle Model of Consumption and Saving', *Journal of Economic Perspectives*, 15(3), 3–22.

Campbell, J.Y. (1991), 'A Variance Decomposition for Stock returns', *Economic Journal*, 101(405), 157–79.

Campbell, J.Y. and Mankiw, N.G. (1990), 'Permanent Income, Current Income, and Consumption', *Journal of Business and Economics*, 8, 269–79.

Campbell, J.Y. and Mankiw, N.G. (1991), 'The Response of Consumption to Income: A Cross-country Investigation', *European Economic Review*, 35, 723–67.

Canzoneri, M. and Gray, J. (1983), 'Two Essays on Monetary Policy in an Interdependent World', *Federal Reserve Board International Finance*, Discussion Paper No. 219.

Carroll, C.D. (1994), 'How Does Future Income Affect Current Consumption?', *Quarterly Journal of Economics*, 109(1), 111–47.

Carroll, C.D. (1997), 'Buffer-Stock Saving and the Life Cycle/Permanent Income Hypothesis', *Quarterly Journal of Economics*, 112(1), 1–56.

Carroll, C.D. (2001), 'A Theory of the Consumtion Function, With and Without Liquidity Constraints', *Journal of Economic Perspectives*, 15(3), 23–45.

Carroll, C.D. and Kimball, M.S. (2001), 'Liquidity Constraints and Precautionary Saving', *NBER Working Paper No. 8496*, Cambridge, MA: National Bureau of Economic Research.

Carroll, C.D. and Samwick, A.A. (1997), 'The Nature of Precautionary Wealth', *Journal of Monetary Economics*, 40(1), 41–71.

Chirinko, R.S. (1993), 'Business Fixed Investment Spending: Modeling Strategies, Empirical Results, and Policy Implications', *Journal of Economic Literature*, 31(4), 1875–911.

Clews, R. (2002), 'Asset Prices and Inflation', *Bank of England Quarterly Bulletin*, Summer, 178–85.

Conference Board (2003), 'Consumer Confidence Index', *Consumer Confidence Survey*, February.

Cooper, R.N. (1985), 'Economic Interdependence and Co-ordination of Economic Policies', in R.W. Jones and P.B. Kenen (eds), *Handbook of International Economics*, Vol. II, London: Elsevier Science Publishers.

Council of Economic Advisers (2004), *Economic Report of the President*, Washington DC: United States Printing Office.

Deaton, A. (1991), 'Saving and Liquidity Constraints', *Econometrica*, 59(5), 1221–48.

Deaton, A. (1992), *Understanding Consumption*, Oxford: Oxford University Press.

Dixit, A. and Pindyck, R. (1994), *Investment under Uncertainty*, Princeton: Princeton University Press.

Dornbusch, R. (1976), 'Expectations and Exchange Rate Dynamics', *Journal of Political Economy*, 84(December), 1161–76.

Dornbusch, R. and Fisher, S. (1980) 'Exchange rates and the Current Account', *American Economic Review*, 70(5), 960–71.

Duisenberg, W.F. (2002), *Testimony to the European Parliament*, October, Brussels, Belgium: European Commission.

Eichner, A.S. (1987), *The Macrodynamics of Advanced Economies*, New York: M.E. Sharpe.

Eisner, R. (1974), 'Econometric Studies of Investment behaviour: A Comment', *Economic Inquiry*, 1281, 91–104.

Fazzari, S. (1993), 'Monetary Policy, Financial Structure, and Investment', chapter 3 in *Transforming the U.S. Financial System: Equity and Efficiency for the 21st Century*, Armonk, New York: M.E. Sharpe.

Fazzari, S. and Peterson, B. (1993), 'Working Capital and Fixed Investment: New Evidence on Financing Constraints', *Rand Economic Journal*, 24, 328–42.

Flavin, M. (1985), 'Excess Sensitivity of Consumption to Current Income: Liquidity Constraints or Myopia', *Canadian Journal of Economics*, 18, 117–36.

Fleming, J.M. (1962), 'Domestic Financial Policies Under Fixed and Under Flexible Exchange Rates', *International Monetary Fund Staff Papers*, 9(November), 369–79.

Friedman, M. (1957), *A Theory of the Consumption Function*, Princeton, NJ: Princeton University Press.

Frowen, S.F. and Karakitsos, E. (1996), 'Monetary and Fiscal Policy Under Conditions of Globalised Money and Capital Markets: Lessons For The UK Personal Sector', *Public Finance*, 51(3), 305–24.

Frowen, S.F. and Karakitsos, E. (1998), 'A Strategic Approach to the Euro Prospects', *Public Finance*, 53(1), 1–18.

Garber, P.M. (2000), *Famous First Bubbles: The Fundamentals of Early Manias*, Cambridge, MA: The MIT Press.

Goodhart, C.A.E. (2001), 'What Weight Should Be Given to Asset Prices in the Measurement of Inflation', *Economic Journal*, 111(472), F335–F356.

Gordon, M.J. (1962), *The Investment, Financing and valuation of the Corporation*, Irwin: Homewood III.

Gordon, R. (2000), 'Does the "New Economy" Measure Up to the Great Invention of the Past?', *Journal of Economic Perspectives*, 14(4), 49–74.

Greenspan, A. (1999), 'Mortgage Markets and Economic Activity', Remarks Before a Conference on *Mortgage Markets and Economic Activity*, Sponsored by America's Community Bankers, Washington DC, November 1999.

Greenspan, A. (2000), 'Testimony of Chairman Alan Greenspan', *The Federal Reserve's Semiannual Report on the Economy and Monetary Policy*, Before the Committee on Banking and Financial Services, U.S. House of Representatives, February 2000.

Greenspan, A. (2002a), 'Economic Volatility', Speech given to a Symposium Sponsored by the Federal Reserve Bank of Kansas City, Jackson Hole, Wyoming.

Greenspan, A. (2002b), 'Issues for Monetary Policy', *Remarks Before the Economic Club of New York, New York City*, December 2002. Available at: http://www.federalreserve.gov/boarddocs/speeches/2002/20021219/ (It should be noted that pages in the text refer to the website document).

Greenspan, A. (2004a), 'Risk and Uncertainty in Monetary Policy', *Remarks by Chairman Alan Greenspan at the Meetings of the American Economic Association*, San Diego, California, January 2004.

Greenspan, A. (2004b), 'Testimony of Chairman Alan Greenspan', *The Federal Reserve's Semiannual Monetary Policy Report to the Congress*, Before the Committee on Financial Services, U.S. House of Representatives, February 2004.

Greenspan, A. (2004c), 'Government-Sponsored Enterprises', *Testimony of Chairman Alan Greenspan*, Before the Committee on Banking, Housing, and Urban Affairs, U.S. Senate, February 2004.

Hamada, K. (1974), 'Alternative Exchange Rate Systems and the Interdependence of Monetary Policies', in R.Z. Aliber (ed.), *National Monetary Policies and the International Financial System*, Chicago: University of Chicago Press.

Hamada, K. (1976), 'A Strategic Analysis on Monetary Interdependence', *Journal of Political Economy*, 84, 677–700.

Hamada, K. (1979), 'Macroeconomic Strategy and Co-ordination Under Alternative Exchange Rate Regimes', in R. Dornbusch and J.A. Frankel (eds), *International Economic Policy*, Baltimore: The John Hopkins University Press.

Hubbard, R.G. (1998), 'Capital-Market Imperfections and Investment', *Journal of Economic Literature*, XXXVI(1), 193–225.

Jappelli, T. and Pagano, M. (1989), 'Consumption and Capital Market Imperfections: An International Comparison', *American Economic Review*, 79(5), 1088–105.

Jorgenson, D. (1971), 'Econometric Studies of Investment Behaviour: A Survey', *Journal of Economic Literature*, 53, 1111–47.

Kaldor, N. (1955), 'Alternative Theories of Distribution', *Review of Economic Studies*, 23.

Kalecki, M. (1943), 'The Determinants of Investment', in his *Studies in Economic Dynamics*, London: Allen and Unwin.

Kalecki, M. (1971), *Selected Essays on the Dynamics of the Capitalist Economy*, Cambridge: Cambridge University Press.

Keynes, J.M. (1936), *The General Theory of Employment, Interest and Money*, London: Macmillan.

Kindleberger, C.P. (2000), *Manias, Panics and Crashes: A History of Financial Crises*, 4th edition, London: John Wiley and Sons.

Kotlikoff, L.J. and Summers, L.H. (1981), 'The Role of Intergenerational Transfers in Aggregate Capital Accumulation', *Journal of Political Economy*, 89(4), 706–32.

Lee, T. (2004), *Why the Markets Went Crazy and What it Means for Investors*, New York: Palgrave Macmillan.

Mankiw, N.G. (2001a), 'The Inexorable and Mysterious Tradeoff Between Inflation and Unemployment', *Economic Journal*, 111(3), C45–C61.

Mankiw, N.G. (2001b), 'US Monetary Policy in the 1990s', *NBER Working Paper No. 8471*, Washington: National Bureau of Economic Research.

Mayer, C. (1994), 'The Assessment: Money and Banking: Theory and Evidence', *Oxford Economic Review*, 10, 1–13.

McConnell, M.M., Peach, R.W. and Al-Haschimi, A. (2003), 'After the Refinancing Boom: Will Consumers Scale Back Their Spending?', *Current Issues in Economics and Finance, Federal Reserve Bank of New York*, 9(12), 1–7.

Minsky, H.P. (1986), *Stabilising an Unstable Economy*, New Haven: Yale University Press.

Modigliani, F. (1988), 'The Role of Intergenerational Transfers and Life Cycle Saving in the Accumulation of Wealth', *Journal of Economic Perspectives*, 2(2), 15–40.

Modigliani, F. and Brumberg, R. (1954), 'Utility Analysis and the Consumption Function: An Interpretation of Cross-section Data', in K.K. Kurihara (ed.), *Post-Keynesian Economics*, New Brunswick, NJ: Rutgers University Press.

Mundell, R.A. (1960), 'The Monetary Dynamics of International Adjustment Under Fixed and Flexible Exchange Rates', *Quarterly Journal of Economics*, 74(2), 227–57. Reprinted as Chapter 11 in R.A. Mundell (1968), *International Economics*, New York: Macmillan, 152–76.

Mundell, R.A. (1963), 'Capital Mobility and Stabilisation Policy Under Fixed and Flexible Exchange Rates', *Canadian Journal of Economics and Political Science*, 29(November), 475–85.

OECD (2000a), 'Monetary Policy in a Changing Financial Environment', *Economic Outlook*, 67(June), Paris: Organisation for Economic Co-Operation and Development.

OECD (2000b), 'House Prices and Economic Activity', *Economic Outlook*, 68(December), Paris: Organisation for Economic Co-Operation and Development.

OECD (2000c), 'Links Between Policy and Growth: Cross-Country Evidence', *Economic Outlook*, 68(December), Paris: Organisation for Economic Co-Operation and Development.

Oliner, S.D. and Sichel, D.E. (2000), 'The Resurgence of Growth in the Late 1990s: Is Information Technology the Story?', *Journal of Economic Perspectives*, 14(4), 3–22.

Robinson, J.V. (1964), 'Kalecki and Keynes', in her *Collected Economic Papers*, 3, Oxford: Basil Blackwell.

Rosenzweig, M.R. (2001), 'Saving Behaviour in Low-Income Countries', *Oxford Review of Economic Policy*, 17(1), 40–54.

Rowthorn, R. (1995), 'Capital Formation and Unemployment', *Oxford Review of Economic Policy*, 11(1), 26–39.

Sachs, J. (1983), 'International Policy Co-ordination in a Dynamic Macro-Model', *NBER Working Paper* 1166, Washington, DC: National Bureau of Economic Research.

Sargan, J.D. (1964), 'Wages and Prices in the United Kingdom: A Study in Econometric Methodology', in P.E. Hart, G. Mills and J.K. Whitaker (eds), *Econometric Analysis for National Economic Planning*, London: Butterworths, pp. 25–63.

Sawyer, M. (1982a), *Macro-Economics in Question*, Brighton: Wheatsheaf Books, and New York: M.E. Sharpe.

Sawyer, M. (1982b), 'Collective Bargaining, Oligopoly and Macro-Economics', *Oxford Economic Papers*, 34(4), 428–48.

Sawyer, M.C. (1985), *The Economics of Michal Kalecki*, London: Macmillan.

Schiller, R.J. (2000), *Irrational Exuberance*, Princeton: Princeton University Press.

Stegman, T. (1982), 'The Estimation of an Acclerator-Type Investment Function with a Profitability Constraint by the Technique of Switching Regressions', *Australian Economic Papers*, 21(2), 379–91.

Stiglitz, J. and Weiss, A (1981), 'Credit Rationing in Markets with Imperfect Information', *American Economic Review*, 71(3), 393–410.

Stiroh, K. (2002), 'Are ICT Spillovers Driving the New Economy?', *Review of Income and Wealth*, 48(1), 33–57.

Temple, J. (2002), 'The Assessment: The New Economy', *Oxford Review of Economic Policy*, 18(3), 241–64.

Tevlin, S. and Whelan, K. (2002), 'Explaining the Investment Boom of the 1990s', *Journal of Money, Credit and Banking*, 35(1), 1–22.

Tobin, J. (1969), 'A General Equilibrium Approach to Monetary Theory', *Journal of Money, Credit, and Banking*, 1(1), 15–29.

Tobin, J. (1978), 'Monetary Policies and the Economy: The Transmission Mechanism', *Southern Economic Journal*, 44(3), 421–31.

Warburton, P. (1999), Debt and Delusion: Central Bank Follies That Threaten Economic Disaster, New York: Allen Lane and Penguin Press.

Zeldes, S. (1989a), 'Consumption and Liquidity Constraints: an Empirical Investigation', *Journal of Political Economy*, 97, 305–46.

Zeldes, S. (1989b), 'Optimal Consumption with Stochastic Income: Deviations from Certainty Equivalence', *Quarterly Journal of Economics*, 104, 275–98.

Index